SYSTEMIC RISK AND THE FUTURE OF INSURANCE REGULATIO

LLOYD'S INSURANCE LAW LIBRARY

Editor-in-Chief
Malcolm A. Clarke

Systemic Risk and the Future of Insurance Regulation
Edited by
Andromachi Georgosouli and Miriam Goldby
(2016)

Lloyd's: Law and Practice
Julian Burling
(2013)

The Law of Liability Insurance
Malcolm A. Clarke
(20155)

Insurance Disputes
Third Edition
The Right Honourable The Lord Mance
Iain Goldrein QC
Robert Merkin
(2012)

Reinsuring Clauses
Ozlem Gurses
(2011)

Insurance Law and the Financial Services Ombudsman Service
Judith P Summer
(2011)

Good Faith and Insurance Contracts
Third Edition
Peter MacDonald Eggers
Simon Picken QC
Patrick Foss
(2010)

Directors' and Officers' Liability Insurance
Adolfo Paolini
Deepak Nambisan
(2009)

Reinsurance Law and Practice and the Law
Barlow Lyde & Gilbert
(20101)

The Law of Insurance Contracts
By Malcolm A. Clarke
(2010)

Compendium of Insurance Law
Robert Merkin
Johanna Hjalmarsson
(2008)

SYSTEMIC RISK AND THE FUTURE OF INSURANCE REGULATION

Edited by
Andromachi Georgosouli and Miriam Goldby

informa law
from Routledge

First published 2016
by Informa Law from Routledge
2 Park Square, Milton Park, Abingdon, Oxon OX14 4RN

And by Informa Law from Routledge
605 Third Avenue, New York, NY 10017

First issued in paperback 2020

Informa Law from Routledge is an imprint of the Taylor & Francis Group, an Informa business

British Library Cataloguing in Publication Data
A catalogue record for this book is available from the British Library

Library of Congress Cataloguing in Publication Data
A catalogue record for this book has been requested

ISBN 13: 978-0-367-73787-0 (pbk)
ISBN 13: 978-0-415-74467-6 (hbk)

Typeset in Plantin by
Servis Filmsetting Ltd, Stockport, Cheshire

TABLE OF CONTENTS

FOREWORD

It is now over seven years since the start of the financial crisis of 2007/8. We are in a new decade and much has happened since then. We should by now have some sense of remove from the events of that time; perhaps a capacity to put what happened then in perspective. Yet I do not believe that we are there yet. Too many individuals and institutions are still experiencing the fallout – can we truly say that we are out of the shadow of the crisis? As I write this, Greece totters on the edge of leaving the Eurozone and the term Grexit has entered the lexicon to describe the risk that Greece may have to leave the European Union itself. Greece is led by the newly elected anti-austerity party, Syriza, a party which is looking to renegotiate the terms of the bailout offered to that country by the other members of the Union in 2012 after Greece faced bankruptcy. The dramatic challenges faced by Greece owe much to what happened in 2007/8. Other countries such as Spain and Italy also know much of the pain that the Greeks have experienced recently and are watching what will happen with interest. The financial crisis and its consequences are still very much with us.

It is also not difficult to see that the financial crisis is still here in other ways. The world is still awash with Quantitative Easing and other emergency financial measures. We can also note the historically low interest rates and ongoing serious challenges of deficit reduction facing many countries that had to spend heavily during the initial phase of the crisis while now faced with a diminished income from battered economies. These and other problems have led to a significant loss of trust in the banking sector in particular.

Perhaps, then, now is not the time to write the history books but it is never too early to ask what are the lessons we need to learn and this book bravely tackles perhaps one of the most challenging topics now under discussion – systemic risk, with the focus on the implications for insurance regulation.

It is now widely acknowledged that the exposure to systemic risk in the financial sector was underestimated or, I suspect in many cases, not at all appreciated prior to 2007. We all know what it is now. Certainly, we have seen what can happen to the wider system when banks such as Lehmann Brothers fail, as it did in September 2008. It is entirely understandable, therefore, that governments and regulators concluded that work needed to be done to identify and address systemic risk where it was found. To date, the main focus has primarily and rightly been on the banking industry.

But what do we say about systemic risk in insurance? Insurance companies are not the same as banks. AIG aside, we did not see any significant failure of insurance companies during the height of the crisis (and AIG's difficulties anyway arose from its non-insurance activities). Insurers do buy reinsurance and are interconnected in that way, but are they truly as interconnected as the banks? And if insurers fail are there the same risks of dislocation to the financial system or the wider economy? Claims only come in slowly and most insurers that cease underwriting are still more than able to meet their liabilities. Does the failure of an insurance company typically have the knock-on risks that a failing bank can?

The International Association of Insurance Supervisors (IAIS), spurred on by the Financial Stability Board and the G20, has now looked at this and taken forward the thinking on what we mean by systemic risk in insurance and how we identify it. I believe work still needs to be done to ensure that the measures taken to address systemic risk in insurance companies are the right ones. We need to ensure that any measures put in place address the alleged mischief of systematic risk but do not act as an undue drag on companies who themselves have an important role to play in mitigating risk in society. We also need to remain watchful of the risk that insurers will be swept along in regulations that are designed and suitable for the banking sector but which sometimes have the appearance of being applied to insurance as an afterthought or without due regard to the particular features of insurance companies.

We also need to ensure that the processes for setting those rules are transparent, take on board considered and fair criticisms and allow for the proposed regimes to be properly tested before being implemented. We need good regulation; that is in the interest of all concerned. But there are a large number of stakeholders involved and increasingly the rules need to be coordinated at a global level. That makes getting it right all the more difficult. The way to achieve the right outcome is by having open processes with an opportunity for all those with an interest to engage and a willingness by the policy makers to listen to and engage constructively with stakeholders. If we have that then we can have some optimism that the end product will be the right one.

No doubt the co-authors of this book will each have their own perspective on these points and the many other difficult questions that arise. Their insights are set out in the chapters that follow. We should be grateful to them for their contributions as we need the very best thinking in this area to ensure that the right outcomes are achieved. That is the case, whether one agrees with all the views expressed or not. This book may be an academic work but no-one should suggest that these issues are of interest only in the academic sphere. How we address these issues will have a real impact on companies, their employees and stakeholders and the economies in which they operate. Given the list of contributors, I take comfort that we are in safe hands in that regard. The chapters come from individuals with established and well deserved reputations in this field as well as from individuals whose fame I am sure will be assured if their offering in this book is indicative of what is to follow.

I am also pleased to see this volume of essays being published because I hope it will further establish the reputation of the editors and the Centre for Commercial Law Study at Queen Mary, where they are based. The links between CCLS and Lloyd's go back a number of years now and those links have strengthened incrementally over the period and continue to strengthen.

We were also very pleased to see CCLS set up its Insurance Law Institute when it was formed in 2012. While there have always been a number of experts in the field, insurance law as a whole is under-served in academia in the UK with a particular historical dearth of expertise in regulation (a few honourable exceptions aside). Given the importance of the insurance industry to the UK and the comparative strength of academic study in this field in other countries, particularly the US and Germany, the imbalance needed to be corrected. CCLS's Insurance Law Institute plays a part in that.

This book, therefore, has much to offer on an important topic and a topic with real consequences for the future shape of insurance regulation. I am sure the diverse articles in this collection will receive the attention and consideration that they deserve.

Sean McGovern
Chief Risk Officer and General Counsel, Lloyd's

PREFACE

The expressions 'systemic risk' and 'financial stability' have surely never been in more widespread use than in the aftermath of the 2008–2009 crisis. The string of failures and bailouts with which the world was faced during the few fateful months when the crisis reached its peak, and the panic that pervaded financial markets, were unprecedented in recent decades and left the world reeling. Since then much energy and many resources have been devoted to reform designed to prevent a repetition of this crisis. But in this flurry of activity, relatively little (albeit increasing) attention has been paid to the insurance industry. In this book we map developments in this field and we attempt to address the question whether and to what extent the reforms which have taken place following the crisis are sufficient to address systemic risks that may be triggered or exacerbated as a result of the future activities of the insurance sector. Taken together, the contributions that make up this collection attempt to provide a varied and multi-faceted perspective on this highly interesting question and, where appropriate, to make proposals for what may require to be done in the future.

The research that ultimately led to the writing of this book developed from the Centre for Commercial Law Studies' June 2013 Roundtable on 'Systemic Risk and the Future of Insurance Regulation', held in the Old Library at Lloyd's and celebrating the launch of the Centre's Insurance Law Institute. Thus we owe a debt of gratitude to many people who participated in and contributed to the organisation of this event. First among them are the event's sponsors, Lloyd's and Informa to whom we are extremely grateful for their generous support. In particular, Kevin Lazarus at Lloyd's and Rebecca Brennan and Alexia Sutton at Informa were unstinting in their support and encouragement. We would also like to thank all of the speakers at the event, including those who, for various reasons were unable to develop their conference contribution into a chapter for this book. They include:

- Sean McGovern (General Counsel, Lloyd's) who kindly gave the Keynote Speech at the event
- Chris Finney (Partner, Cooley LLP)
- Daniel Haefeli (Head of Insurance and Finance, Geneva Association)
- Professor Rosa Lastra (CCLS)
- John Maroney (IAIS, Principal Administrator)
- Andrew Mawdsley (EIOPA, Head of the Financial Stability and Information Unit)

- Professor Patricia A. McCoy (Liberty Mutual Insurance Professor of Law, Boston College, USA)
- Professor Philip Rawlings (CCLS)
- Professor Steven Schwarcz (Director of the Interdisciplinary Global Capital Markets Center, Duke University, USA) who presented a paper he co-wrote with Professor Daniel Schwarcz (University of Minnesota); and
- John Breckenridge (Manager, Insurance Specialists and Prudential Support, Prudential Regulation Authority).

We would also like to thank Ms Katherine Zaim, Events Manager at CCLS, and Ms Kay Smith, Hospitality and Events Sales Manager at Lloyd's, who provided us with invaluable organisational support for the event.

In addition to Sean McGovern, who kindly agreed to write the Foreword to this book, and Chris Finney, Rosa Lastra, Patricia McCoy, Philip Rawlings and Steven and Daniel Schwarcz, all of whom spoke at the event, we are also very happy to be able to add to the list of contributors to this book, early career researchers Ms Anat Keller and Dr Louise Steinberg, to whom we extend our warm thanks for their contribution.

We are extremely grateful to Alexia at Informa Law from Routledge and also to Joshua Wells, Ashlie Jackman and Paula Divine at Informa for their understanding, patience and assistance.

Andromachi Georgosouli and Miriam Goldby
Centre for Commercial Law Studies, Queen Mary, University of London
February 2015

AUTHORS' BIOGRAPHICAL NOTES

Mr Chris Finney: Chris Finney is a partner in Cooley's Business department in London and he advises insurers, reinsurers, (re)insurance distributors, alternative fund managers, crowd funding platform providers, payment service providers, pay-day lenders and asset managers on UK and European regulatory issues. He is an Independent Adjudicator for the UK Financial Conduct Authority and the High Court sanctioned Card Protection Plan Redress Scheme and he is a member of various professional associations including the City of London Law Society, the City of London Solicitors' Company and the British Insurance Law Association.

Dr Andromachi Georgosouli: Dr Andromachi Georgosouli is a senior lecturer in law at the Centre of Commercial Law Studies QMUL, a member respectively of the Insurance Law Institute and the Institute of Regulation and Ethics at CCLS QMUL, the convenor of the seminar series New Voices in Commercial Law and the yearly Roundtable in Financial Law and Regulation. Prior to joining CCLS in January 2012, she was a lecturer in law at the Law School University of Leicester and Deputy Director of the School's Centre for European Law and Internationalisation. She has written extensively on institutional and policy aspects of the post-crisis reform agenda of financial regulation pertaining to the regulation of the financial network. She has been a regular contributor (upon invitation) to conferences and roundtables in the UK, the USA and more recently in Asia. Currently, she is a research visitor at the George Washington University Law School and at the International Monetary Fund.

Dr Miriam Goldby: Dr Miriam Goldby is a senior lecturer in Shipping, Insurance and Commercial Law, Deputy Director of the Insurance Law Institute, and convenor of the MA by Research programme at the Centre for Commercial Law Studies, QMUL. Prior to joining CCLS she conducted research as a Visiting Scholar at George Washington University in Washington DC, USA. Between September 2007 and December 2010 she held a lectureship post at the University of Surrey where she taught Contract Law, Commercial Law and Banking Law. She read for her PhD degree at University College London where she also held the post of teaching fellow between January 2004 and August 2007, and taught on the LLM Banking Law and LLM International Trade Law courses. She has written extensively on various areas of commercial and financial law, including maritime law, money laundering, and financial regulation.

Ms Anat Keller: Ms Anat Keller is a qualified solicitor, a teaching associate at CCLS, QMUL and a teaching fellow at the Faculty of Law, University College London. She holds an LLM in Corporate and Commercial Law from the London School of Economics and Political Science and she is currently reading for her PhD degree at CCLS under the supervision of Professor Philip Rawlings. Her thesis research provides an analysis of the functioning of the European Systemic Risk Board (ESRB) as the macro-prudential supervisor of the financial system within the EU.

Professor Rosa María Lastra: Professor Rosa María Lastra is a Professor in International Financial and Monetary Law at the Centre for Commercial Law Studies, QMUL. She is a member of Monetary Committee of the International Law Association (MOCOMILA), a founding member of the European Shadow Financial Regulatory Committee (ESFRC), an associate of the Financial Markets Group of the London School of Economics and Political Science, and an affiliated scholar of the Centre for the Study of Central Banks at New York University School of Law. From 2008 to 2010 she was Visiting Professor of the University of Stockholm. She has served as a consultant to the International Monetary Fund, the European Central Bank, the World Bank, the Asian Development Bank and the Federal Reserve Bank of New York. From November 2008 to June 2009 she acted as Specialist Adviser to the European Union Committee (Sub-Committee A) of the House of Lords regarding its Inquiry into EU Financial Regulation and responses to the financial crisis. Prior to coming to London, she was an Assistant Professor of International Banking at Columbia University School of International and Public Affairs in the City of New York (1993–1996). She is the author of several books including *Sovereign Debt Management* (Oxford University Press, 2014, co-edited), *International Law in Financial Regulation and Monetary Affairs* (Oxford University Press, 2012, co-edited), *Cross-Border Bank Insolvency* (Oxford University Press, 2011, edited), *Legal Foundation of International Monetary Stability* (Oxford University Press, 2006, authored), *Central Banking and Banking Regulation* (FMG of the LSE, 1996, authored), *The Reform of the International Financial Architecture* (Kluwer, 2001, edited) and *Bank Failures and Bank Insolvency Law in Economies in Transition* (Kluwer, 1999, co-edited), and the author of numerous articles in internationally refereed journals.

Professor Patricia A. McCoy: Professor Patricia A. McCoy is the inaugural Liberty Mutual Insurance Professor of Law at the Boston College Law School in Boston, USA and before joining the Boston College Faculty, she was the Director of the Insurance Law Centre at the University of Connecticut School of Law. In 2010 and 2011, she joined the US Department of the Treasury, where she helped form the new Consumer Financial Protection Bureau (CFPB), and, as the CFPB's first assistant director for mortgage markets, oversaw the Bureau's mortgage policy initiatives. After receiving her law degree from UC Berkeley, Professor McCoy clerked for the late Hon Robert S Vance on the US Court of Appeals for the Eleventh Circuit and was a partner at Mayer Brown in Washington, DC, specialising in complex securities, banking and constitutional litigation. Professor McCoy's research interests focus on the nexus between financial products, consumer welfare, and systemic risk, analysed through the lens of law, economics, and empirical methods. In 'A Tale of Three Markets: The Law and Economics of Predatory Lending' in the *Texas Law Review* in 2002, Professor McCoy was among the first to raise alarms about the dangers of subprime loans. She has three books to her credit, the most recent being *The Subprime Virus* with Kathleen Engel, published by Oxford University Press in 2011. The author of numerous book chapters and articles, she has testified before Congress and been quoted in the *New York Times*, *Wall Street Journal*, and *The Washington Post* and on National Public Radio. Previously, Professor McCoy was a Visiting Scholar at the MIT Economics Department and served on the Federal Reserve's Consumer Advisory Council and on the board of the Insurance Marketplace Standards Association. In 2012, the American Law Institute named her as an Adviser to the Third Restatement on Consumer Contracts. She currently sits on the Advisory Committee on Economic Inclusion of the Federal Deposit Insurance Corporation.

Professor Philip Rawlings: Professor Philip Rawlings is the inaugural Roy Goode Professor of Commercial Law and Director of the Insurance Law Institute at CCLS. He is a member of the committee of the British Insurance Law Association, of the editorial boards for the journals *International Corporate Rescue* and *Journal of Financial Perspectives*, and of the advisory board for Palgrave Macmillan's Corporate and Finance Law series of books. He is also a member of the Institute of International Financial Law at CCLS. Before joining CCLS in 2011 he was Professor of the Law of Finance at University College London. Previously, he held posts at the University of Warwick, Brunel University and Aberystwyth University. He has been Visiting Professor at Université Panthéon-Assas (Paris II), and is an associate of the Chartered Institute of Bankers (now the IFS). He is a contributing editor to *Benjamin's Sale of Goods* (8th edition, Sweet & Maxwell, 2011) and he is the author/co-author of more than ten books and 50 papers on, among other things, the law of insurance, banking and sales, as well as on legal history and criminal justice. Among his books are: *Insurance Law: Doctrines and Principles* (3rd edition, Hart, 2011, with Lowry and Merkin); *Insurance Law: Cases and Materials* (Hart, 2004, with Lowry); *Policing: A Short History* (Willan, 2002); and *Crime and Power* (Longman, 1999). Among current research projects are papers on the history of insurance regulation in the UK, on cyber insurance and on fraudulent insurance claims, along with continuing responsibility for the first three chapters of *Benjamin's Sale of Goods*.

Professor Daniel Schwarcz: Professor Daniel Schwarcz is an Associate Professor of Law and a Solly Robins Distinguished Research Fellow at the University of Minnesota School of Law. His research primarily focuses on consumer protection and regulation in property/casualty and health insurance markets. His articles have been published, or accepted for publication, in the *University of Chicago Law Review*, *Virginia Law Review*, *Minnesota Law Review*, *North Carolina Law Review*, *William and Mary Law Review*, and *Tulane Law Review*. Additionally, he is the editor of a book entitled, *The Law and Economics of Insurance* and recently joined the casebook, *Abraham's Insurance Law and Regulation*. In 2011, his article, 'Reevaluating Standardized Insurance Policies', received the Liberty Mutual Prize for an exceptional article on insurance law and regulation. Professor Schwarcz serves as a Funded Consumer Representative to the National Association of Insurance Commissioners and has served as an expert witness in multiple insurance-related disputes. Professor Schwarcz earned his AB, *magna cum laude*, from Amherst College and his JD, *magna cum laude*, from Harvard Law School. He clerked for Judge Sandra Lynch on the United States Court of Appeals for the First Circuit and practiced at the law firm Ropes & Gray. He subsequently spent two years as a Climenko Fellow and Lecturer on Law at Harvard Law School.

Professor Steven L. Schwarcz: Professor Steven L. Schwarcz is the Stanley A. Star Professor of Law & Business at Duke University and Founding Director of Duke's interdisciplinary Global Capital Markets Centre (now renamed the Global Financial Markets Centre). His areas of research and scholarship include insolvency and bankruptcy law; international finance, capital markets, and systemic risk; and commercial law. He holds a bachelor's degree in aerospace engineering (*summa cum laude*) and a Juris Doctor from Columbia Law School. Prior to joining the Duke faculty, he was a partner at two leading international law firms where he represented top banks and other financial institutions in structuring innovative capital market financing transactions, both domestic and international. He is the author of numerous peer-refereed articles and his book *Structured Finance, A Guide to the Principles of Asset Securitization* (3rd edition) helped pioneer the field of asset securitization and is one of the most widely used in this field. Professor Schwarcz has been the Leverhulme Visiting Professor at the University of Oxford, Visiting Professor at the University of Geneva Faculty of Law, Senior Fellow at The University of Melbourne Law School, and an adviser to the United Nations. He has given numerous endowed or distinguished public lectures, including at The University of Hong Kong, the University of Oxford (the Leverhulme Lectures 2010) and Georgetown University Law Centre. He has served as an expert at meetings of the World Economic Forum. He also has given numerous keynote speeches, including at annual conferences of the European Central Bank and the Asian Securitisation Forum. Additionally, Professor Schwarcz has testified before the US Congress on topics including systemic risk, securitisation, credit rating agencies, and financial regulation and has advised several US and foreign governmental agencies on the financial crisis and shadow banking. He is a Fellow of the American College of Bankruptcy, a Founding Member of the International Insolvency Institute, a Fellow of the American College of Commercial Finance Lawyers, Business Law Advisor to the American Bar Association Section on Business Law, and Senior Fellow of The Centre for International Governance Innovation (CIGI).

Dr Louise Steinberg: Dr Louise Steinberg is a teaching associate at CCLS, QMUL and a member of the Centre's Insurance Law Institute. She holds a PhD in Insurance Regulation from King's College and an LLM in Banking Law and International Financial Regulation from University College London. Since being admitted as a solicitor in 1990 she has practised commercial law at Freshfields and Clifford Chance. She is a member of the British Insurance Law Association and the Financial Services Lawyers Association.

TABLE OF CASES

TABLE OF STATUTES AND CONVENTIONS

United Kingdom

United States

European Union

Treaties

Regulations

International Instruments

CHAPTER 1

Introduction

The increasingly complicated nature of financial markets means that we are more than ever exposed to the adverse consequences of shocks and crises.[1] This was the case about eight years ago when the financial crisis started; this is the case even today after five years of reform. Of course, a difference between now and then is that we have become more sophisticated in our understanding of how the financial system behaves and how to respond to it. But the fact remains that there are limitations on what we can actually do. For example, an advanced legal framework for the regulation of systemic risk is already in place, but the attempt to anticipate risk is inherently futile, as certain types of risk cannot actually be foreseen. This claim is hardly new. In the field of economics, Frank Knight was the first to note the difference between risk and uncertainty as early as 1921.[2] Situations involving risk are those in which it is possible to assign a probability to the occurrence of a hazardous event in the future. Situations of uncertainty are those in which no such assignation is possible. Financial regulation is concerned with both situations. For example, financial crises are recurring events: we know that they are coming but we do not know how and when.[3]

This book attempts to provide a discussion of policy developments that have been occurring in the field of financial regulation, in particular macroprudential policy and its significance for the insurance sector. While much has been written on recent developments in financial regulation, including macroprudential policy in general, not much attention has been paid to the implications of this wave of regulatory reform for the insurance industry and markets. Insurance regulation as a whole is an area that has not been sufficiently explored and this book represents an effort to begin to address this gap in the academic literature. Addressing this gap is particularly important in view of the immense importance of the insurance sector to Western economies.

Within the context of recent reforms, the received wisdom on the regulation of insurance has begun to face challenges. The bailout of a large international financial conglomerate, American International Group (AIG), by the United States Federal Reserve drew attention to one way in which insurers' activities can be significant

1 S. Schwarcz, 'Regulating complexity in financial markets' (2010) 87(2) *Washington Law Review* 2011 (arguing that complexity is one of the major challenges for financial regulation).

2 F. Knight, *Risk, Uncertainty and Profit* (New York: Harper and Row, 1965 copyright 1921).

3 R. Shiller, *Finance and the Good Society* (Princeton: Princeton University Press, 2012) 11–112. [AQ Number span ok?]

contributors to systemic risk.[4] The dissection of AIG's crisis has formed the underlying narrative of the reforms to insurance regulation that have been suggested and adopted following the crisis. Part of the purpose of this book is to examine these reforms, focusing specifically on reform adoption and implementation programmes in the EU and UK as well as the US, and to provide some commentary on how they might contribute to reaching the goal of financial stability. But bearing in mind that no crisis is ever identical to the ones that preceded it, this book also attempts to look beyond the insurance industry's past role as a contributor to systemic risk and to focus also on how insurance business is evolving and what its role might be in the future.

The reform of insurance regulation has been the subject of controversy for quite some time. A key driver of the reform has been the need to maintain financial stability by taking better control of systemic risk.[5] Although there is a general consensus in favour of measures that aim to ensure a stable financial system, there is a lot of debate as to whether the insurance business is actually systemic. The book aims to shed light on the interface between systemic risk and the nature of the insurance business and to offer a critical and engaging analysis of what this interaction is telling us about the rationale and merits of the reform currently shaping the future of insurance regulation. Accordingly, the book focuses on insurance regulation but it approaches its subject matter from macro-prudential and systemic-risk perspective. It is not the purpose of this volume to offer a comprehensive comparison between insurance and banking and securities regulation. Similarly, a comparative analysis of the EU/UK and the US regimes falls beyond the scope of this volume, although some comparative elements are considered to the extent that such consideration advances the aims of the discussion.

The book was conceived as an edited collection including contributions from speakers and other participants in the Centre for Commercial Law Studies' June 2013 Roundtable on 'Systemic Risk and the Future of Insurance Regulation', held at Lloyd's and celebrating the launch of the Centre's Insurance Law Institute. The speakers and participants who have contributed to this book come from academia and legal practice. Their diverse backgrounds and years of experience have given us a rich and multi-textural approach to the topic, ensuring the consideration of many different perspectives. We are immensely grateful to all contributors and we hope that the result is a rounded understanding of this very important topic, which is bound to generate much interest and attention in the coming years.

Philip Rawlings's chapter, 'What can history tell us about insurance regulation?' gives the historical background to insurance regulation while attempting to analyse the raison d'être behind its flaws and shortcomings. Typically, discussions of the history of regulation simply provide a chronology of responses to different crises and pay no attention to the pre-regulatory era or the compromises or dead ends when proposals were rejected or the silences when a problem did not lead to regulation.

---

4 See, e.g., W. K. Sjostrom, Jr, 'The AIG Bailout' (2009) 6 *Washington and Lee Law Review* 943 and S. E. Harrington, 'The Financial Crisis, Systemic Risk, and the Future of Insurance Regulation' (2009) 76(4) *Journal of Risk and Insurance* 785.

5 See notably, A. Turner, *Economics After the Crisis – Objectives and Means* (Cambridge MA: MIT Press, 2012).

What history can tell us is that regulation involves negotiation over the existence and nature of the problem and the response, including whether anything needs to be done, or, indeed, can be done. This is shaped by the intellectual context and the available material resources: what is it possible to think and do in light of contemporary ideas about the economy and the proper role of government and the financial and bureaucratic resources available? Even those whose interest is solidly in the here and now can find, in a study of the history, an insight into how change occurs; insurance regulation provides a particularly good laboratory because its history stretches back to the sixteenth century.

Rosa María Lastra's chapter 'Macro-prudential supervision, systemic risk and insurance companies' gives an introductory examination and analysis of systemic risk and the related concept of macroprudential policy and supervision. Ongoing discussions are trying to identify the powers and instruments macroprudential authorities should have. Given the lack of a commonly accepted theoretical paradigm on the definition of systemic risk, this is no easy task. Systemic risk refers to the risk or probability of breakdown of the entire financial system, as opposed to breakdowns in individual parts or components. But a widely accepted definition is still missing. All classes of financial intermediaries, markets and infrastructures can be systemically important at some level. Any risk (not just credit risk but liquidity risk, interest rate risk, exchange rate risk, etc.) can grow to systemic proportions when its negative impact extends beyond an individual institution. It will then affect or threaten to affect by contagion other institutions, often creating a disruption in the monetary or financial system and, depending on the severity of the downturn, eventually mutate into economic paralysis (halt in production). What makes a crisis systemic in nature has generally been understood as being not so much the trigger event (*causa proxima*) but the transmission mechanisms, domestically and internationally. If the linkages are strong, the potential for systemic instability increases. The ability of the financial system to withstand unforeseen shocks is recognised by many economists and central banks as the key indicator of financial stability, and macro-prudential policy and supervision has been viewed as an essential ingredient towards enhancing this ability.[6] The chapter explains the challenges inherent in the effective development of macro-prudential policy and its implementation, as well as its significance for the effective regulation of insurance companies. Many of the issues raised are developed in greater depth in subsequent chapters.

In Chapter 4, 'Systemic risk in insurance: common thinking errors and their resolution', Chris Finney observes that while many insurance market professionals do not believe that insurance and insurers are systemic or that the near collapse of AIG is sufficient to justify the sweeping changes that are being made to the way insurance and insurers are regulated, policymakers clearly have the opposite view.

6 This ability of the financial system to 'withstand' is currently enshrined in the concept of resilience that is attached to several definitions of the financial stability. See, for instance, G. Shinasi, Defining Financial Stability (Washington DC: IMF Working Paper WP/04/187) and A. Clarke and A. Large, Macroprudential Policy: Addressing the Things We Don't Know (Washington: G-30 Occasional Working Paper No. 83, 2011). For a comprehensive discussion of the correlation of stability and resilience as attributes of the financial system, see A. Georgosouli, 'Financial Resilience' (CCLS, Working Paper April 2014 unpublished).

He uses AIG as a case study to analyse whether the instincts of insurance market professionals are right. The chapter draws attention to some of the flaws in the regulatory narrative, which have allowed or encouraged professional perceptions to differ to the extent that is apparent in the markets today. It is at least possible that the thinking errors described in this chapter have two causes: (a) a misunderstanding of '*operational risk*'; and (b) communication by policymakers and insurance regulators that has been so poor that it has failed to engage and persuade insurance market professionals. If policymakers really want to prevent '*another*' AIG, and they really want to protect consumers from the '*operational risks*' inherent in the insurance business, they are more likely to achieve their objectives if operational risk is properly understood and mitigated. They are more likely to achieve that, if insurance market professionals have a better understanding of the regulatory narrative than policymakers have managed to deliver so far. If that is right, it seems to suggest that a coherent regulatory approach to, and a clearer and more consistent regulatory narrative about, systemic risk in insurance is desirable, if not essential. It also seems to suggest that regulators have a lot more work to do before moving on.

Seeking to go beyond the lessons to be learnt from the past, Daniel Schwarcz and Steven L. Schwarcz, in their chapter 'Anticipating new sources of systemic risk in insurance', point out that, to date, much of the analysis of systemic risk in insurance has focused on the particular role of insurers in the recent financial crisis, assuming this experience represents the only pattern by which insurance might contribute to or trigger systemic risk. However, such a historically bound, narrow perspective, is exactly what caused regulators and policymakers to overlook the partly unprecedented pattern of events leading to that crisis. They argue that the dynamic nature of the insurance industry and its regulation, as well as the increasing complexities and interconnections of finance and insurance, can potentiate systemic risk in novel and unexpected ways, and that insurers' interlinkages to the larger financial system and their potential vulnerability to tail-end events are not simply the product of individual firms, that are 'too big to fail' such as AIG. Instead, there exist pervasive correlations among individual insurance companies in their financial strategies, product design, and risk mitigation strategies, among others. These correlations stem from common economic features of insurance, insurance regulatory restrictions that apply to insurers, shared suppositions and strategies that are embedded within the culture of insurance executives and managers, and rational herding behaviour among firms. Whatever their source, these correlations mean that the insurance industry and its activities can distort markets in non-obvious ways which substantially contribute to systemic risk. Ultimately, these conclusions suggest the need for a regulatory structure that is adapted to anticipating, measuring, and mitigating existing and newly emerging sources of systemic risk in insurance.

In a similar vein, Miriam Goldby and Anat Keller, in Chapter 6, 'Oversight of systemically relevant insurance practices within the EU: the role of macro prudential supervision', attempt to identify examples of emerging EU-wide trends and practices in the insurance industry which have the potential, in future, to cause systemic complications. They argue that in order to achieve the aims of macro-prudential supervision, practices prevalent in the insurance sector which increase interconnectedness and common exposures, thereby constituting a potential source of systemic risk, need to be addressed. Taking as a case study the European Systemic Risk Board, the prime example of a macro-prudential supervisory body that has cross-border competence, and therefore the ability, in theory, to address trends that transcend national boundaries which may threaten financial stability, the chapter attempts to assess the extent to which macro-prudential supervisory bodies set up in the wake of the recent crisis are equipped to address such risks.

Patricia A. McCoy's chapter, 'Stealth federal regulation of insurance in the United States' examines the ESRB's counterpart in the US, the Financial Stability Oversight Council (FSOC), and provides an assessment of the inroads it is making into the past model of insurance regulation in the US, which has always been largely state-based. This model has been remarkably enduring to date, in part because the traditional rationales for a greater federal role – consisting of efficiency, solvency and consumer protection concerns – have not succeeded in overcoming state regulation. However, the 2008 financial crisis, the federal government's bailouts to the insurance sector, and the need for a coordinated international approach to containing systemic risk changed the terms of the state versus federal regulation debate to the detriment of the states. As a result, the federal government is making new inroads into insurance regulation in the areas of international cooperation and systemic risk. As this chapter discusses, FSOC has embraced two different models of systemic risk, including a vague, unconventional and highly expansive second model, in its insurance company systematically important financial institution designations to date. To the extent that FSOC continues to expand and build on that novel theory of systemic risk, the federal government is likely to become more immersed in solvency standards for the insurance industry generally, particularly for internationally active US insurers and groups.

The discussion takes an international turn, in the next chapter ('The emerging special recovery and resolution framework of G-SIIs and its effectiveness'), where Andromachi Georgosouli examines the effectiveness of the Insurance Resolution Framework (IRF) for Systemically Important Insurance firms with global presence. The chapter draws attention to some difficulties of the envisaged IRF and makes preliminary recommendations on how some of them might be addressed. In particular, the discussion focuses on: (a) the International Association of Insurance Supervisors (IAIS) designation criteria; (b) the ongoing resolvability assessments; (c) the limitations of the Recovery and Resolution Plans; (d) some challenging aspects of the mandatory bail-ins for G-SIIs; (e) issues concerning international coordination and information sharing; and (f) the provision of Insurance Guarantee Schemes as an instrument for the containment of systemic risk triggers in the insurance sector. The exploration of the likely effectiveness of the IRF brings to the surface a range of factors that bear on the orderly recovery and resolution of insurers in general and G-SIIs in particular, most notably the level of competition in specific insurance sectors and the features of certain insurance contracts. For example, in relation to the latter, Georgosouli argues the expediency of reintroducing mandatory restrictions on the relaxation of withdrawal barriers is worthy of consideration at least in relation to certain types of insurance contracts as a tool that promises to guard the insurance industry from runs akin to bank runs. Other key themes that emerge from the analysis and which also impact on the effectiveness of the

IRF include the optimal level of administrative discretion, its bearing on standard setting, the importance of having in place a comprehensive system of data resource management at a global level, and the key role of culture and cognitive challenge in improving situational awareness under circumstances of uncertainty.

Continuing on the international theme, Chapter 9 on 'The international regulation of systemic risk: the role of the leading international organizations, groups and standard-setting bodies in shaping the post-crisis reform of insurance regulation', by Louise Steinberg, considers the role of international organisations, groups and standard-setting bodies in framing the regulations that apply to insurance market participants across nation states, particularly those designed to address systemic risk. As systemic risk manifested itself across financial markets in the 2008/2009 financial crisis, an international regulatory response was necessary and the G20 has taken the lead in efforts to design and coordinate this response. With the support of the FSB, the IMF and the IAIS in particular, the G20 has shaped a regulatory reform programme designed to effect legislative and regulatory changes across member states and beyond. The relationships between and among these organisations and groupings afford an insight into how laws regulating financial markets are made internationally and applied domestically by individual nation states.

CHAPTER 2

What can history tell us about insurance regulation?

Philip Rawlings

2.1 Why history?

Governments seem as addicted to the regulation of financial services as smokers are to cigarettes – perhaps more so since there is at least the prospect of weaning smokers off their dependence. Might history allow us to understand this addiction? The history of regulation is generally seen as an interesting (or not) introduction to the main issues of describing and discussing current regulation, and it is, therefore, reduced to a simple chronology, which tells us little. A more nuanced history may allow us to understand something about why regulation takes a particular form and why it changes. It should, at least, enable us to take a step back. Regulation typically involves negotiation over the existence and nature of the problem and the response, including whether anything is thought necessary or feasible. All of this is shaped by the intellectual context and the available material resources: what is it possible to think and do in light of contemporary ideas about the economy and the proper role of government and the available financial and bureaucratic resources?

2.2 Regulation in the early modern period

Regulation of insurance in England began with attempts in the sixteenth and seventeenth centuries to introduce registration of policies, establish jurisdiction over disputes and to set down a code of insurance law. These initiatives were driven by the desire to generate revenue and by conflicts between different courts and between lawyers and merchants anxious to wrest control over an increasingly lucrative source of litigation.[1] In the eighteenth century the state's spiralling appetite for funds to finance a series of wars led to regulations requiring underwriters and brokers to document insurance in ways that allowed the imposition of stamp duty.[2] Obviously, this legislation yielded revenue and, as a by-product, stipulated certain contractual formalities, but it also acknowledged the size and importance of the market. Two other developments – the South Sea Act 1720 and the law on insurable interest – demonstrate how the state began to recognise in the eighteenth

1 V Barbour, 'Marine Risk and Insurance in the Seventeenth Century' (1929) 1(4) *Journal of Economic and Business History* 561; D Ibbetson, 'Law and Custom: Insurance in Sixteenth-century England' (2008) 29 JLH 291; CG Lewin, *Pensions and Insurance before 1800: A Social History*, East Linton: Tuckwell Press, 2003, chap. 5.

2 For a summary, M Hopkins, *A Manual of Marine Insurance*, London, 1867, 89–104.

century that insurance could play a role in public policy and that this justified regulation.

The South Sea Act 1720 was passed during a period of intense financial speculation with the aim not of stopping that speculation but of channelling the flood of capital into certain companies by banning any new joint-stock companies, unless incorporated by royal charter or Act of Parliament (s. 18).[3] The Royal Exchange Assurance and the London Assurance were both granted royal charters and the Act privileged them further by prohibiting other corporations, societies and partnerships from offering marine insurance (s. 12). The companies secured their advantages with a promise, embodied in the statute, to pay £300,000 to the Crown. But the Act presented the restriction on competition as a benefit to policyholders because it would allow the establishment of properly capitalised insurers which would improve the resilience of the market and remove the uncertainty over the payment of claims that supposedly existed. Two provisions appeared to reinforce these aims. Under the first the Royal and the London were required to 'cause such a stock of ready money to be provided and reserved, as shall be sufficient to answer, from time to time, all just demands upon their policies of assurance for any losses whatsoever which shall happen' (s. 4). The second was that if a claim was not paid the policyholder could sue in debt for double damages secured on the relevant company's assets.[4] However, the lack of monitoring and enforcement mechanisms meant these provisions bore no fruit. Moreover, while the Act prevented the formation of new marine insurance companies for more than 100 years, it did not result in the Royal and the London cornering the market because individual underwriters could still issue policies (s. 12), which allowed them to continue their domination of marine insurance, far outstripping the Royal and the London. This was no accident. The subscription market was well established, which meant there were vested interests, but, more importantly, the country's economic and military dependence on shipping led the Attorney General and the Solicitor General to warn that 'the Experiment in a thing of this Nature, if it should prove amiss, would be of the utmost Consequence to the Trade of this Nation'.[5]

The other major theme of eighteenth-century insurance legislation involved regulation of the contract and, in particular, the requirement that policyholders have an interest in the insured subject matter. In part this arose out of the state's military ambitions, but it was also rooted in what could broadly be called the

3 The Act did not affect existing companies: 6 Geo. I c18; J Carswell, *The South Sea Bubble*, London: Cressett Press, 1960; HJ Paul, *The South Sea Bubble: An Economic History of its Origins and Consequences*, Abingdon: Routledge, 2011. The idea that the Act responded to the bursting of the bubble persists: *R (On the application of the Project Management Institute) v Minister for the Cabinet Office* [2014] EWHC 2438 (Admin) at [2].

4 Repealed 8 Geo I c 15; s. 25, 21 Geo I c 20, s. 43. See J Lowry and PJ Rawlings, 'Insurers, Claims and the Boundaries of Good Faith' [2005] MLR 82.

5 *Special Report from the Committee Appointed to Inquire into, and Examine the several Subscriptions for Fisheries, Insurances, Annuities for Lives, and all other Projects carried on by Subscription*, London, 1720, 28. Mutual associations of shipowners (early P & I clubs) were largely unhindered by the Act where they did not involve members carrying liability for non-payment by other members. They expanded rapidly when premiums rose during the Napoleonic Wars in the early 1800s: *Report; with minutes of evidence, and accounts, from the Select Committee on Marine Insurance*, 1810 (226), 8, 55–57. Compare *Harrison v Miller* (1796) 2 Esp 513 with *Lees v Smith* (1797) 7 TR 338.

professionalisation of insurance. The legislation registered a distinction between insurance and gaming, but it is worth noting that the courts had already engaged in this area. Wagers were enforceable at common law, except if they involved gaming prohibited by statute or were contrary to morality or public policy,[6] but the courts distinguished them from insurance on the basis of the nature of the contract and the intentions of the parties: 'Policies of insurance are of two sorts; either upon interest, or by way of wager. Where it is upon interest, it has been solemnly determined that it is merely a contract of indemnity, and therefore ought to be so framed that the party can only recover in case of a loss really sustained, and to the precise amount of that loss.'[7] In addition, public policy considerations reinforced the requirement of an insurable interest, at least in respect of property insurance. In a case concerning fire insurance, Lord Hardwicke explained in 1743, 'If the insured was not to have a property at the time of the insurance or loss, any one might insure upon another's house, which might have a bad tendency to burning houses.'[8] A few years later, Lord Mansfield agreed: 'This rule was calculated to prevent fraud; lest the temptation of gain should occasion unfair and wilful losses.'[9] It is also worth noting that some insurers developed their own insurable interest requirements: early life schemes seem to have been constructed largely around the idea that benefits would go to relatives, and it was one of the terms of life policies issued by The Society of Equitable Assurances on Lives and Survivorship in 1762.[10]

Parliament intervened in insurable interest through the Marine Insurance Act 1746 and the Life Assurance Act 1774. Writers have largely taken at face value the explanations given in these statutes that they were reactions to moral outrage at gaming, but closer examination of the legislation suggests a rather more complex reasoning. Neither statute adopted the simple expedient of prohibiting gaming contracts. Both required an insurable interest, but their treatment of the issue is not comprehensive and there is no clear definition of insurable interest. Indeed, these statutes could be said to have muddied this area. The courts appeared to be developing a general requirement of insurable interest (at least in property insurance), but the legislation referred to particular types of insurance, raising the question as to whether an insurable interest was required in those policies not mentioned in the legislation.[11] The 1746 Act stated, first, that certain maritime risks (broadly those involving British marine adventures) could only be covered if there were an insurable interest, and, second, that other risks (broadly those involving foreign marine risks) could be covered without an insurable interest. This rather undermines the gaming explanation, but the reasons for the distinction become clearer when it is realised that the Act was passed in the middle of a largely naval war and

6 *Da Costa v Jones* (1778) 2 Cowp 729, 734. For early decisions to the contrary: *Goodart v Garrett* (1692) 2 Vern 269; JA Park, *System of the Law of Marine Insurances* (6th edn), London, 1809, 346–347. For legislation, see, e.g., 9 Ann c 14; *Jones v Randall* (1774) 1 Cowp 37, 39.

7 *Kulen Kemp v Vigne* (1786) 1 TR 304, 309, Buller J.

8 *Sadlers' Company v Badcock* (1743) 1 Wils KB 10. See also, *Lynch v Dalzell* (1729) 4 Bro PC 431.

9 *Godin v London Assurance Co* (1758) 1 Burr 489, 492.

10 ER Mores, *A Short Account of the Society for Equitable Assurances on Lives and Survivorships; Established by Deed*, London, 1762, 21 (rule VI).

11 E.g. there was no insurable interest in *Carter v Boehm* (1766) 3 Burr 1905, which established the duty of utmost good faith.

was regarded as being of assistance in that struggle.[12] It was believed – following the sort of argument put forward by Hardwicke and Mansfield – that encouraging insurance without insurable interest rendered foreign shipping more vulnerable to barratry.[13] The usual explanation for the 1774 Act is that it was the result of outrage at *Earl of March v Pigot*,[14] which involved betting on the lives of people, but there had been criticism for at least 25 years of this form of gambling, the Act was rushed through in two months in 1774, which was three years after the case, the jury and the King's Bench (including Lord Mansfield) enforced the wager without apparent comment, and one struggles to find expressions of outrage concerning this case in contemporary newspapers. The better explanation is that the 1774 Act was a reaction to another financial bubble which burst to spectacular effect in 1772–1773.[15] Nevertheless, it was doubtless influenced by the wish to separate insurance from the moral criticism associated with gaming and can be seen as part of a broader professonalisation in the market, alongside developments such as the creation of a membership structure at Lloyd's, greater emphasis on risk calculation particularly in the burgeoning fire and life markets and in judicial recognition of the duty of disclosure, and the proliferation of texts on insurance practice and insurance law.

2.3 A change of focus

There were criticisms of the restrictions imposed by the 1720 Act, particularly as rising premiums during the long war with France (1793–1815) made this market more attractive to investors and more burdensome to merchants. Nevertheless, the Act survived until 1824–1825.[16] The delay was because of opposition from vested interests, including the Royal, the London and Lloyd's, and because many were unconvinced of the benefits of a free market – the disastrous South Sea Bubble and more recently the crash of 1772–1773 were still part of the collective memory.[17] Reform eventually came with the coincidence of an economic boom and a government that favoured a freer market. Greater prosperity also brought rapid growth in non-marine insurance, particularly life insurance, with more than 400 offices opening in the first half of the nineteenth century and total cover growing fifteenfold.[18] But this prompted concern over the stability of some of these companies and fears of fraud, which seemed to have been realised when the promoters of the

12 G Clark, 'Insurance as an Instrument of War in the 18th Century' (2004) 29(2) *The Geneva Papers on Risk and Insurance* 247.

13 There was inconsistency in that insurance without interest could be taken out on British privateers (vessels engaged in war but commissioned by private persons) probably because it was believed this would encourage people to undertake such ventures. The other controversy was that London insurers were allowed to insure enemy ships because, it was argued, a prohibition would drive business to rival centres: *Commons Journal*, 6 Apr 1741, 700. Lord Hardwicke (*obiter*) thought the practice was not illegal: *Henkle v Royal Exchange Assurance Co* (1749) 1 Ves Sen 317, 320; *Planche v Fletcher* (1779) 1 Dougl 251, 253–254; N Magens, *An Essay on Insurances*, London, 1755, vol. 1, 28. This practice was not contrary to common law until *Furtado v Rogers* (1802) 3 Bos & Pul 191, 198.

14 (1771) 5 Burr 2802.

15 See PJ Rawlings, 'The Confused History of Insurance Regulation', forthcoming.

16 Marine Assurance Act 1824 (5 Geo IV c114).

17 J Marryat, *Observations upon the Report of the Committee on Marine Insurance*, London, 1810, 61.

18 TL Alborn, *Regulated Lives: Life Insurance and British Society, 1800–1914*, Toronto: University of Toronto Press, 2009, 20, 22, 53.

Independent and West Middlesex Assurance vanished in 1841 with £250,000. The subsequent Gladstone inquiry concluded that defects in the law needed to be addressed 'for the furtherance of the system of Life Assurance, so important to the well-being of the nation at large',[19] but the Joint-Stock Companies Act 1844 was concerned with general company structure and not the particular problems of insurance. While the statute made it easier to form such companies,[20] it did little to address the problem of the separation between ownership and management which allowed managers to pursue their own interests rather than those of their shareholders or policyholders.

The failure of the Sea, Fire and Life Assurance Company in 1850 brought a demand for a fresh inquiry from James Wilson, later Financial Secretary to the Treasury in the Earl of Aberdeen's government. He emphasised the importance of life assurance and argued that this and its special nature justified regulation.

> 'He knew of nothing in the history of modern inventions, or in the progress of modern ingenuity, which, in a social point of view, was of greater importance than the establishment of these offices, calculated, as they were, to win the people to provident habits, and to present an easy and facile mode of making a provision for those who came after them'.[21]

Since the life business involved individuals, who were 'actuated by the best feelings of human nature', making provision for others, the companies were 'a sacred trust for the future'.[22] Moreover, Wilson pointed out that life companies were major investors, holding around £150 million in capital and receiving annual premiums of £5 million: 'those funds which were accumulated for the benefit of private individuals became in the meantime useful instruments of public utility.'[23] He argued that the 1844 Act had been abused by promoters drawing in subscribers without any intention of going further than the provisional stage of registration.[24] The accounts required by the Act were largely worthless in relation to life companies because they did not show whether there were sufficient assets to meet liabilities that might not arise for several years.[25]

The report of the committee, which Wilson chaired, proposed that new life companies should deposit £10,000 to show good faith and provide security to policyholders, and that life companies should be obliged 'to make such annual returns, and ... afford such other tests as could be given without an undue interference with

19 *First Report of the Select Committee on Joint Stock Companies; together with the minutes of evidence (taken in 1841 and 1843), appendix and index*, 1844 (119), vii. Generally, R Harris, *Industrialising English Law: Entrepreneurship and Business Organisation, 1720–1844*, Cambridge: Cambridge University Press, 2000.

20 The 1720 Act did not prevent the formation of companies, but made them unwieldy and created uncertainty around the legal rights and liabilities of 'shareholders'.

21 Commons Debates, 8 Mar 1853, vol. 124, c. 1321. Also, R Vincent, *Life Assurance as bearing on Social Economy*, London, 1850.

22 *Ibid*, cc. 1323–24.

23 Commons Debates, 8 Mar 1853, vol. 124, c. 1321. Thomas Sotherton MP estimated capital of £350 million: *ibid*, c. 1332. Most investment was in government securities, mortgages and loans on personal security to policyholders: Commons Debates, 15 Jun 1813, c. 643; *Drake v Symes* (1859) John 647, 649; *Life Assurance Companies: Statements of Account and of Life Assurance and Annuity Business*, HC 273 (1884–85), 276.

24 Commons Debates, 8 Mar 1853, vol. 124, cc. 1327–28, 1323.

25 *Ibid*, c. 1331, Thomas Chambers MP.

their business, for the purpose of securing one safe and uniform system, by which a reasonable security may be afforded for the respectability and solvency of Insurance Companies'.[26] These proposals came to nothing.[27] The report did not provide a clear idea about the form the accounts should take, but, more importantly, opinion remained divided as to the role of the state (if any) in business and in protecting individuals. Indeed, for some, the failure of insurers demonstrated the effectiveness of the market,[28] and obliged policyholders to exercise care: 'every man must look after his own affairs, for they could not be safely left to any one else.'[29]

2.4 The Life Assurance Companies Act 1870

While fraudulent insurers may have attracted most of the attention, by emphasising the importance of the life sector, the Wilson committee raised broader questions about the resilience of companies and the nature of the information available to policyholders and, in so doing, challenged the effectiveness of market discipline. Yet, it took another scandal to produce legislation. This time it was difficult to ignore because it involved one of the largest life companies in the world, the Albert Life Assurance Company, which failed in 1869. Another huge company, the European Assurance Society, was also on the brink, eventually collapsing in 1871.[30] The earlier scandals that had led to the Gladstone and Wilson committees involved smaller companies and had principally affected shareholders, whereas the failure of the Albert and the European threatened confidence among policyholders in the life market. Both had expanded through acquisitions – between them taking over 69 life offices – a strategy that often involved the payment of large sums to shareholders of target companies and was driven less by the quality of those companies than by the commission senior officers would receive on the insurance business acquired.[31] The failure of these two companies also highlighted the problem identified by the Wilson committee of valuing life company assets and liabilities because both had received favourable actuarial reports shortly before they collapsed.[32] Moreover, corporate insolvency laws had proved defective; indeed, the first task was to pass special legislation appointing arbitrators with almost unlimited discretion to settle affairs.[33]

This time opposition to regulation was muted. The Life Assurance Companies Act 1870[34] took much from the Wilson report. The principal approach involved coupling a gatekeeping measure to restrict access to the life market with something later dubbed 'freedom with publicity', which aimed 'to give parties every facility for

26 *Report from the Select Committee on Assurance Association*, HC 1852–53 (965), para. 7.

27 Wilson introduced bills in 1857 and 1859, but only managed to remove the exemption from registration granted to life offices by the Companies Act 1857.

28 Commons Debates, 8 Mar 1853, vol. 124, c. 1331.

29 *Ibid*, c. 1330.

30 *Daily News*, 23 Aug 1869, 26 Aug 1869; T Alborn, *Regulated Lives: Life Insurance and British Society 1800–1914*, London: University of Toronto Press, 2008, 60–63.

31 *The Maitland Mercury & Hunter River General Advertiser*, 30 Oct 1869.

32 T Alborn, *Regulated Lives: Life Insurance and British Society 1800–1914*, London: University of Toronto Press, 2008, 60–63.

33 Arbitration Acts 1871–1875 (34 & 35 Vict c. 31, 37 & 38 Vict c 58 (Albert); 35 & 36 Vict c 145, 36 & 37 Vict c. 9, 38 & 39 Vict c157 (European)).

34 33 & 34 Vict c 62. There were amending statutes in 1871 and 1872.

investigation, but that investigation they should conduct for themselves'.[35] The Act restricted access to the market by obliging new life companies to deposit £20,000 in the Court of Chancery (s. 3). This was meant to show good faith and that the companies had access to funding.[36] Significantly, existing companies were not required to deposit funds. This was presumably to avoid imposing burdens retrospectively, but it revealed the limitations of the Act since it did not address the events that led to its enactment – the failure of established companies. What had happened was the rearticulation of the problem as one of bubble or mushroom companies, which were fraudulent or had inadequate funds. The principal beneficiaries of this measure were, therefore, not policyholders but those who would otherwise have been sufficiently foolish or greedy to invest in the shares of bubble companies. Other provisions did, however, apply to all life companies. Life insurers had to separate receipts in respect of life and annuity business from other insurance (s. 4). This fund was security for the life policyholders and annuitants and, on exceeding £40,000, any initial deposit made by the company would be returned (s. 3). Life offices were obliged to publish an actuarial report on their financial condition every five years (s. 7) and to provide regular information to the Board of Trade, although it had no obligation to check for accuracy (s. 8).[37] These transparency measures might have helped those contemplating life assurance, but were less useful to existing policyholders. The Act did give them some limited rights. Amalgamation or transfer of a life office could only be undertaken with the sanction of the court, which could not be given if it was opposed by a tenth of the policyholders (based on the total assured) (s. 14). A policyholder or shareholder could petition if the company were 'insolvent' (s. 21), which, in essence, involved taking a 'snapshot of the company's current financial position' based on its existing assets and liabilities,[38] but, leaving aside the difficulty of how policyholders or shareholders might learn of the insolvency, any intervention would come too late to save the company.

The lack of bureaucratic resources but, more importantly, contemporary opinion as to the proper role of the state precluded supervision by government.[39] Robert Lowe, the Chancellor of the Exchequer, who broadly supported the legislation, remarked:

> 'The difficulty really amounts to this—the returns of the affairs of companies are wanted; but if you trust to the companies to make their own returns, you may be quite sure they will strain every nerve to keep back all that they wish you not to know. If, on the other hand, you trust to a Government audit or inspection, then you mix the Government up in the concern; and, although a man may be given only a limited function, yet the inevitable result will be that he will give the company a spurious, false, and unfair credit, as having the weight, and probably the guarantee of the Government behind.'[40]

35 Commons Debates, 23 Feb 1870, vol. 199, c. 741, GB Gregory MP. See T Alborn, *Regulated Lives: Life Insurance and British Society 1800–1914*, London: University of Toronto Press, 2008, ch. 2.

36 *Ibid*, 29 Jun 1870, vol. 202, c. 1171.

37 *Ibid*, 23 Feb 1870, vol. 199, c. 752.

38 Broadly codifying *In re European Life Assurance Society* (1869) LR 9 Eq 122. See P Watson, 'Inability to Pay Debts: Beyond the Point of No Return?' [2013] JBL 212.

39 This does not mean state intervention was unknown: PJ Rawlings, '"Without Feeling and Without Remorse"? Making Sense of Employers' Liability and Insurance in the Nineteenth Century' (2013) 126 BILA Journal.

40 See note 35, c. 752.

The 1870 model's main objective was merely to improve the efficiency of the market without undermining the responsibility of policyholders (and shareholders) to exercise caution. Yet, even though the ambition of the Act was severely restricted, the willingness to legislate was a significant step in that it acknowledged the public interest in insurance, and the characterisation of the underlying problem as bubble companies made it easier to roll the 1870 model out to other sectors as new insurance markets developed.

The extension of regulation beyond life insurance began with employers' liability policies. Prior to 1880, employers were, broadly speaking, not liable for the negligence of their employees, but legislation in that year changed this, creating a demand for cover that led to the formation of a large number of new insurance companies. Fears about their robustness eventually led to the Employers' Liability Insurance Companies Act 1907,[41] which, with some adjustment, adopted the 1870 model; in 1909, regulation was extended to other sectors.[42] This legislation attracted support from the largest insurance companies and their powerful allies in Parliament because they stood to gain from regulation which, as companies established before the statutes, would have little negative impact on them but would both limit competition and boost public confidence in insurance. Interestingly, however, Lord Hamilton, first chairman of the Employers' Liability Assurance Corporation, which was a leader in its field, seemed to acknowledge a new objective when, in a speech to the House of Lords on the 1909 bill, he said it aimed to protect the public, 'who ... would otherwise be unable to look after themselves and investigate the stability of the insurance companies'.[43] What this meant was unclear since he added that 'the Bill does not strike out any new line in regard to the control of insurance by the State'.[44] The 1907–1909 statutes retained the idea of 'freedom with publicity' – that protection of policyholders would be achieved not by extending their rights but by providing them with information and restricting market access to those companies able to demonstrate good faith through the deposit scheme. The Board of Trade was given no special powers of inspection beyond those available under ordinary company law,[45] but it was not entirely impotent. It could require accounts to be redrafted if they were inadequate and produced annual reports setting out the Board's views on that issue. Moreover, the Board's authority grew with the acquisition of expertise and, in particular, was boosted by the establishment of the Government Actuary's Department.[46] But such limited formal powers

41 Rawlings, *ibid*; Commons Debates, 7 Aug 1907, vol. 180, c. 197, Sir Hudson Kearley. Returns in 1911 indicated that 78 companies, one Lloyd's syndicate and 38 employers' mutual associations offered cover: *Employers' Liability Insurance Companies*, HC 121 (1911).

42 E Gore-Browne, *The Law Relating to Assurance Companies Under the Assurance Companies Act 1909*, London, 1909. It was extended to other sectors: e.g. Road Traffic Act 1930; Air Navigation Act 1936. Lloyd's came under a series of statutes (1871–1982), which, broadly, allowed self-regulation: J Burling, *Lloyd's: Law and Practice*, London: Informa Law, 2014.

43 Lords Debates, 30 Jun 1909, vol. 2, c. 1026.

44 *Ibid*, c. 1028.

45 Companies (Consolidation) Act 1908, ss 108–114.

46 The GAD originated in the Chief Actuary to the National Health Insurance Joint Committee (1912), becoming the Government Actuary in 1917 and the Department in 1919: CD Daykin, 'The Decreasing Role of the Government Actuary's Department in the Supervision of Insurance' (1992) 119 JIA 313.

as were gradually acquired before the Second World War were largely concerned with insolvency.[47]

It is clear that, at least, as far as life companies went, their quality and resilience did improve as a result of the statutory provisions on transparency, the growing authority of the Board of Trade, consensus among company actuaries on the methods of valuing the assets and liabilities of insurers, improvements in the investment of funds by insurers, and the creation of large companies through mergers and acquisitions.[48] After the failure of Briton Medical & General in 1886, no life insurer collapsed for almost 90 years. There was, however, greater fragility elsewhere, particularly in new sectors such as motor insurance, which expanded rather too rapidly after legislation in 1930 made liability cover compulsory.

2.5 Insurance and welfare

The regulation of insurance acknowledged the importance to public policy of the sector. This was reinforced in the twentieth century by its role in the modern welfare state. Insurance is, of course, about shifting the risk of loss from the policyholder, but it is also about providing for others – life and liability insurance are obvious examples of this. The regulation of employers' liability insurance benefited those employers who took out cover and indirectly protected employees because they were more likely to receive their compensation. The flaw was that the legislation extending liability was not matched by any compulsion to take out insurance. The recognition of the role private insurance could play in achieving this welfare objective of compensating accident victims led to the acceptance, from the 1930s, of the idea that those engaged in certain activities, such as motorists, aviators and employers, should be obliged to cover their liability for injury.[49] But this intervention in the market required the state to regulate terms of cover and create direct rights of action for victims against insurers to prevent compensation from being swallowed by the tortfeasor's insolvency. As will be seen, the acknowledgement of a public interest in these sectors blurred the boundary between state and business and could bring criticism of the regulator when an insurer failed.

The socio-economic importance of insurance – which drove regulation – was not only because it provided a way of shifting the burden of caring from the state to private insurers, but also because it supplied a model for welfare provision (which, paradoxically, had the effect of shifting the burden back on to the state, even if this was not its goal). Shrugging off the hated Poor Law, which, since its reform in 1834, had been constructed around notions of punishment exemplified by the workhouse, the modern welfare state drew on the model of cheap cover against the exigencies of life and work for those on low incomes that had been developed by friendly societies, which were mutual associations, and by industrial assurance companies, such as Prudential Assurance. The state welfare system established in the twentieth

47 Assurance Companies (Winding Up) Act 1933–1935.

48 T Alborn, *Regulated Lives: Life Insurance and British Society 1800–1914*, London: University of Toronto Press, 2008, ch. 2.

49 E.g. Road Traffic Act 1930, s. 35(1); Air Navigation Act 1936, Pt III; Workmen's Compensation (Mines) Act 1934, s. 3; Employer's Liability (Compulsory Insurance) Act 1969, s. 1(1).

century under the National Insurance Act 1911 and the Beveridge Report of 1942 was based on the insurance idea of benefits based on contributions.[50]

2.6 Supervision

The landslide victory enjoyed by the Labour Party at the 1945 election was seen as an endorsement for a radical programme of social and economic reform. Coal mining, iron and steel making, electricity and gas production and distribution, telecommunications, railways and the Bank of England were scooped up into state ownership. There was strong support for nationalising other parts of the financial sector and, indeed, the failure of a number of motor insurers in the 1930s had led Sir Stafford Cripps, who was the Labour Opposition spokesperson at that time, to talk of 'the impossibility, once we reach the stage of compulsory insurance, of carrying on with private insurance companies'.[51] On his appointment to the Board of Trade in the post-war government, Cripps rejected the idea and acknowledged the industry's contribution to invisible exports, which made it 'an asset of very great value in our economy, especially at the present time'.[52] Motor insurers did, however, agree to implement a proposal made by the Cassel Committee (1937) to cover victims of uninsured drivers through the establishment of the Motor Insurers' Bureau,[53] and the government introduced a significant reform of regulation.

The Assurance Companies Act 1946 shifted away from the gatekeeping model of the 1870 Act and sought to address concerns that the Board of Trade could not intervene before an insurer became insolvent. This meant that, while regulation was still characterised as 'freedom with publicity', there was a new focus on the continued monitoring of solvency. The Act abolished the deposit requirement, which had been the cornerstone of the 1870–1909 statutes, replacing it with an obligation to maintain a minimum level of paid-up share capital and a solvency margin of £50,000 or a tenth of annual premium income (s. 3). Breach constituted insolvency, triggering the Board's powers to seek to wind up a company. These rules did not apply to life businesses where the perceived need for greater flexibility meant that each company had a solvency margin set by its actuary.[54] One problem with the new provisions was that what constitutes 'solvency' may be more difficult to define than 'insolvency' and makes the powers necessary to ensure solvency hard to define. There was also the danger that unrealistic expectations might develop as to the Board's role, and that these could fuel criticism and lead to frequent trips to Parliament for further measures. This prospect was, inadvertently perhaps, present in a statement by Cripps when he suggested an ambitious aim for regulation wanting 'to make as certain as possible that there are no failures of British assurance companies in the future which would, of course, entail great losses to policy holders'.[55]

50 *Social Insurance and Allied Services. Report by Sir William Beveridge*, Cmnd 6404 (1942).

51 Commons Debates, 25 Jul 1935, vol. 304, c. 2166.

52 *Ibid*, 12 Nov 1945, vol. 415, c. 1824. Nationalisation did not vanish: *Labour Believes in Britain: A Statement on Policy for Discussion at the Labour Party Conference*, London: Labour Party, 1949.

53 *Board of Trade Report of the Committee on Compulsory Insurance*, Cmd 5528 (1936–1937); Commons Debates, 1 Jul 1946, vol. 424, cc. 1772–73. It was later extended to untraced motorists.

54 This was only changed by EU's First Life Directive of 1979 (see Insurance Companies Act 1982).

55 Commons Debates, 12 Nov 1945, vol 415, c. 1823.

The next major reconsideration of the aims and methods of insurance regulation was forced by the scandal surrounding the collapse of several cut-price motor insurers in 1966–1967 – Fire, Auto and Marine Insurance, London & Cheshire Insurance and London & Midland Insurance – and the investigation into two others.[56] These companies had grasped the opportunity provided by the rapid growth in car ownership and the rather uncompetitive approach to motor insurance taken by the industry; but their failure left more than 400,000 motorists without cover. The Board of Trade was immediately attacked for failing to prevent the collapses: an Opposition MP, Anthony Grant, remarked: 'In view of the fact that by statute companies of this kind have to file their accounts with the Board of Trade, surely some responsibility must rest upon the President of the Board of Trade.'[57] The Board protested that it did not have the power to intervene, but the affair seemed to realise Robert Lowe's warning in 1870 that the regulator might come to be seen as responsible for the solvency insurance industry.

The Companies Act 1967 extended the scope of supervision by introducing tougher rules on solvency, reinsurance, fit and proper persons, and accounting. Reluctance to intervene in policy terms (outside compulsory insurance) remained, and the DTI (the Department of Trade and Industry, as the Board became in 1970) continued to subscribe to the objective of 'freedom with publicity': 'we have always maintained that insurers should remain free to determine the terms on which they will do business with their clients and the manner in which they will ensure their ability to meet claims when they arise.'[58] But again this failed to deflect criticism when another cut-price motor insurer, Vehicle and General, collapsed in 1971.[59] The Insurance Companies Amendment Act 1973, which emerged, partly, as a result of that event, continued to focus on the regulator rather than on the rights of policyholders, aiming to 'strike a proper balance between, on the one hand, allowing the industry so much freedom that it can be exploited by rogues, and on the other hand, creating for the industry such shackles that it cannot give efficient, competitive and forward looking service to consumers here and abroad'.[60] The Act brought further measures on solvency, the quality of senior staff, actuarial investigations, takeovers and advertising, but little on consumer rights.[61] The DTI could intervene where, among other situations, it was 'desirable for protecting policy holders or potential policy holders ... against the risk that the company may be unable to meet its liabilities, or, in the case of long term business, to fulfil the reasonable expectations of policy holders' (1973 Act, ss 12(1)(a), 21).[62] However, this did not empower policyholders; it was a test for determining the strength of a company

56 *Ibid*, 25 Jan 1967, cc. 282–83; J Connell with D Sutherland, *Fraud: The Amazing Career of Dr Savundra*, London, 1978.

57 *Ibid*, 4 Jul 1966, c. 41.

58 Commons Debates, 14 Nov 1968, c. 740, Edmund Dell MP, Board of Trade.

59 *Report of the Tribunal appointed to inquire into certain issues in relation to the circumstances leading up to the cessation of trading by the Vehicle and General Insurance Company Limited* (HL 80/HC 133), 1972. See also, *Linked Life Assurance. Report of the Committee on Property Bonds and Equity-Linked Life Assurance*, Cmnd 5281 (1973).

60 Commons Debates, 21 May 1973, c. 118. The British Insurance Association rejected a proposal to become the regulator: Lords Debates, 8 Feb 1973, c. 1157.

61 Although s. 45 established a cooling-off period in long-term insurance.

62 Also, Insurance Companies Act 1982, ss 37(2)(a), 45(1).

by looking at its likely liabilities to policyholders.[63] One minister spoke of his wish 'to raise the management control of the less good companies to the standard of the best.'[64] Yet, significantly, he also boasted that levels of staff responsible for supervision were lower than in most rival jurisdictions.[65]

The confusion as to the appropriate regulatory objectives and methodology arose again during debates on the Policyholders Protection Act 1975. This statute, which followed the collapse of the Nation Life in 1974, provided important protection to policyholders in the shape of guarantees on an insurer's insolvency,[66] and further illustrated the acceptance of insurance as fundamental to the socio-economic life of the nation. During the debates, Peter Shore, the minister who introduced the bill, declared 'my main objective, in supervising the industry, is to see that insurance companies do not fail'.[67] A few years later, in 1981 a minister in a different government, Reginald Eyre, while warning that failures of insurance companies could not be entirely prevented, accepted 'Government responsibility for a systematic approach'.[68] It was unclear how all of this fitted with the idea of 'freedom with publicity', and, indeed, such ministerial statements came back to bite government when The Equitable Life Assurance Society ran into difficulties. This insurer revolutionised life insurance in the eighteenth century by adjusting cover and premiums to estimates of life expectancy, and it became a world leader in the nineteenth century. By the 1990s it had 1.5 million policyholders and around £28 billion in funds. Then in 2000 a failure to hedge promises made to certain investors forced it to close to new business and to reduce payments on existing policies. The conclusion of the subsequent inquiry by the Parliamentary and Health Service Ombudsman that the regulators had failed and that, therefore, the government should provide compensation was based on, among other things, statements by ministers as to their role in supervision.[69] Such criticism and the further attempts at the refinement of regulation it brought seemed an identification, perhaps even an acceptance, of the regulator's responsibility. Nevertheless, it did not constitute a criticism of the idea of regulation; it merely triggered the search for better regulation – and, perhaps, a better regulator.

Matters outside the industry also affected insurance regulation. The comprehensive overhaul of financial regulation in the mid-1980s did not lead the DTI to lose its role, although its supervision became more intensive; but the structure was dramatically changed in 1997. There had been growing criticism of regulation

63 Parliamentary and Health Service Ombudsman, *Equitable Life: A Decade of Regulatory Failure: Part Two: The Regulatory Regime: Fourth Report, Session 2007–2008*, HC 815-11 (2008), 90–91. The phrase 'reasonable expectations of policy holders' seems to come from Ronald Skerman, Chief Actuary of Prudential ('A Solvency Standard for Life Assurance Business' (1966) 92 *Journal of the Institute of Actuaries* 75), although its true origins lie in nineteenth-century actuarial practice: C Daykin, 'Address by the President of the Institute of Actuaries: Turning Promises into Reality' (1995) 1 *British Actuarial Journal* 5. But see *Equitable Life Assurance, Society v Hyman* [2002] 1 AC 408.

64 Lords Debates, 8 Feb 1973 vol. 338, c. 1159, the Earl of Limerick (DTI).

65 *Ibid*, c. 1197.

66 *Fourth Report of the Parliamentary Commissioner for Administration*, HC 485 (1975–1976).

67 Commons Debates, 18 Jul 1975, c. 1941.

68 *Ibid*, 2 Feb 1981, c. 103.

69 Parliamentary and Health Service Ombudsman, *Equitable Life: A Decade of Regulatory Failure*, HC 815 (2008). For the government's compensation: see www.gov.uk/equitable-life-payment-scheme.

following various scandals in the financial services industry in the 1980s and 1990s, some of which involved insurance companies, but the principal driver was the decision of the new Labour government to give the Bank of England independent control of monetary policy. That, in turn, led to the Bank losing responsibility for banking supervision. The creation of a single financial regulator was justified on the basis that the industry was no longer made up of single enterprise firms but comprised financial conglomerates and that regulation should reflect this change.[70] The Financial Services Authority (FSA) proved only a brief chapter in the history of regulation and its fate revived issues about the nature of regulation and what it could achieve. Both regulation and the FSA were held partly to blame for the financial crisis of 2008, while the idea that the financial sectors are not really distinguishable has meant that solutions have been rolled out to all sectors. Thus, a crisis in the banking sector leads to new rules for insurers. This has been criticised by many in the insurance industry who see the new measures as detrimental (expensive, restrictive) and as punishing a sector that was not responsible for the crisis.[71]

The focus of regulation on, broadly, the ability of insurers to meet claims and the reluctance to intervene in the relationship between insurers and policyholders left brokers largely untouched, even though they have played a key role in shaping the industry.[72] The European Economic Community (EEC) did introduce limited measures,[73] but UK reform was eventually shaped mainly by domestic concerns about the quality of brokers.[74] In 1977, a government white paper identified the problem of matching 'maximum availability of the product, and expertise and integrity in those who sell it'.[75] But more than a limited measure of statutory regulation was successfully resisted by this powerful part of the industry, although the government justified its decision not to regulate on the basis of its lack of resources – which might also be construed as an unwillingness to commit: 'the Government does not currently have officials with the expertise and knowledge of insurance broking to which the BIBC [British Insurance Brokers' Council] has access; such people would be difficult to find and train.'[76] The Insurance Brokers (Registration) Act 1977 merely banned unregistered people from calling themselves brokers without prohibiting them from undertaking this work and left regulation to the brokers themselves. That situation survived the radical restructuring of financial regulation under the Financial Services Act 1986 and even the establishment of FSA. It was only in 2005 that the FSA took on this function.

Domestic issues have been the primary driver of insurance regulation in the UK, but the financial crisis of 2008 highlighted the international nature of much of the financial services industry and the interdependence of domestic economies. In

70 Commons Debates, 20 May 1997, vol 294 c. 510.

71 The collapse of AIG is not seen as spoiling this argument since (it is argued) that resulted from activities outside its insurance business.

72 A proposal to control brokers was rejected during the passage of the 1973 Act: Lords Debates, 8 Feb 1973, c. 1167.

73 E.g. The Insurance Companies (Intermediaries) Regulations 1974, SI 1974/902 (also SI 1974/1051, SI 1976/521). See also Insurance Companies Amendment Act 1973, s. 43.

74 Commons Debates, 7 Mar 1975, cc. 1962–2056.

75 Department of Trade, *Insurance Intermediaries*, Cmnd 6715 (1977), para. 3.

76 *Ibid*, para. 9. BIBC was an industry body.

truth, concerns about (in particular) London's ability to compete as an international centre have always played a role so that, for example, right back to 1870, the shape of regulation has often been influenced by the perceived need to undercut the rules of rival jurisdictions.[77] As has been seen, in the mid-eighteenth century, London insurers justified writing policies on enemy shipping on the ground that otherwise rival centres would benefit. By the late twentieth century, however, although this consideration remained important, there was a recognition that the international nature of insurance companies (as well as the possibility of them moving to a more favourable regulatory environment) required some regulatory harmonisation between countries. Thinking on these issues was decisively influenced by work on solvency in the Insurance Committee at the Organisation for European Economic Co-operation (OEEC) from the late 1950s,[78] at its successor, the Organizations for Economic Cooperation and Development, and much later at the International Association of Insurance Supervisors (1994). Even more directly influential for the UK was membership of the EEC in 1973. The goal of a single market in insurance services led to greater harmonisation of the laws of the member states, but it also brought more emphasis on consumer rights and protection than had been typical of UK legislation. Progress remained slow and was often met with stiff resistance from the industry, in spite of initiatives such as the Statements of Insurance Practice and the Insurance Ombudsman Bureau (1981), which had an effect on the conduct of business without changing the law.[79] However, the FSA took greater interest in consumer protection,[80] and, indeed, what was characterised as its failure to give sufficient focus to the traditional objective of monitoring the business was one of the criticisms made in the wake of the financial crisis.

2.7 What does history tell us about regulation?

Surveying such a broad area in such a relatively limited space inevitably means much is left unsaid, but the intention was to discuss why and how regulation arises and changes rather than to provide a detailed description of the regulatory statutes from 1870.[81] Moreover, in keeping with the theme of the book, this chapter has focused on what might now be called microprudential and macroprudential risks. Nevertheless, an attempt has been made to give some flavour of the other issues involved in shaping regulation. Descriptions of the development of insurance regulation (including, in some respects, this one) tend to depict regulation as a response to a problem designed to eliminate or reduce the likelihood of the problem

---

77 R Pearson and M Lönnborg, 'Regulatory Regimes and Multinational Insurers before 1914' (2008) 82 *Business History Review* 59.

78 C Campagne, *Minimum Standards of Solvency for Insurance Firms*, OEEC: Paris, 1957; *Minimum Standards of Solvency for Insurance Firms*, OEEC: Paris, 1961.

79 J Lowry and P Rawlings, '"That Wicked, That Evil Doctrine…": Reforming the Law on Disclosure in Insurance Contracts' (2012) 75 MLR 1100.

80 The FSA developed increasingly stiff conduct of business rules, some of which entitled consumers to bring an action for loss (e.g. ICOBS 8.1R).

81 R Ford, 'History: A History of Insurance Regulation in the UK' in J Burling and K Lazarus (eds), *Research Handbook on International Insurance Law and Regulation*, London: Edward Elgar, 2012. For further discussion, see PJ Rawlings, 'The Confused History of Insurance Regulation', forthcoming.

reappearing. This excludes regulation, such as revenue collection or welfare policy, which does not arise from problems with the insurance industry, but, nonetheless, has an impact on it, if only in that such legislation may help embed insurance into the socio-economic infrastructure and make it more important to government policy. Even if regulation responds to a problem in the industry, it is unlikely to be a straightforward process whereby the problem leads inexorably to the solution. Why does one problem lead to regulation and another does not? Why is one solution preferred to another? Why is a solution later discarded and a new one put in its place? The identifications of the problem, its cause and solution are entwined, and the process works, at least partly, in reverse because it is limited by the range of possible solutions as determined by material (finance, bureaucracy), intellectual (philosophical and economic theories), political and cultural contexts that are neither clear nor uncontested. The open market was rejected in 1720 because this served certain interests but also because many did not regard it as an effective economic approach; one aim of the 1870 Act was to facilitate the market, although regulation to achieve this invited further regulation resulting in a more restricted market.

New regulation is also shaped by the old. Partly, this may be because it is difficult to think in new ways and a model that seems to work (even if it is defective) is likely to be less controversial than something that is untested. The old system may be stretched and patched, until it breaks down. Even when it comes to be discarded because it is believed to have failed in some fundamental way or because there is practical advantage in depicting it as having failed (it may, for example, be a way in which a new government ascribes blame for failure to a previous government), the new approach is likely to be defined in terms of not being the existing model, even though it may draw on that model.[82] Regulation is often influenced by those who are regulated. This is not just because it responds to some problem with the regulated businesses. The need for state intervention (at least in the financial sector) identifies this industry as important and that gives insurers importance, which empowers them – as, of course, does their wealth and ability to organise and lobby. Moreover, there has been an assumption over the last 200 years that regulation is about keeping certain corrupt practices out of the market; it is not really concerned with the vast bulk of insurers. Insurers may express concern at what seems to undermine their competitiveness, but they also support regulation because it narrows the market, favours existing companies and may boost confidence among customers. Indeed, in a curious view of how public policy should be enforced, certain aspects of regulation, such as insurable interest, depend on the parties – or, more accurately, the insurer – bringing the defect to notice by refusing a claim. There is, perhaps, a sense that the criticism of post-2008 reforms coming from insurers is an expression of resentment at some loss of this influence.

The decision to initiate or reform regulation is an assertion that things will change and problems will be avoided or mitigated – in short, that regulation works. It is hard to turn back from this position. Thus, a crisis is not taken to mean that *regulation*

82 E.g. the statutory structure for, and many of the rules adopted by, the Prudential Regulation Authority and the Financial Conduct Authority draw on pre-crisis legislation and FSA rules: PJ Rawlings, 'All Change: The Fall of the FSA and the Further Rise of the Bank of England' (2011) 30(4) *US Banking & Financial Services Policy Report* 16.

does not work, but rather that *this* regulation (or *this* regulator) does not work. Even though the regulations, the regulator and the government are likely to be blamed for failures, the solution is regarded as resting with them. As the financial crisis showed, government cannot detach itself by appointing an independent regulator because it can hardly shrug off responsibility for an activity regarded as sufficiently important to require statutory regulation. Once embarked upon, this is a journey with no prospect of a conclusion – just a series of staging posts. To an extent Robert Lowe was alive to some of these problems in 1870, but it is too late to challenge the view that regulation works and there are political dangers in trying to convey the realistic message that regulation cannot provide a lasting solution.

CHAPTER 3

Macro-prudential supervision, systemic risk and insurance companies

Rosa María Lastra

3.1 Introduction

This chapter examines the regulatory and institutional issues related to the management of systemic risk and the concept of macro-prudential supervision from the perspective of insurance companies. Following a revisionist analysis of these notions, the chapter considers the specificity of the insurance business and concludes by arguing that international cooperation and coordination of policies is necessary for realising effective domestic and regional institutional frameworks in the supervision of insurance companies.

3.2 Defining systemic risk in the financial system

Systemic risk refers to the risk or probability of breakdown of the entire financial system, as opposed to breakdowns in individual parts or components.[1] A widely accepted definition, however, is still missing, which complicates the search for adequate instruments to prevent and contain it.

Any risk (not only credit risk but liquidity risk, interest rate risk, exchange rate risk, etc.) can grow into systemic proportions when its negative impact extends beyond an individual institution, affecting or threatening to affect by contagion other institutions (externalities) often creating a disruption in the monetary or financial system and which depending on the severity of the downturn – will then mutate into economic paralysis (halt in production). Systemic risks seldom occur alone; they usually spread to other risks like fire.

The debate about systemic risk is ubiquitous in the aftermath of the global financial crisis. Before the crisis, systemic risk was often associated with size and banking (the transmission mechanisms of a bank failure trigger contagion). However, after the crisis, a consensus has emerged that all classes of financial intermediaries, markets and infrastructures can be systematically important. This means that concerns about systemic risk are also relevant for securities and insurance markets. This seismic change in the understanding of systemic risk has fundamental regulatory implications, as evidenced by a flurry of national, EU and international initiatives.

Systemic risk can be defined as the risk that the failure of one significant financial

1 Steven L. Schwarcz, 'Systemic Risk' (2008) 97(1) *Georgetown Law Journal*, 198.

institution can cause or significantly contribute to the failure of other significant financial institutions as a result of their linkages to each other.[2]

At the EU level, the 'Lamfalussy Report' in 1990 defined systemic risk as 'the risk that the illiquidity or failure of one institution, and its resulting inability to meet its obligations when due, will lead to the illiquidity or failure of other institutions'.[3] But systemic risk is also related to 'the relative propensity of payment and settlement systems to transmit exposures suddenly or unexpectedly from one participant to another – and from one market to other markets – in ways that increase the difficulty all participants will have in managing and containing their exposures'.[4]

Article 2 of the Regulation No. 1092/2010 defines systemic risk as 'a risk of disruption in the financial system with the potential to have serious negative consequences for the internal market and the real economy. All types of financial intermediaries, markets and infrastructures may be potentially systemically important to some degree'.[5] Systemic risk looms large in the regulation of banking and financial institutions.[6]

The ability of the financial system to withstand unforeseen shocks is recognised by many economists and central banks as the key indicator of financial stability. In negative terms financial stability is the absence of instability/crisis. In positive terms the achievement of this objective encompasses a variety of elements such as good supervisory techniques, adequate capital and liquidity, competent and honest management, internal controls, early warning systems, effective regulation, transparency, accountability and an efficient payment system.

What makes a crisis of a systemic nature is not so much the trigger event (*causa proxima*) but the transmission mechanisms, domestically and internationally. If the linkages are strong, the potential for systemic instability increases. If the connections are weak, there is less of a threat of systemic risk. No chain is stronger than its weakest link.

The loss of confidence in an institution or market (whether informer or uninformed, rational or irrational) will undermine the functioning of that institution or market. Interestingly, the resolution of crisis also presents a psychological component: the mere belief that the problem has been solved will bring investors back to the market. It is not so much the ability to lend but the willingness to do so that really counts in the resolution of a financial crisis.

As Alexander noted, 'systemic risk often occurs because banks have an incentive to under-price financial risk, which can lead to too much of it being created in the

2 Hal S. Scott, 'The Reduction of Systemic Risk in the United States Financial System' (2010) 33(2) *Harvard Journal of Law and Public Policy*, 673. The author implies that 'the threat of systemic risk (whether real or imagined) results in both the need for government bailouts at taxpayer expense and in an increase in moral hazard'. See also Ian Ayres and Joshua Mitts, 'Anti-herding Regulation', Yale Law & Economics Research Paper No. 490. Available at: http://ssrn.com/abstract=2399240.

3 Bank for International Settlements, 'Report of the Committee on Interbank Netting Schemes of the central banks of the Group of Ten Countries (Lamfalussy Report)', Basel, November 1990, 6–7.

4 Ibid. at 7.

5 Article 2 of the Regulation (EU) No. 1092/2010 of the European Parliament and of the Council of 24 November 2010 on European Union macro-prudential oversight of the financial system and establishing a European Systemic Risk Board.

6 Daniel Tarullo, 'Regulating Systemic Risk', speech at '2011 Credit Markets Symposium', Charlotte, North Carolina, 31 March 2011.

financial system'.[7] Schwarcz observed: 'once a failure occurs, there may already be economic damage, and it may be difficult to stop the failure from spreading and become systemic'.[8]

In 2001, the Report 'Core Principles for Systemically Important Payment Systems' defined systemic risk as 'the risk that the inability of one of the participants to meet its obligations, or a disruption in the system itself, could result in the inability of other system participants or of financial institutions in other parts of the financial system to meet their obligations as they become due'.[9]

Successful financial regulation should be based on a coherent understanding of the relationship between microeconomic risk, macroeconomic contagion, and macroeconomic consequences.

In the UK regulatory system, the new Financial Conduct Authority (FCA) is entrusted with the responsibility for market conduct of all those that provide financial services to the public (this covers both prudentially significant institutions and all other financial service providers), whereas the Prudential Regulation Authority (PRA) is established and charged with the prudential regulation of the prudentially significant firms, including banks, investment firms[10] and insurance companies.[11]

The PRA has been busy since its inception publishing framework papers on its delegated responsibilities. Of particular importance for the subject of our study is the paper defining the PRA approach to the supervision of insurance companies.[12]

The efficient regulation of systemic risk in global financial markets may require a multilateral framework treaty setting out broad standards of good regulatory practice. In this regard, it has been proposed to replace the notion of 'systemically important institutions' with that of 'systemically important platforms'.[13] Such platforms would only be directly accessible to a group of 'officially recognized financial institutions' that would have to comply with special regulatory requirements and would be directly supervised by the central bank. The status of 'officially recognized financial institution' could be revoked by the central bank if these special regulatory requirements were not satisfied. In this view, traditional prudential regulation is targeted at financial firms (institution-based).

---

7 Kerfn Alexander, Rahul Dhumale and John Eatwell, 'Managing Systemic Risk. The Rationale for International Financial Regulation', in Kern Alexander, Rahul Dhumale and John Eatwell (eds), *Global Governance of Financial Systems The International Regulation of Systemic Risk* (Oxford University Press 2005) 15.

8 Steven L. Schwarcz, 'Keynote Address: Ex Ante Versus Ex Post Approaches to Financial Regulation' (2011) 15(1) *Chapman Law Review*, 258.

9 Bank for International Settlements, Committee on Payment and Settlement Systems, 'Core Principles for Systemically Important Payment Systems', January 2001, 5.

10 Anita A. Anand, 'Is Systemic Risk Relevant to Securities Regulation?' (2010) 60 *University of Toronto Law Journal*, 980.

11 Simon Debbage and Stephen Dickinson, 'The Rationale for the Prudential Regulation and Supervision of Insurers', *Bank of England Quarterly Bulletin* 2013, 216–217.

12 See The PRA's approach to insurance supervision, June 2014. Available at: www.bankofengland.co.uk/publications/Documents/praapproach/insuranceappr1406.pdf.

13 Jean-Charles Rochet, 'Systemic Risk: Changing the Regulatory Perspective' (2010) *International Journal of Central Banking*, 273.

3.3 Prudential supervision and the insurance market

Prudential supervision plays an important role in the pursuit of the soundness of the financial system by helping ensure that financial institutions (banking and non-banking institutions) act prudently.[14]

Prudential supervision relates to three distinct types of service providers: (1) systemic infrastructures such as central counterparties and payment and settlement systems; (2) prudentially significant firms such as deposit takers and insurers; and (3) other financial service providers such as most investment firms, insurance brokers, and fund managers.[15]

In the insurance market, prudential supervision protects the consumers of insurance policies, but can also increase moral hazard on the financial condition of the firms.[16] It is noteworthy that a rationale for the regulation of the insurance industry is to diminish the insurer's ability (or that of its intermediaries) to distort its promises at the moment of selling its products, and/or to default on its duties (by insolvency or deficient sinister compensation).[17] In this regard, the insurance functions of safety nets and moral hazard are relevant issues; ill-designed safety nets can be a significant cause of financial instability if they fail to counteract the loss of market discipline that they induce (the 'moral hazard' problem).[18] A macro-prudential orientation in financial stability policies requires safety nets whose structure and functioning address systemic risk. [19]

Insurers are in the business of dealing with uncertainty. Frank Knight's (1921) classic distinction between risk and uncertainty is often cited in academic articles in order to distinguish both concepts, which are often used interchangeably. Knight argued that risk represents a quantity susceptible of measurement, while uncertainty is immeasurable. This raises an important question: are regulators and supervisors today facing systemic risk or rather incalculable, systemic uncertainty?[20] The authorities certainly face imperfect information problems, namely moral hazard and adverse selection.

The International Association of Insurance Supervisors (IAIS) has stated that for

---

14 Isaac Ofoeda, Joshua Abor and Charles K.D. Adjasi, 'Non-bank financial institutions regulation and risk-taking' (2012) 20(4) *Journal of Financial Regulation & Compliance*, 435–436.

15 Benjamin Geva, 'Systemic Risk and Financial Stability: The Evolving Role of the Central Bank' (2013) 28(10) *Journal of International Banking Law and Regulation*, 413.

16 Typically, consumer protection calls for conduct of business regulation. However, in the case of insurance policyholder protection, the assumption seems to be that this group of consumers is better protected through prudential supervision the purpose of which is to ensure the soundness and solvency of the insurance firm.

17 See Fernando Castagnolo and Gustavo Ferro, 'Could we Rely on Market Discipline as a Substitute for Insurance Regulation? (2013) 21(11) *Journal of Financial Regulation & Compliance*, 5–6. The authors observe that 'the regulation of the insurance market is based on the existence of market failures which affect the social welfare maximization otherwise achieved under perfect competition'.

18 John Breckenridge, James Farquharson and Ruth Hendon, 'The Role of Business Model Analysis in the Supervision of Insurers' (2014) *Bank of England Quarterly Bulletin* Q1, 49–50.

19 Prudential supervision may act as a system of implicit insurance premia, including: (1) financial requirements on a range of banking activities; (2) prompt declaration of insolvency; (3) imposition of costs on depositors by way of limited coverage; and (4) imposition of *ex post* direct costs on owners.

20 Frank Knight, *Risk, Uncertainty, and Profit* (Boston, MA: Hart, Schaffner & Marx; Houghton Mifflin Co. 1921).

traditional insurers the 'time horizon is a key dimension of potential systemic risk'.[21] The IAIS adds that because insurance if different from other types of financial intermediation, solutions for addressing systemic insurance risk need to be tailored to its sector-specific features.[22]

Insurers have a distinct business model.[23] As noted by Julian Adams, Deputy Head of the PRA and Executive Director of Insurance, the insurance sector's 'inverted production cycle' characterised by 'the upfront accumulation of premiums and the deferred nature of payment of liabilities' could mean that insurers face different challenges compared to banks.[24]

One particular source of major concern for insurers is the set of activities included under non-traditional non-insurance (NTNI) by the IAIS.[25] These riskier activities encompass instruments that expose insurers to credit risk (e.g. credit default swaps) and maturity transformation. In order to tackle the risks associated with these activities, financial standard-setting bodies such as the IAIS aim to continue to develop prudential requirements (capital and higher loss absorbency) for insurers.

As stated earlier, one important lesson from the 2007–2009 financial crisis is that insurers can also be systemically important. This means that the failure or financial distress of these entities can produce negative externalities and spillover effects that can cause disruptions to both the real and the financial economies, across jurisdictions. The case of American International Group (AIG) is a noteworthy example.[26]

The Financial Stability Board (FSB) framework on Global Systemically Important Financial Institutions (G-SIFIs) has been extended to insurers.[27] These entities have been called 'Global systemically important insurers' (G-SIIs). G-SIIs are defined as insurance-dominated conglomerates, insurance groups and any insurers whose distress or disorderly failure (because of their size, complexity and interconnectedness) would cause significant disruption to the global financial system and financial stability.[28]

However, insurance companies are resisting their classification as SIFIs. A

---

21 'Systemic Risk and the Insurance Sector' the IAIS, 25 October 2009. Available at: http://hb.betterregulation.com/external/Systemic%20Risk%20and%20the%20Insurance%20Sector.pdf, 1

22 International Association of Insurance Supervisors, 'Global Systemically Important Insurers: Initial Assessment Methodology', 18 July 2013.

23 The IAIS also notes that the distinct business model of insurance means that the policy solutions for systemically risky activities will likely differ between sectors. See 'Systemic Risk and the Insurance Sector' the IAIS, 25 October 2009. Available at: http://hb.betterregulation.com/external/Systemic%20Risk%20and%20the%20Insurance%20Sector.pdf

24 Julian Adams, 'Global systemically important insurers: issues, policies and challenges after designation', speech at The Geneva Association, 24 March 2014, 2. 'MetLife Sues over Being Named Too Big to Fail' Mary Williams Walsh, 13 January 2015. Available at: http://dealbook.nytimes.com/2015/01/13/metlife-to-fight-too-big-to-fail-status-in-court/.

25 International Association of Insurance Supervisors, 'Global Systemically Important Insurers: Policy Measures', 18 July 2013, 13–14.

26 Daniel Schwarcz and Steven L. Schwarcz, 'Regulating Systemic Risk in Insurance' (2014) 81(4) *University of Chicago Law Review*, 1570–1572.

27 Financial Stability Board, 'Key Attributes of Effective Resolution Regimes for Financial Institutions', October 2011.

28 International Association of Insurance Supervisors, 'Global Systemically Important Insurers: Policy Measures' (note 25) 3. The designation of G-SIIs is based on five main criteria: (a) size; (b) global activity; (c) interconnectedness; (d) the degree of engaging in NTNI activities; and (e) substitutability. Available at: www.financialstabilityboard.org/wp-content/uploads/r_141106a.pdf.

noteworthy recent example is provided by MetLife which has sued the Financial Stability Oversight Council in the US to fight its designation as 'systemically important', [29] making it the first financial company to go to court over the issue since the entry into force of the Dodd Frank Act 2010.

3.4 Macro-prudential supervision: policies and objectives

A consensus has emerged after the crisis regarding the difference between macro- and micro-prudential supervision. According to the House of Lords Report on the Future of EU Supervision and Regulation:[30]

> 'macro-prudential supervision is the analysis of trends and imbalances in the financial system and the detection of systemic risks that these trends may pose to financial institutions and the economy. The focus of macro-prudential supervision is the safety of the financial and economic system as a whole – the prevention of the materialization of systemic risk. Micro-prudential supervision is the day-to-day supervision of individual financial institutions. The focus of micro-prudential supervision is the safety and soundness of individual institutions and also consumer protection. The same or a separate supervisor can carry out these two functions. If different supervisors carry out these functions they must work together to provide mechanisms to counteract macro-prudential risks at a micro-prudential level.'

From an institutional perspective, the exercise of macro-prudential supervision is given to either newly created councils for financial stability, such as the Financial Stability Oversight Council in the US[31], or to the central bank, such as the Bank of England in the UK, where the Financial Policy Committee is in charge of this task.[32]

In the EU, the European Systemic Risk Board shares macro-prudential supervisory responsibilities with national authorities and, following the entry into force of the Single Supervisory Mechanism (SSM) Regulation,[33] also with the European Central Bank for those Member States that participate in the Banking Union and fall under the SSM.[34] Given the lack of a commonly accepted theoretical paradigm on the definition of systemic risk, this is no easy task.[35]

---

29 'MetLife Sues over Being Named Too Big to Fail' Mary Williams Walsh, 13 January 2015. Available at: http://dealbook.nytimes.com/2015/01/13/metlife-to-fight-too-big-to-fail-status-in-court/.

30 House of Lords, 'The Future of EU Financial Regulation and Supervision', Vol. I, London, 17 June 2009.

31 Edward V. Murphy, 'Financial Stability Oversight Council: A Framework to Mitigate Systemic Risk' Congressional Research Service Report R42083, 21 March 2013, 1–2 and 4–6. Available at: http://fas.org/sgp/crs/misc/R42083.pdf. It is underlined that 'the FSOC is expected to facilitate communication among existing financial regulators intending to identify sources of financial instability that cross agency regulatory jurisdiction, or that reside in gaps in the financial regulatory framework'.

32 HM Treasury, 'Remit and Recommendations for the Financial Policy Committee', Letter from the Chancellor, George Osborne to the Governor of the Bank of England Mervyn King, 30 April 2013.

33 Article 5 of Council Regulation (EU) No. 1024/2013 of 15 October 2013 conferring specific tasks on the European Central Bank concerning policies relating to the prudential supervision of credit institutions [2013] OJ L287/63 (SSM Regulation).

34 Eilís Ferran, 'European Banking Union: Imperfect, but it can Work', University of Cambridge Faculty of Law Research Paper No. 30/2014. Available at: http://ssrn.com/abstract=2426247. See also Eilís Ferran and Valia Babis, 'The European Single Supervisory Mechanism' (2013), University of Cambridge Faculty of Law Research Paper No. 10/2013. Available at: http://ssrn.com/abstract=2224538.

35 Financial Stability Board, 'Policy Measures to Address Systemically Important Financial Institutions', 4 November 2011.

Macro-prudential supervision is generally an inductive rather than deductive process that follows a top-down approach, working out the desirable safety standard for the system as a whole and, from there, deriving that of the individual institutions within it.[36] The focus of macro-prudential supervision is the safety of the financial and economic system as a whole; it consists of the analysis of trends and imbalances in the financial system and the detection of systemic risks that these trends may pose to financial institutions and the economy.[37]

In contrast, micro-prudential supervision focuses on strengthening individual financial institutions with a view to protecting their creditors, particularly depositors and investors.[38] In this regard, macro-prudential supervision is analogous to the oversight of the forest, whereas micro-prudential supervision is analogous to the oversight of individual trees.[39]

Macro-prudential policies are designed to deal with two types of systemic risk: (a) 'resiliency risks', which reflect a concentration of risk that can arise at a point in time when the interconnectedness and similar exposures of financial institutions and markets reduce the resiliency of the financial system to shocks and stresses; and (b) 'procyclical risks' which accumulate over time and reflect the tendency of financial system to procyclical behaviour that exacerbates economic booms and busts.[40]

By addressing systemic risk, macro-prudential policy endeavours to contribute to financial stability.

The macro-prudential objective can be defined as limiting the costs to the economy from financial distress, including those that arise from any moral hazard induced by the policies pursued, whereas the micro-prudential objective can be seen as limiting the likelihood of failure of individual institutions.[41] In this light, the 2011 HM Treasury Report 'A New Approach to Financial Regulation: Building a Stronger System' explained that 'macro-prudential policy seeks to augment the existing regulatory framework by focusing on systemic risk. Systemic risk can be broadly defined as risks to the stability of the whole or a large part of the financial sector'.[42]

Prudential supervision plays an active role in the regulation of SIFIs 'whose disorderly failure, because of their size, complexity and systemic interconnectedness, would cause significant disruption to the wider financial system and economic

36 See Geva (note 15) 408.

37 House of Lords, 'The Future of EU Financial Regulation and Supervision', Vol. I, London, 17 June 2009, 12.

38 Paul Jenkins and Gordon Thiessen, 'Reducing the Potential for Future Financial Crises: A Framework for Macro-Prudential Policy', in Canada Commentary No. 351 (Toronto: C.D. Howe Institute, May 2012) 2.

39 Rosa María Lastra, 'Systemic Risk, SIFIs and Financial Stability' (2011) 6(2) *Capital Markets Law Journal*, 198.

40 Steven L. Schwarcz, 'The Functional Regulation of Finance', Paper presented at Third CCLS Roundtable on Financial Regulation: 'Financial Markets: Impossible To Govern?' London, 26–27 June 2014, 38–39.

41 Andrew Crockett, 'Marrying the Micro- and Macro-prudential Dimensions of Financial Stability', Basel, 21 September 2000, 2.

42 HM Treasury, 'A New Approach to Financial Regulation: Building a Stronger System' (February 2011).

activity'.[43] It could also play a significant role on G-SIIs, in particular with regard to the creation of a Special Resolution Regime (SRR) for insurers.[44]

The emerging SRR for G-SIIs is based upon three pillars: (1) the identification of those activities that bear the potential of triggering systemic risk in the event of the disorderly failure of the insurer; (2) the designation of certain insurers with global presence as G-SIIs; and (3) the adoption of policy measures that are geared towards the recovery of the financially distressed G-SII or – where this is no longer feasible – its orderly resolution.

As Georgosouli notes in Chapter 8, a special resolution regime has two chief objectives.[45] The first one is to ensure that the resolution of the financially distressed G-SII will not cause systemic disruption and will not increase costs for taxpayers. The second one is to protect vital economic functions by having in place mechanisms where shareholders and unsecured creditors absorb losses in a manner that respects the hierarchy of claims in liquidation.

The main goals of the SRR are: (1) ongoing resolvability assessments; (2) recovery and resolution plans; (3) mandatory bail-ins; and (4) a soft law framework for coordinating measures for the orderly recovery and resolution of G-SIIs (while the provision of run-off powers and policyholder protection are some of the features that separate the insurance-SRR from the special recovery and resolution regimes applicable to non-insurance SIFIs). However, the success of this proposed framework will depend on policy and legal reforms at domestic and regional level, the progress of harmonisation and the willingness of the relevant authorities to share burdens and cooperate at a global level ideally by legally committing themselves to a forward-looking plan of action.[46]

3.5 Concluding remarks

The changing structure of global financial markets not only has resulted in a substantial increase in cross-border trade in financial services and portfolio capital flows but has also introduced a higher level of risk in financial transactions that may impact systemic stability.[47]

The 'collapses' of Northern Rock, Royal Bank of Scotland, Bear Stearns, Lehman Brothers and American International Group revealed failures by the authorities entrusted with the task of supervising them.[48] These failures evidenced that not

43 Financial Stability Board, 'Reducing the Moral Hazard Posed by Systemically Important Financial Institutions – the FSB Recommendations and Time Lines', 20 October 2010, 1.

44 Financial Stability Board, 'Global Systemically Important Insurers and the Policy Measures that Will Apply to Them', 18 July 2013.

45 Andromachi Georgosouli, 'The Emerging Special Recovery and Resolution Framework of G-SIIs and its Effectiveness', in A. Georgosouli and M. Goldby (eds) *Systemic Risk and the Future of Insurance Regulation* (Informa Law from Routledge, 2015), chap. 8.

46 Financial Stability Board, 'Key Attributes of Effective Resolution Regimes for Financial Institutions', 15 October 2014.

47 Kern Alexander, 'Bank Capital Management and Macro-Prudential Regulation – A Law and Finance Perspective' (2012) 24 *Journal of Banking Law*, 331.

48 Marc Labonte, 'Systemically Important or "Too Big to Fail" Financial Institutions', Congressional Research Service Report R42150, 19 September 2014, 34–36. Available at: www.fas.org/sgp/crs/misc/R42150.pdf.

only banking institutions, but derivatives markets, securities firms and insurance companies can also be a source of systemic risk. In response to these deficiencies there has been a significant switch from a principles-based regime towards a more intrusive and systemically-oriented regulatory approach.

In the UK this change was well documented in the 'The Turner Review' which signalled: (1) a radical shift in supervisory style from focusing on systems and processes, to focusing on key business outcomes and risks and on the sustainability of business models and strategies; (2) a different approach to the assessment of approved persons, with a focus on technical skills as well as probity; and (3) an outstanding increase in resources devoted to sectoral and firm comparator analysis, enabling the FSA (now defunct, and replaced by the Bank of England/PRA and the FCA) to better identify firms which are outliers in terms of risks and business strategies and to identify emerging sector wide trends which may create systemic risk.[49]

The domain of financial stability has expanded from the need to ensure sound banking (both with regard to individual institutions and with regard to the banking and payment system as a whole) to the need to ensure sound finance (encompassing all financial institutions and the financial system as a whole). It is not 'what you do' that worries the authorities but the systemic implications of what you do. Therefore, whether it is banking, securities or insurance, the authorities will want to monitor the systemic implications of different lines of financial business.

The institutional challenges involved in creating arrangements at the international, regional, and domestic levels (both with regard to micro-prudential supervision as well as macro-prudential supervision) represent a momentous shift towards the development of a systemic regulatory approach.[50] However, substantial international cooperation and coordination of policies is still necessary in order to achieve effective frameworks for systemic risk control.

49 Financial Services Authority, 'The Turner Review. A Regulatory Response to the Global Banking Crisis', March 2009, 88–92. The major features indicated are the need for *ex ante* macro-prudential analysis, the intensity of supervision and effective regulation, combining prudential supervision with conduct of business compliance.

50 See Article 70 ('Transmission of information to central banks, monetary authorities, payment systems overseers and the European Systemic Risk Board') of the Directive 2014/51/EU of the European Parliament and of the Council of 16 April 2014 amending Directives 2003/71/EC and 2009/138/EC and Regulations (EC) No. 1060/2009, (EU) No. 1094/2010 and (EU) No. 1095/2010 in respect of the powers of the European Supervisory Authority (European Insurance and Occupational Pensions Authority) and the European Supervisory Authority (European Securities and Markets Authority). The Directive 2014/51/EU (so-called 'Omnibus II') has replaced Directive 2009/138/EC (so-called 'Solvency II') by introducing specific rules on 'risk-based capital requirements across all EU Member States'.

CHAPTER 4

Systemic risk in insurance: common thinking errors, and their resolution

Chris Finney

4.1 Introduction

Many insurance market professionals do not believe that insurance and insurers are systemic. They do not therefore believe that the near collapse of American International Group (AIG) is sufficient to justify the sweeping changes that are being made to the way insurance and insurers are regulated. Policymakers clearly have the opposite view.

This chapter uses AIG as a case study to analyse whether the instincts of insurance market professionals are right. It does this by describing and then analysing the arguments that are most commonly used to rebut the assertion that change is required to prevent '*another AIG*'. This chapter also draws attention to some of the inconsistencies and flaws in the regulatory narrative, which have allowed or encouraged professional perceptions to differ to the extent that is apparent in the market today.

4.2 An introduction to thinking errors

Psychologists, psychiatrists and cognitive behavioural psychotherapists sometimes encourage their clients to identify and challenge their '*thinking errors*':[1] the traps we can all fall into, if we focus on the negative, and ignore the positive; take things personally, when they are not; and jump to conclusions about ourselves, without thinking things through. Left unchecked, thinking errors can make us unhappy. They can also make us ill.

4.3 Some common thinking errors

Before AIG failed, it was widely accepted, by insurance regulators and market professionals alike, that insurers could not experience a '*run*';[2] and they could not be systemic.

1 See, for example, *Cognitive Therapy of Anxiety Disorders. A Practice Manual and Conceptual Guide*, Adrian Wells, published by John Wiley & Sons, 1997.

2 '*Run*' is a reference to '*a run on the bank*'. A run on the bank occurs when so many depositors try to withdraw money from their bank accounts that the bank does not have enough liquidity to settle their claims when made. In these circumstances, the bank may be '*cash flow insolvent*' (it cannot pay its debts as they fall due), even though its assets are greater than its liabilities, and it therefore remains solvent on a capital basis.

Today, many of those working in the regulatory community seem to accept, almost as an article of faith, that insurers can experience runs, and they can be systemic. Having reached these conclusions, policy makers, supervisors and regulators are changing their approach to insurers. They are also changing the prudential and other obligations that insurers are required to meet and they are doing these things to reduce the risk that '*another*'[3] systemic insurer will come so close to failure that it will cause other failures,[4] unless it is rescued by the state.

At the same time, it is not unusual to hear insurance market professionals argue that insurers are not systemic; they do not experience runs; and that whilst it is true that several insurers or insurance groups have collapsed suddenly, or come perilously close to doing so, that is almost always about '*operational risk*' ('*the risk of loss arising from inadequate or failed internal processes, personnel or systems, or external events*'[5]), and not insurance or insurers as such. On this analysis, insurance market professionals would also argue that today's insurance regulators do not understand insurance; having failed to anticipate and prevent runs and collapses in the banking sector, they are being over-zealous by trying to prevent imaginary runs and collapses in the insurance sector too.

Each of these arguments has merit; but which is more likely to be right? Which is more likely to be based on, or at least to include, thinking errors?

4.4 What does systemic risk mean?

AIG argued that systemic risk was '*the risk imposed by inter-linkages and interdependencies in a system or market, which could potentially bankrupt or bring down the entire system or market if one player is eliminated, or a cluster of failures occurs at once. Systemic financial risk occurs when contingency plans that are developed individually to address selected risks are collectively incompatible [and/or] where every element that once appeared independent is connected with every other element*'.[6]

Professor Cummins of Temple University[7] has suggested[8] that systemic risk is '*the risk that an event will trigger a loss of economic value or confidence in a substantial*

---

3 In this context, '*another*' is a reference to AIG.

4 These failures could be self-reinforcing, and they may have an adverse effect on '*main street*'. If one insurer fails, it may cause the failure of other banks and financial and non-financial institutions. Any or all of these things could adversely affect the (so called) '*real economy*'. Although it is not always the case, when policy makers, regulators and market professionals refer to '*main street*' and the '*real economy*' they are usually referring to: (i) consumers, and businesses operating outside the financial services sector; and (ii) the non-financial services part of national and international economies.

5 See recital 33 to Directive 2009/138/EC of the European Parliament and of the Council of 25 November 2009 on the taking up and pursuit of the business of insurance and reinsurance, as amended (Solvency II). An operational risk might be or include an internal fraud, an overbearing CEO who runs the business with little or no effective challenge from the board, and the risk that a change of law will materially affect the value of the firm's assets and liabilities to its detriment. Operational risk has caused insurers to fail, or to come perilously close to doing so. Recent examples include: The Independent Insurance Company Limited; The Equitable Life Assurance Society; HIH Insurance Limited and Quinn Insurance.

6 See 'AIG Draft – February 26, 2009 (Strictly Confidential) AIG: is the Risk Systemic?' Available at: http://abcnews.go.com/images/Business/aig_systemic_090309.pdf

7 Professor J. David Cummins is the Joseph E. Boettner Professor of Risk, Insurance, and Financial Institutions, at the Fox School of Business, Temple University, Philadelphia PA, US.

8 By reference to statements made by the G-10 (2001) and the World Economic Forum (2008).

segment of the financial system serious enough to have significant adverse effects on the real economy'. Professor Cummins has also suggested that systemic financial risk involves '*a system-wide financial crisis*'; '*a sharp decline in asset values and economic activity*'; the '*spread of instability throughout the financial system*'; and an impact that is sufficient '*to adversely affect the real economy*'.[9]

The Financial Stability Board (the FSB) has argued that[10] a '*systemic event*' occurs when there is '*disruption to the flow of financial services that is … caused by an impairment of … the financial system; and … has the potential to have serious negative consequences for the real economy*'.[11] On the FSB's analysis, the main criteria for assessing an institution's systemic importance are size, a lack of product substitutability, and interconnectedness. Larger firms that are heavily interconnected with other firms, and firm's offering unique products that other firms rely on to a significant extent, are therefore more likely to be systemic than firms that do not.[12]

Although the AIG definition may seem exaggerated[13] and self-serving,[14] it draws our attention to some important systemic risk features, which the other definitions seem to miss. For example, post-crisis, it is now clear that '*systemic financial risk [can] occur … when contingency plans that are developed individually to address selected risks are collectively incompatible*' and when things '*that once appeared independent [turn out to be] connected*'. The significance of this should not be underestimated. It becomes apparent in at least two ways. First, it seems clear that banking regulations and insurance regulations are developed separately by experts in their respective fields and that very few people are able to understand and influence the shape of both regimes. That can generate material tension and inconsistency between them, for example, when it comes to measuring and mitigating identical risks.[15] Second, it

9 See 'Systemic Risk and the Insurance Industry', J. David Cummins, Temple University, The Brookings Institution Conference on Regulating Non-Bank SIFIs, 9 May 2013.

10 See para. 7 of the 'Guidance to Assess the Systemic Importance of Financial Institutions, Markets and Instruments: Initial Considerations' – Report to the G-20 Finance Ministers and Central Bank Governors, Prepared by Staff of the International Monetary Fund and the Bank for International Settlements, and the Secretariat of the Financial Stability Board, October 2008.

11 For these purposes, '*disruption to the flow of financial services*' includes situations where some financial services are temporarily unavailable, or their cost increases sharply; '*the financial system*' includes firms that manufacture savings and investment products, as well as those offering payment services; and '*serious negative consequences for the real economy*' suggests that there is something about a firm that will cause '*significant disruption to the rest of the financial system and the real economy*', if it fails.

12 See paras 11 and 12 of the report referred to in footnote 9. This may have been what the International Association of Insurance Supervisors had in mind when it proposed that the primary criteria for identifying a Global Systemically Important Insurer (G-SII) should be size, global activity, interconnectedness, the degree of engaging in non-traditional and/or non-insurance activities and substitutability (see 'G-SIIs: Initial Assessment Methodology', published by the International Association of Insurance Supervisors in July 2013).

13 For example, a systemic risk '*could … bankrupt or bring down the entire system … if one player is eliminated*'.

14 AIG used this definition when it was seeking to persuade the United States' Federal Government that AIG was systemic, and that it was therefore both necessary and desirable for the government to provide substantial financial support to secure its future. This support eventually reached $184.6 billion – see 'AIG's Benmoshe joins list of financial crisis players putting pen to paper', published in the *Wall Street Journal* on 27 October 2014.

15 See, for example: (i) 'The Implications of Financial Regulatory Reform for the Insurance Industry', Oliver Wyman August 2011; (ii) IMF Working Paper WP/11/187 'Possible Unintended Consequences of Basel III and Solvency II', published by the International Monetary Fund, 2011; (iii) 'Solvency II and Securitisation: Significant Negative Impact on European Market – Special Report', Fitch ratings, 30

is also widely accepted that asset classes that have long appeared to be uncorrelated are correlated in some circumstances. Put simply, it used to be thought that if the value of some asset classes fell, others would rise, so a well-diversified portfolio would protect most investors against market volatility. However, during the recent crisis, it became apparent that sometimes apparently uncorrelated assets classes fall together. In practice, this has made it difficult or impossible for banks to strengthen their balance sheets by raising more capital from insurers (even though insurers have traditionally been the most significant investors in bank equity and bank debt). It has also made it difficult or impossible, at least in some circumstances, to reduce insurers' market and counterparty risks by encouraging a diverse investment strategy. Each of these things still helps, but neither is the panacea it once appeared to be.

Professor Cummins' definition is also useful because it reminds us (for example) that '*a loss of economic value or confidence [can be] serious enough to have significant adverse effects on the real economy*'.[16]

We may therefore come to regret the fact that most of the regulatory community has coalesced around the FSB's relatively narrow definition,[17] even if at least some regulators and policy makers are prepared to read and apply the FSB's definition together with three additional factors: (i) '*time*' and '*speed*';[18] (ii) the availability of '*transmission mechanisms*';[19] and (iii) a focus on activities rather than institutions.[20]

April 2012; and (iv) 'Basel Accords versus Solvency II: Regulatory Adequacy and Consistency under the Post-Crisis Capital Standards, Working Paper on Risk Management and Insurance No. 132', University of St Gallen, October 2013.

16 Many of the banks that collapsed during the financial crisis did so because consumers and market counterparties lost confidence in them. Northern Rock is just one example: consumers queued for hours to withdraw their savings and the bank ran out of liquidity because demand increased significantly and wholesale market counterparties refused to lend cash and/or to enter into liquidity swaps with the bank, in each instance for fear that it would collapse. In the event, this fear of collapse caused or contributed to the collapse that followed.

17 This definition has been accepted by (for example) the G-20 finance ministers, the Central Bank Governors, the International Monetary Fund, the Bank for International Settlements and the International Association of Insurance Supervisors. (See p. 23 of 'Systemic Risk in Insurance: An analysis of insurance and financial stability. Special Report of the Geneva Association Systemic Risk Working Group', published by the Geneva Association in March 2010.)

18 The International Association of Insurance Supervisors has argued that time and speed should be included in the FSB's definition of systemic risk to reflect '*the critical role that timing (speed) plays in whether an event transmitted into the financial system can be absorbed by the system*'. The Geneva Association agrees. See p. 24 of 'Systemic Risk in Insurance: An analysis of insurance and financial stability. Special Report of the Geneva Association Systemic Risk Working Group'.

19 The Geneva Association has endorsed the time and speed additions suggested by the International Association of Insurance Supervisors (see footnote 18), and noted that there must also be at least one '*transmission mechanism*' available before a risk crystallising in one part of the financial system can have an impact on another part of that system, or on main street. See p. 33 of 'Systemic Risk in Insurance: An analysis of insurance and financial stability. Special Report of the Geneva Association Systemic Risk Working Group'.

20 The aim of the Geneva Association '*is not to argue that the [FSB's] criteria are wrong, or that they do not apply to insurers*', but to show that the FSB criteria need to be applied '*to activities and not to institutions*'. For example, '*Applying the criteria blindly to whole institutions risks adding an additional regulatory burden on system-stabilising institutions whilst potentially missing some institutions carrying out activities which do pose a systemic risk*'. See p. 24 of 'Systemic Risk in Insurance: An analysis of insurance and financial stability. Special Report of the Geneva Association Systemic Risk Working Group'.

4.5 Can insurance and insurers be systemic?

4.5.1 Traditional insurance products and the traditional insurance business

The focus on activities rather than institutions has encouraged policy makers to use the terms '*traditional*' and '*non-traditional*' to describe their '*indicator and judgment based approach*' to systemic insurance and insurers. We may also come to regret these labels for the confusion they will cause.

At its simplest, an insurer carrying on '*traditional insurance business*' effects and carries out '*traditional insurance products*'; and products are '*traditional*' if they include an '*insurable interest*',[21] a carefully defined '*claims trigger*',[22] and '*policyholder entitlements*'.[23] Most life and general insurance policies have these features and are therefore regarded as '*traditional insurance products*'.

Insurers carrying on traditional insurance business fund themselves using ordinary debt and equity; they are usually cash-flow positive, with little need for substantial leverage. Most traditional insurers rely on well-developed enterprise-risk management (ERM) and asset-liability management (ALM) programmes, and modern actuarial techniques, to help them predict and manage their cash flow requirements.[24] They also use a mix of reinsurance and hedging products to spread their insurance and investment risk.

Most traditional insurers insure large numbers of policyholders against a pool of well-diversified risks. The traditional insurer collects premiums, which it invests in the hope of generating positive investment returns and a cash-flow that matches the rate at which claims will arise. Claims on traditional insurance policies tend to be idiosyncratic: a claim on one policy or a large number of policies in one location does not necessarily mean there will be claims on other policies or in other locations. They also tend to be disconnected from ordinary economic and business cycles; as well as being made and settled over extended periods of time. It is therefore unusual (but not impossible[25]) for a traditional insurer carrying on traditional insurance business to experience a '*run*' or significant '*cash-flow stress*',

21 In other words, the person who buys the protection, or will benefit from it, has an actual or legally presumed pecuniary or financial interest in the insured life, property or risk. See also the discussion about whether Credit Default Swaps are contracts of insurance, below.

22 An uncertain event that will trigger the insurer's obligation to pay money or provide services for the benefit of the policyholder or his beneficiaries, if the event occurs.

23 The benefits due under the terms of the policy, even if they are not necessarily due to the person who owns the legal title to the policy. There is more information about each of these things in, for example, Chapter 6 of the Financial Conduct Authority's Handbook of rules and guidance. Available at: http://fshandbook.info/FS/html/FCA/PERG/6. See also the Financial Services and Markets Act 2000 (Meaning of 'Policy' and 'Policyholder') Order 2001, SI 2001/2361.

24 In fact, they are effectively required to do so. See, for example: (i) chapters two and three of Directive 2002/83/EC of the European Parliament and of the Council of 5 November 2002 concerning life assurance, as amended (the Consolidated Life Directive); and (ii) Title I, chapter IV of Directive 2009/138/EC of the European Parliament and of the Council of 25 November 2009 on the taking-up and pursuit of the business of insurance and reinsurance, as amended (Solvency II).

25 For example, policyholders using their policies as savings vehicles may cancel them as a way of 'withdrawing' the current value of their policy in cash; in times of panic or deep recession, that could generate cash-flow stress or a run. But this is relatively rare. Arguably, a life policy which includes an investment or savings product is not a traditional insurance policy, in any event. See also '4.7.2 *That insurers do not experience runs and cash-flow stress, and AIG did not experience these things either*' below.

and it is extremely unusual for a modern traditional insurance business to fail for lack of liquidity alone.

4.5.2 Non-traditional insurance and non-insurance business

The line between traditional and non-traditional insurance is sometimes difficult to draw. For example, a traditional life insurance policy may include non-traditional features, which begin to change the status of the product without making it entirely non-traditional. Examples include life policies with embedded Guaranteed Annuity Rates (GARs)[26] and Guaranteed Investment Returns (GIRs).[27]

Mortgage guarantee, trade credit, and financial guarantee insurance are almost certainly '*non-traditional insurance products*' because of their likely correlation with business and economic cycles, and the increased risk of large numbers of correlated claims. So are alternative risk transfers (ARTs),[28] insurance-linked securities (ILS)[29] and finite reinsurance,[30] even though many of these products have been

---

26 See, for example, *Equitable Life Assurance Society v Hyman* [2002] 1 AC 408:

> '*The need to plan for retirement is ... a high priority. One of the most attractive methods of ... saving ... has been life assurance policies with profits ... It is, however, a fact of life that the level of ... retirement benefits is dependent on variable ... annuity rates. ... the Society ... sold policies containing guaranteed minimum annuity rates. ... this may have seemed to investors an attractive way of reducing uncertainties in retirement. Against this background a dispute arose out of the decisions of the ... Society of calculating final bonuses so as to allocate to a with-profits policyholder, whose policy contains provision for guaranteed annuity rates ("GARs"), a different final bonus ... depending on whether the policyholder ... elects: (a) to take the annuity to which the guaranteed annuity rates apply ...; or (b) ... an alternative benefit ... calculated at current rates ...*' *per* Lord Steyn.

27 A with-profits policy with a guaranteed investment return is a with-profits insurance contract which guarantees a minimum investment return regardless of the performance of the assets in the underlying with-profits fund. A contract that includes a GIR is therefore especially valuable from a policyholder's perspective, and expensive to honour from an insurer's perspective, when investment returns were poor. A with-profits policy might include a GAR, a GIR, both or neither. Other types of guarantee also exist. See, for example, *Phoenix Life Assurance Ltd v Financial Services Authority* [2013] EWHC 60 (Comm), where the court was concerned with the meaning and effect of: '*... a "Nominal Capital Sum" (or "NCS"); (ii) A MAR ...: a guarantee that Phoenix would convert the policyholder's fund into an annuity at a rate no less favourable to the policyholder than a specified minimum annuity rate ... (iii) A GMP ...: a guarantee of annuities for the policyholder and his surviving spouse of no less than ... a Guaranteed Minimum Pension revalued to State Pension Age ...*'.

28 ART mechanisms are used to transfer insurable risks to the capital markets. They may include '*risk securitization through catastrophe bonds, insurance-linked securities and reinsurance sidecars, trading of risk through industry loss warranties and weather derivative contracts and transforming capital market risks into reinsurance through transformer vehicles*'. See, for example, http://www.artemis.bm/library/what_is_alternative_risk_transfer.html.

29 At its simplest, an insurer will create ILS by establishing a special purpose vehicle (the SPV), transferring specified risks to that vehicle and paying it a premium. The SPV then issues bonds to capital markets investors, before investing the premium and bond issue receipts. If the risks crystallise, the premium, bond issue receipts, and investment returns are used to pay the insurer; if they do not, these assets are used to pay investment returns to the bond investors. The risks and associated bonds may be used to create (so called) catastrophe bonds, mortality bonds, industry loss warranties, insurance futures and redundant reserve securitisations.

30 Finite reinsurance means '*reinsurance under which the explicit maximum loss potential, expressed as the maximum economic risk transferred, arising both from a significant underwriting risk and timing risk transfer, exceeds the premium over the lifetime of the contract by a limited but significant amount; together with at least one of the following features: (a) explicit and material consideration of the time value of money; and (b) contractual provisions to moderate the balance of economic experience between the parties to the reinsurance over time to achieve the target risk transfer*' – see art. 210(3) of the Directive 2002/83/EC of the European Parliament

available in the market for so long that they might be regarded as *'traditional'* for other purposes.

4.6 AIG – a practical example

4.6.1 An insurance group just like any other?

The business that eventually became AIG began life as C V Starr, a general insurer, in Shanghai in 1919.

By the end of 2006, the last full year of trading before its financial position began to deteriorate, AIG had become one of the largest publicly traded companies,[31] and the largest publicly traded insurer,[32] in the world. The AIG group had more than $1 trillion of assets, and more than 76 million customers, in more than 130 countries worldwide. Its annual revenue was more than $100 billion, and almost 90% of its net revenue was generated by its insurance and reinsurance businesses. This group included more than 70 US and 175 non-US insurers and reinsurers. It also included consumer and insurance-premium finance companies, a professional advisory services business, a major aircraft leasing company, an asset manager, a private bank, and AIG Financial Products (AIGFP).

Although the AIG group was larger and more complex than other insurance groups, in many respects, it was just like any other. To keep its overall costs of capital down, AIG issued subordinated debt at holding company level, and invested the proceeds in its subsidiaries. Group companies relied on each other for at least some of their insurance and reinsurance needs. They also entered into intra-group loans, asset management contracts and other business arrangements. Many of the AIG insurers held shares in other group companies, and these shares were used to meet at least part of the insurers' regulatory capital requirements. Some of the larger subsidiaries provided guarantees for the benefit of the creditors of the smaller subsidiaries and, crucially, the AIG holding company guaranteed AIGFP's Credit Default Swaps (CDSs) and derivatives portfolios.

At the same time, AIG's life and annuity insurers had invested heavily in corporate bonds, treasuries, gilts, and mortgage backed securities (MBS); and 12 of AIG's life insurers were participating in a securities lending programme through an affiliated lending agent, AIG Securities Lending Corp (AIGSLC). Like many other life insurers, the AIG participating insurers were lending equities, high quality corporate bonds, treasuries and gilts to third-party banks and broker-dealers in return for a fee and collateral, which AIGSLC invested in the hope of generating investment returns.

---

and of the Council of 5 November 2002 concerning life assurance, as amended (the Consolidated Life Directive); and (ii) Title I, Chapter IV of Directive 2009/138/EC of the European Parliament and of the Council of 25 November 2009 on the taking-up and pursuit of the business of Insurance and Reinsurance, as amended (Solvency II).

31 Congressional Oversight Panel, June Oversight Report, 'The AIG Rescue, its Impact on Markets, and the Government's Exit Strategy', June 2010.

32 See p. 6 of 'The Financial Crisis, Systemic Risk and the Future of Insurance Regulation', by Scott E. Harrington PhD, an Issue Analysis; a Public Policy Paper of the National Association of Mutual Insurance Companies, September 2009.

4.6.2 What went wrong?

When AIGFP started to write CDSs in 1998, it was extremely cautious. It restricted itself almost entirely to offering CDSs against highly rated corporate bonds. It also used the group's insurance underwriting expertise to analyse every credit default risk it was offered, before declining to accept anything that was too complex, too risky, or too likely to put the group's AAA rating at risk.[33]

However, as the business grew, AIGFP came under internal pressure to generate higher profits to help the group maintain its share price and dividend growth. AIGFP also began to experience pricing pressure as its competitors commoditised, standardised and '*mass produced*' similar products before offering them to the market at a lower cost than AIGFP could manage. AIGFP's response was to write CDSs on less highly rated and unrated corporate debt, as well as on MBS and other forms of Collateralised Debt Obligations (CDOs), where the competitive pressures were lower and the premiums and risks were higher. This continued until the end of 2005, when AIGFP stopped writing some classes of derivative because it thought the quality of its underwriting had fallen too far.

In the beginning, AIGFP also hedged itself against the downside risk of almost every contract it entered into. But as its business grew, it hedged less. So, whilst other CDS issuers almost always bought protection against the risks they were taking, AIGFP did not.

There were at least three reasons for this. Although AIGFP was taking more risk than before, it still saw itself as extremely cautious. AIGFP's CDSs were usually in a '*second loss position*' on the '*super-senior*' tranches of highly rated CDOs; the underlying loans were geographically and financially diverse; and AIGFP's models suggested that the chance of it being required to make a payment on a CDS were less than 0.15%, even in highly stressed scenarios.[34] AIGFP relied on the same three reasons when, having decided to stop writing some derivatives because its underwriting standards had fallen too far, it decided not to hedge or reduce the (excessive) risks it had already taken. This was strange because AIGFP knew that, whilst its models were good at predicting the risk of default on the debts supporting the securities its CDSs were backing, they did not reflect the risk that these securities would fall in value and be downgraded; that AIG would be downgraded; or that, if either or both of these things happened, they would generate collateral calls against AIGFP, and therefore against AIG.

On 14 March 2005, Maurice 'Hank' Greenberg, AIG's Chairman and Chief Executive Officer of more than 37 years, was forced to step down following allegations that he had been involved in a fraud that overstated AIG's earnings and misrepresented its regulatory capital position. Greenberg was the only person who really understood the complexity of, and the interconnectedness within, the AIG

---

33 See, for example, R. Boyd *Fatal Risk: A Cautionary Tale of AIG's Corporate Suicide* (Chichester: Wiley, 2011).

34 This is why, in August 2007, Joseph Cassano, AIGFP's chief operating officer, was able to describe its CDS business as largely risk-free: '*It is hard for us, without being flippant, to even see a scenario within any kind of realm of reason that would see us losing $1*' – see, for example, 'How Mayfair Office brought down AIG', published in *The Guardian* on 2 March 2009.

group. His loss exposed material failings in the group's internal systems and controls and ratings downgrades quickly followed. These downgrades automatically triggered collateral calls from AIGFP's CDS counterparties, which AIG was obliged to meet.

The ousting of Greenberg has been controversial. One reason is that Greenberg insists that he knew that AIGFP needed to hedge and reduce the derivative risks it had already taken. Greenberg claims that he would therefore have ensured that AIGFP completed a hedging and risk reduction programme in the second half of 2005.[35] There does not seem to be much evidence to support these assertions; but if they are true, they would have made a significant difference to what happened next for two reasons. First, AIGFP may have succeeded in its attempts to de-risk its derivatives portfolio before the risks it had already taken started to crystallise and that might have saved the group from the near collapse that followed. Second, because if Greenberg had still been AIG's CEO, he might have stopped AIGSLC from aggressively expanding its securities lending business in the second half of 2005, before investing its counterparties' cash-collateral in sub-prime MBS, because he knew that AIGFP had stopped writing sub-prime-related CDSs due to the risks in the sub-prime market.

Be that as it may, on 1 January 2006, and in common with other insurance and reinsurance groups, AIG switched from '*mark-to-model*'[36] to '*mark-to-market*'[37] accounting. This exacerbated the losses that AIG appeared to suffer between the autumn of 2006 and the end of 2009, as property values fell, borrowers defaulted on their loans, and the value and ratings of the AIGFP CDS-backed securities fell.

In the summer of 2007, AIGFP received the first in a series of collateral calls linked to the falling value and ratings of these securities. In the beginning, AIG was able to use its models and a lack of liquidity in the securities' markets to argue that the relevant securities were worth more than its counterparties suggested and that values would correct upwards as liquidity returned. This enabled AIG to post collateral at much lower levels than its counterparties wanted.[38] But, as the number of

35 See, for example, 'Ex-Chairman of AIG says Bailout Has Failed', published in the *New York Times*, 2 April 2009.

36 A firm taking a '*mark-to-model*' approach will use internal assumptions and financial models to value its assets and liabilities for accounting, risk and other purposes; and these assumptions are likely to depend, at least in part, on the assumption that the original purchase price was reasonable, even if it was agreed in a highly illiquid market. The '*mark-to-model*' approach has the benefit of stability (*cf* the description of '*mark-to-market*' in footnote 37). However, if the assumptions and models are consciously or unconsciously flawed, the firm, its investors and its policyholders will necessarily be relying on inaccurate pricing information. For this reason, the '*mark-to-market*' approach is now preferred, although '*mark-to-model*' is still regarded as appropriate if there is no current liquid market in the relevant assets.

37 A firm taking a '*mark-to-market*' approach will value its assets and liabilities using current market information, if the market is sufficiently liquid for this to be appropriate. '*Mark to market*' therefore gives a more 'realistic' view of the value of the firm's assets and liabilities, and is more likely to reflect 'fair value'. However, if markets are volatile, and the firm '*marks to market*', the value of its assets and liabilities will also be volatile. In regulatory terms, this is regarded as prudent because regulated firms are required to hold enough regulatory capital to be able to meet their regulatory capital obligations at all times (i.e. regardless of the value of its assets and liabilities as they change over time). A firm '*marking to market*' is therefore likely to be required to hold more assets than if it was '*marking to model*' instead.

38 For example, in August 2007, Goldman Sachs asked AIG to post $1.5 billion of collateral but AIG eventually posted $450 million instead. In October 2007, Goldman Sachs asked for an additional $3 billion of collateral; AIG eventually posted $1.5 billion.

collateral calls increased, securities' values fell; more securities were downgraded; and other CDS issuers publicly acknowledged these facts. AIG was compelled to accept its counterparties' demands in full because, if it did not, it would appear unwilling or unable to meet its obligations, and that would effectively close the group to new business.

In the fourth quarter of 2007, AIG was forced to recognise an unrealised market valuation loss of $11.25 billion on a tranche of AIGFP CDS-backed securities. Collateral calls followed – each call adding to the liquidity stress at AIG holding company level.

In February 2008, AIG told the markets that its external auditor had reported, in November 2007, that material weaknesses in the way AIGFP valued its CDS portfolio meant that AIG could not rely on the financial information it was receiving from its subsidiary. This prompted more collateral calls. In the first quarter of 2008, AIG posted $7 billion of cash collateral.

In May 2008, AIG reported an unrealised loss of $5.9 billion on its CDS portfolio; Standard and Poor's downgraded AIG from AA to AA-. Each of these developments prompted collateral calls. In the second quarter of 2008, AIG was required to post an additional £13 billion of cash collateral.

In September 2008, Standard and Poor's expressed concern about the liquidity stress being experienced at AIG holding company level and downgraded AIG to A-. More collateral calls followed, so that by the end of 2008, AIG had posted £31.5 billion more.

As the sub-prime crisis deepened, AIGSLC's counterparties started to close out their positions, before demanding the return of their collateral; AIGSLC found it difficult to meet these demands. Eventually, losses on the MBS-collateral investments and an increasingly illiquid MBS market, meant that AIGSLC could not meet its borrowers' demands without selling its MBS investments at a significant loss, if it could sell them at all. This forced the AIG parent to honour AIGSLC's collateral-return commitments, which created even greater liquidity stress within the group. '*By the end of August 2008, AIG had provided $3.3 billion ... to help plug the shortfall*'. But this was wholly inadequate: '*between September 12 and September 30 2008 securities lending counter-parties demanded that AIG return ... $24 billion.*' Eventually, it became clear that the AIGSLC securities lending programme had been '*reckless*' in at least three ways: (a) its scale (at its peak, AIGSLC had $76 billion of securities out on loan); (b) the amount of collateral AIGSLC required in return for the securities it was lending out (market practice suggested that 100% to 105% was appropriate, with the value of the collateral rising and falling as the value of the securities changed over time but, for competitive reasons, AIGSLC often accepted collateral worth less than 100%, before asking AIG to post the rest); and (c) because AIGSLC invested up to 60% of the collateral it received in MBS, and left it there too long. It also became clear that if AIGFP had not brought AIG to the brink of collapse, the securities lending programme would have brought it to that point in any event.[39]

39 See, for example, pp. 34 to 36 and 231 of the Congressional Oversight Panel, June Oversight Report, 'The AIG Rescue, its Impact on Markets, and the Government's Exit Strategy', June 2010.

4.7 Where were the thinking errors?

4.7.1 The problems at AIG had nothing to do with insurance and insurers

In fact, about 10%[40] of all CDSs *would be* contracts of insurance under both UK law, and under the law of the US, if a UK '*legal fiction*' and a specific US legal provision had not been created to change this.[41]

A contract of insurance is a binding promise by one party, to make a payment or provide a benefit to another, if a pre-defined event occurs, in circumstances where the promise is given in return for a payment; and the pre-defined event is: (a) uncertain (either as to whether or when it will occur); *and* (b) adverse to the interests of the benefit receiving party.[42]

A CDS has the same features. The only material difference is that, in a CDS, the defined event will not always be adverse to the interests of the benefit receiving party.

If the benefit receiving party *invests* in debentures and takes a CDS to protect himself against the risk that the debenture issuer will default on its coupon and other obligations, the CDS will be insurance. However, if the benefit receiving party buys the CDS for 'risk and return' purposes *without investing* in the underlying securities as well, the defined event will not (or will not necessarily) be adverse to his interests. The CDS will probably not therefore be a contract of insurance.

In other words, some CDSs are contracts of insurance, and their status varies depending on the circumstances of the protection buyer, rather than the identity of the protection issuer or the terms of the CDS itself.

When CDSs were developed in the 1990s, this analysis, which correctly reflected the law at the time, had the potential to create significant practical difficulties, especially if it was read alongside two long-standing European and US legal principles: that for consumer protection reasons: (a) only insurers are lawfully permitted to carry on insurance business; and (b) insurers are expressly prohibited from carrying on anything other than insurance business and business that is closely related to it. If these principles were retained and applied to CDSs, a CDS protection buyer would be obliged to buy insurance-CDS and non-insurance-CDS from different providers. Insurers (at least) would be required to investigate the securities holding status

40 On 7 October 2008, Eric R Dinallo, Superintendent of the New York State Insurance Department, told the US House of Representatives Committee on Oversight and Government Reform that CDS '*… is often … called insurance in the sense that you are buying insurance against the default of [a] bond … There are probably $60 trillion of credit defaults swaps. An overwhelmingly high percentage are … naked credit default swaps. What that means is you enter into a contract with a party. Neither of you own any exposure … You're just taking a bet … And the Governor has said that he's willing to regulate the piece that we can, which is the insurance piece, that original 10% we can easily call an insurance product. We can regulate that because it is an insurance transaction…*'

41 See footnote 44 below.

42 *Prudential v Commissioners of Inland Revenue* [1904] 2 KB 658. See also PERG 6.3.4G. Arguably, the requirement for the defined event to be adverse to the interests of the insured reflects, and has the same effect as, the legal requirement that at least some types of contract of insurance will only be valid and enforceable if they are entered into by reference to, and they protect, the insured's insurable interest in the insured life, property or risk.

and intentions of their insured;[43] and CDS buyers would be required to cancel one type of contract and enter into another if they bought a CDS for 'risk and return' purposes, and then bought the underlying securities.

CDS issuers did not want to be regulated; regulators did not want to regulate them. So CDS issuers argued, and regulators accepted, that the fact that the pre-defined event would not always be adverse to the interests of the benefit receiving party meant that CDSs were not contracts of insurance and should not be regulated as if they were (even though this was only partially true).[44] This may have seemed sensible at the time. After all, the primary purpose of regulation was to protect consumers[45] and most CDSs were 'non-insurance' contracts between well-advised wholesale institutions. A CDS breach would almost certainly not have a material adverse effect on '*consumers*', '*main street*' or the '*real economy*'. Intervening in and seeking to regulate even a small part of a nascent CDS market could not therefore be justified in the risk-based, free market and '*light touch*' regulatory environment that prevailed at the time.[46]

In this sense then, the problems at AIG (or at least the problems that began in AIGFP) were to do with insurance (or at least, insurance-CDSs) and they were to do with insurers (because AIGFP was part of a major insurance group).

The problems at AIG were also to do with insurance and insurers for a second and more obvious reason too. Twelve of AIG's life assurance companies and their affiliate (AIGSLC) were operating a '*reckless*' securities lending programme (see above). So reckless, in fact, that the AIGSLC securities lending programme created 'a *$[21] billion-plus cash drain on [the AIG life insurers'] operations, a shortfall that may have threatened the solvency of these units in the absence of government assistance*', and certainly contributed to a '*double-death spiral*' within the group.[47]

43 Because they could only lawfully enter into a CDS if they were sure that the protection buyer had an insurable interest to protect.

44 In the UK, Robin Potts QC advised the International Swaps and Derivatives Association (ISDA) that credit derivatives (including CDSs) were not contracts of insurance because they did not depend on the existence of an insurable interest, and this was accepted by a grateful Financial Services Authority for policy reasons. In the US, the Commodity Futures Modernization Act 2000 was used to make sure that CDSs were not gambling contracts, insurance contracts or securities, and were not, therefore, regulated products. See, also, the evidence of Eric R. Dinallo, Superintendent of the New York State Insurance Department, to the US House of Representatives Committee on Oversight and Government Reform of 7 October 2008.

45 Regulation is now also concerned with financial stability. See, for example, s. 2B of the Financial Services and Markets Act 2000; recitals 16 and 141 and art. 28 of Directive 2009/138/EC of the European Parliament and of the Council of 25 November 2009 on the taking-up and pursuit of the business of Insurance and Reinsurance (Solvency II).

46 The crisis has demonstrated the fallacy of this approach; CDSs are beginning to be regulated. See, for example, the (so-called) EMIR or European Market Infrastructure Regulation (Regulation 648/2012/EU of the European Parliament and of the Council of 4 July 2012 on OTC derivatives, central counterparties and trade repositories) and Regulation 236/2012/EU of the European Parliament and of the Counsel on short selling and certain aspects of credit default swaps.

47 In the original quote, this figure is put at $15 billion, but later reports describe the actual exposure as being $21 billion. See p. 19 of the Congressional Oversight Panel, June Oversight Report, 'The AIG Rescue, its Impact on Markets, and the Government's Exit Strategy', June 2010; see also the evidence of Senator Richard C. Shelby to the Hearing before the Committee on Banking, Housing, and Urban Affairs in the United States Senate on 'What Went Wrong with American International Group': '*In total, AIG's life insurance companies suffered approximately $21 billion in losses related to securities lending in 2008. More than $17 billion in Federal Assistance has been used to recapitalize the State-regulated insurance companies to ensure*

The problems at AIG therefore seem to have been related to insurance and insurers.

4.7.2 Insurers do not experience runs and cash-flow stress, and AIG did not experience these things either

The most commonly advanced argument in support of this thinking error is that catastrophes are relatively rare; when they occur, it takes many years for claims to emerge, be investigated, settled and paid. There is, of course, some truth in this. Even so, a significant number of general insurers have experienced a '*claims run*' resulting in failure.

For example, the 2001 terrorist attacks on the World Trade Centre created insurance losses which exceeded the capital of Japanese Taisei Fire & Marine Insurance Company Limited. This brought the company to the point of collapse, before it was rescued by Sompo Japan Insurance in 2002.[48]

The Canterbury earthquakes of 2010 and 2011 created so many insurance claims that they pushed Western Pacific Insurance Limited into liquidation. This forced the New Zealand government: (a) to assume the insurance liabilities of AMI Insurance Limited; and (b) to inject capital into the state-owned Earthquake Commission when its insurance liabilities exceeded its capital resources.[49]

Accelerating, panic-driven, surrender demands have also caused '*runs*' on, and the failure of, general,[50] and life and annuity[51] insurers.

In AIG's case, policyholders in Asia began to cash in their life and annuity policies which put a strain on the cash flow positions of AIG's Asian businesses. It also began to affect local bond and equity markets. The authorities feared that these runs would be repeated in the US. If they were, the consequences would be severe because AIG had written more than 81 million life policies, and those policies had a face value of more than $1.9 trillion.[52] The US authorities' particular concerns included that policyholders would cash their policies in and then find they could not obtain equivalent cover for a competitive price, if they could obtain that cover at all. The authorities were also concerned that policy costs would increase, product

they are able to pay their policyholders' claims. In addition, the Federal Reserve had to establish a special facility to help unwind AIG's securities program.' The first death spiral was formed when the holding company began to suffer liquidity difficulties, the rating agencies downgraded it, generating collateral calls which added to the liquidity stress, prompting additional ratings downgrades and more collateral calls.

48 See, for example, p. 10 of 'Ratings Direct: What May Cause Insurance Companies to Fail – And How This Influences Our Criteria', Standard & Poor's, 13 June 2013.

49 Ibid. at p. 11.

50 For example, in 1999, GenAmerica Financial Corp, General American Life Insurance Co, ARM Financial Group Inc, Integrity Life Insurance Co, and RGA Reinsurance Co, all failed as a result of accelerating surrender demands. See, for example, p. 7 of 'Ratings Direct: What May Cause Insurance Companies to Fail – And How This Influences Our Criteria', Standard & Poor's, 13 June 2013.

51 These assurers were First Executive Corp, Executive Life Insurance Co of CA, First Capital Holding Corp, Mutual Benefit Life Insurance Co, Monarch Life Insurance Co, Kentucky Central life Insurance Co and Confederation Life Insurance Co. See, for example, p. 8 of 'Ratings Direct: What May Cause Insurance Companies to Fail – And How This Influences Our Criteria', Standard & Poor's, 13 June 2013.

52 See p. 9 of 'AIG Draft – February 26, 2009 (Strictly Confidential) AIG: is the Risk Systemic?' Available at: http://abcnews.go.com/images/Business/aig_systemic_090309.pdf.

availability would fall and that AIG would be forced to make asset sales into a falling market to cover policyholder withdrawals, which would undermine AIG's capital position, and drive prices down still further. It would also undermine market confidence, because it tended to suggest that banking sector problems had contaminated the insurance sector as well.

AIG did, therefore, at least begin to experience a run, in some parts of its business. It also experienced some run-related cash flow stress. It did not, however, seem to experience the runs that the US authorities had feared

4.7.3 Insurers are not systemic

When it first became apparent that AIG would have a systemic impact if it failed, the systemic risk seemed to be coming from AIGFP's CDS and derivatives portfolio. The US government therefore (seemed) to structure an AIG rescue that would protect AIGFP's counterparties from the consequences of AIG's failure.[53] However, the US Government's reasoning changed over time, and it eventually claimed that it intervened because AIG's insurers were systemic too.[54] This also seems credible: for example, the AIG group included AIG Commercial Insurance (AIGCI); and American International Underwriters (AIU). AIGCI insured more than 180,000 US companies employing more than 106 million people. It also paid approximately $18.3 billion in US claims in 2008 and was the second largest US investor in US municipal bonds. If AIGCI had failed, it would have materially reduced the capacity of the commercial insurance market and sharp premium increases would have followed. It is also likely to have materially and adversely affected the US municipal bond markets, which were weak and falling, and would have fallen further if AIGCI had become a forced seller of bonds as well.[55] At the same time, AIU was a leading risk carrier in financial lines, covering 70% of the top 50 international banks and insuring 20% of the global aviation market. Its failure is likely to have removed so much capacity from these markets that rate increases would have been inevitable and some businesses would have been left uninsured.[56]

53 This made sense because the largest CDS counterparties, and the largest beneficiaries of the US Government's AIG intervention aid were Goldman Sachs (which received $12.9 billion); Société Générale ($11.9 billion); Deutsche Bank ($11.8 billion); Barclays ($8.5 billion); Merrill Lynch ($6.8 billion); Bank of America ($5.2 billion); UBS ($5 billion); BNP Paribas ($4.9 billion); HSBC ($3.5 billion); and Dresdner Bank AS ($2.6 billion).

54 The New York Federal Reserve was concerned that AIG might not be able to pay insurance claims and, because it '*was providing insurance policies to households across the country ... if AIG had defaulted, you would have seen a ... failure of a set of insurance companies that touched Americans ... and, of course, savers across the world*'. This was surprising because, when the New York Federal Reserve intervened in September 2008, it insisted that AIG's insurance subsidiaries were solvent and liquid as a result of state insurance supervision. In November 2009, the inspector general of the US Troubled Assets Relief Programme, Neil Barofsky, disclosed that the New York Federal Reserve did not believe, when it intervened to save AIG in September 2008, that AIGFP's CDS and the risks to its CDS counterparties, posed a systemic risk. Nor did it intervene to save AIG's counterparties. In fact, '*the financial condition of the [AIG] counterparties was not a relevant factor*' according to Timothy Geithner, President of the New York Federal Reserve at the time of the AIG bailout, and subsequently, the US Treasury Secretary. Quoted in 'AIG and Systemic Risk', in the *Wall Street Journal Europe*, 24 November 2009.

55 See 'AIG Draft – February 26, 2009 (Strictly Confidential) AIG: is the Risk Systemic?'. Available at: http://abcnews.go.com/images/Business/aig_systemic_090309.pdf

56 Ibid.

It does, therefore, seem that at least two of the AIG insurers were systemic; history includes other examples.[57]

4.7.4 The AIG company that caused the problems was neither regulated nor supervised

Whilst it is true that AIGFP was not regulated as a solo entity, it was part of the AIG group that was regulated by the US Office of Thrift Supervision (OTS). In fact, the OTS recognised that whilst CDSs were unregulated products, '*they absolutely, positively fell within a company that OTS regulated and [it] very much understood the risks of the profile of the credit default portfolio*' too.[58] As a result, when the OTS became the regulator of AIG's holding company in 2000, it began to conduct risk-focused reviews of AIG's businesses, including AIGFP. In 2004, it made recommendations about risk management oversight, financial reporting transparency and corporate governance to AIG's senior management and board. In 2006, it began holding annual supervisory college meetings with AIG's key national and international regulators, to enable information sharing and co-ordinated action. In 2007, as the housing market deteriorated, it increased its surveillance of AIGFP, recommending that it review its modelling assumptions, and improve its systems and controls. Then, in 2008, when AIG revealed PricewaterhouseCoopers' concerns about the weaknesses in AIGFP's CDS valuation processes, it tried to force AIG to manage the risks in AIGFP's CDS portfolio; called for a remediation plan; and, eventually, prohibited some group companies from entering into transactions with others, unless notice had been given to the OTS and it had no objections to them.

Even so, because the OTS is thrift regulator, its focus was on the AIG deposit-taking subsidiaries,[59] rather than the wider group; it supervised from the bottom up, rather than the top down. It did not therefore '*fully foresee the potential losses that transactions undertaken by [AIGFP] posed to the holding company*'.[60]

From a European perspective, it is perhaps a surprise that AIGFP was not regulated by one or more of the 50 state insurance regulators that were responsible for supervising AIG's US insurers and reinsurers or by the US Securities and Exchange Commission, which was responsible for regulating many of AIG's US financial services and asset management businesses. However, the US does not have (or at least did not have) laws akin to the European Union's Insurance

57 For example: (a) HIH was regarded as systemic because it insured such a large proportion of the Australian medical profession that when it collapsed, operations had to be cancelled because the alternative was to ask uninsured surgeons to carry out unlawful operations; and (b) Quinn Insurance was regarded as systemic because it insured such a large proportion of the two–four-partner sector of the UK legal profession that when it collapsed, some firms were left uninsured.

58 Congressional Oversight Panel, June Oversight Report, 'The AIG Rescue, its Impact on Markets, and the Government's Exit Strategy', June 2010, p. 42.

59 Principally, AIG Federal Savings Bank, or AIG FSB.

60 Scott Polakoff, Testimony before the Subcommittee on Capital Markets, Insurance and Government Sponsored Enterprises, House Committee on Financial Services, US House of Representatives, 18 March 2009; referred to in a Congressional Research Service Report for Congress: 'Systemically Important or "Too Big to Fail" Financial Institutions', by Marc Labonte, Specialist in Macroeconomic Policy, 30 July 2013.

Groups Directive[61] or its Financial Conglomerates Directive,[62] which would have required group supervision over and above that required by the US thrift legislation. Whether that would have made a material difference is a moot point. But the OTS oversight does at least put the lie to the thinking error that AIGFP was neither regulated nor supervised, even if it was not regulated or supervised as well as it should have been: '*The Office of Thrift Supervision ..., a federal agency that regulates the US thrift industry, was specifically charged with overseeing the parent and it failed to do so. Whether the OTS or a more coherent regulatory framework could have prevented the build-up in risks that the company's own management team failed to understand is unlikely, but this does not obscure the point that AIG's holding company regulator had the power and the duty to spot and require the company to curtail its risk*' and that it failed sufficiently to do so.[63]

4.7.5 *AIG's problems arose in London, where regulation was lax, whilst the US state = regulatory system has ensured that no insurer had failed for more than a century*

This thinking error seems to have emerged and been promulgated during the negotiations between the European Union and the US about 'Solvency II equivalence'.[64]

This debate had an inauspicious start. Solvency II will apply to almost all European insurers; it is intended to enhance European policyholder protection and European financial stability, as well as re-establishing a single European market in insurance. As the new regime was developed, European policy makers began to consider how best to protect European policyholders against the risks they might face if they were directly or indirectly exposed to a third-country insurer. Eventually, the concept of 'Solvency II equivalence' emerged. If an insurer or reinsurer was in a Solvency II equivalent jurisdiction, it would be treated in one way; if it was not, it would be treated in another (generally less favourable) way instead. The term 'Solvency II *equivalence*' seemed pejorative, and some third countries reacted badly to it. In particular, it became common for senior US policy makers to describe Solvency II as a two decades old '*experiment*', which may (or may not) improve policyholder

---

61 Directive 98/78/EC of the European Parliament and of the Council of 27 October 1998 on the supplementary supervision of insurance undertakings in an insurance group.

62 Directive 2002/87/EC of the European Parliament and the Council on the supplementary supervision of credit institutions, insurance undertakings and investment firms in a financial conglomerate.

63 See p. 16 of the Congressional Oversight Panel, June Oversight Report, 'The AIG Rescue, its Impact on Markets, and the Government's Exit Strategy', June 2010.

64 '*Solvency II*' is a reference to Directive 2009/138/EC of the European Parliament and of the Council of 25 November 2009 on the taking up and pursuit of the business of Insurance and Reinsurance (Solvency II). '*Solvency II equivalence*' matters in three different ways: (i) if a European insurer has a third-country subsidiary, the subsidiary's contribution to the insurer's group capital will be calculated differently depending on whether or not the third country is Solvency II equivalent; (ii) if a European insurer has a third-country parent, the identity of the group regulator will vary depending on whether or not the parent is in a Solvency II equivalent jurisdiction; and (iii) if a European insurer takes its reinsurance from a third-country reinsurer, the regulatory value of the reinsurance in the insurer's hands will vary, depending on whether or not the reinsurer is in a Solvency II equivalent jurisdiction. In almost every case, there is no prejudice if the subsidiary, parent or reinsurer is in a Solvency II equivalent jurisdiction, but there could be significant prejudice if it is not. See, for example, art. 172 and Title III of the Directive 2009/138/EC of the European Parliament and of the Council of 25 November 2009 on the taking up and pursuit of the business of Insurance and Reinsurance (Solvency II); and Title III of the draft Commission Delegated Regulation supplementing the Solvency II Directive.

protection. At the same time, it was often said, the US had not experienced an insurance failure for more than a century, it did not therefore need, and it was rather arrogant to assume that it ought, to be tested for Solvency II equivalence (as if it was somehow defective, and would never '*measure up*').[65]

There is at least some truth in the first part of this thinking error. For example, AIGFP's problems did arise and first became apparent in London.[66] Other actual and potential systemic risks also emerged and crystallised in London.[67] But that does not necessarily mean that UK regulation is lax; or that other systemic risks will necessarily crystallise there. In fact, since the Financial Services Authority was abolished, and the Prudential Regulation Authority and the Financial Conduct Authority were established, in April 2013, the UK seems to have been widely regarded as one of the most conservative, enforcement-led and challenging regulatory regimes in Europe. It is also one of the most widely respected.

At the same time, there is plainly no truth in the second part of this thinking error.[68]

---

65 These comments were made at national and international conferences, including at meetings of the National Association of Insurance Commissioners (NAIC) in the US; and at the second ICIR/EIOPA International Conference on Global Insurance Supervision, which took place at the Goethe University Frankfurt, Germany on 6 and 7 September 2012. The nearest reported equivalent of these comments seems to be those made by Kevin McCarty, president of the NAIC: '*I don't mean to suggest we don't have anything to learn from the process. But I don't think that Europe necessarily is the only place you can learn anything from. No disrespect to the EU but I think it's kind of interesting, at best, they would want to make a comparison to a system [Solvency II] that isn't in place yet. It's a theoretical system … measured up against a system that's been tried and tested for decades.*' See, for example, 'US blow to Brussels over insurance rules', *Financial Times*, 29 April 2012.

66 See, for example, 'Behind Insurer's Crisis: Blind Eye to a Web of Risk', '*In the case of AIG the virus exploded from a freewheeling little 277 person unit in London, and flourished in a climate of opulent pay, lax oversight and blind faith in financial risk models*', *New York Times*, 27 September 2008.

67 For example: (a) JP Morgan incurred trading losses of $5.8bn, and was fined more than $1.2bn, after the (so-called) 'London Whale' made unauthorised derivatives trades from his desk in London. For more information, see http://lexicon.ft.com/Term?term=London-whale; and (b) UBS suffered an unauthorised trading loss of $2.3bn, after Kweju Adoboli allegedly '*fraudulently gambled*' away the bank's money. For more information, see 'Adoboli jailed for UK's biggest bank fraud', *Financial Times*, 20 November 2012. In fact, of course, these problems are not unique to London, for example: (a) Société Générale incurred trading losses of $7.2 billion, and was fined €4 million by the French Regulator, due to the unauthorised trading positions Jérôme Kerviel took until early 2008 which saw him amass unauthorised trades of $68.5 billion. For more information, see, for example 'St Jérôme', published in *The Economist* on 24 May 2014, and 'Ex-Trader's Pilgrimage Culminates in Jail Cell', published in the *New York Times* on 18 May 2014; and (b) 'The Fabulous Fab' Fabrice Tourre, a former Goldman Sachs trader, misled and defrauded investors in a subprime mortgage product, resulting in the SEC suing both Goldman Sachs and Tourre himself. Goldman Sachs settled with the SEC for $550 million and Tourre was ordered to pay more than $825,000 in civil fines and return of bonus payments, For more information, see, for example 'Big Fine Imposed on ex-Goldman Trader Tourre in SEC case', published on Reuters (US) on 12 March 2014.

68 See, for example, fns 50 and 51. Other significant US insurance and reinsurance failures include footnotes (i) Hartford Financial Services Group Inc, which received $3.4bn of Troubled Asset Relief (TARP) funding from the US authorities in 2009, after making a loss of $2.75bn in 2007 (see 'Hartford gets $3.4 billion in TARP funds', published by Reuters in New York, 12 June 2009); (ii) the Lincoln Financial Group, which raised $2bn by issuing new debt and equity, before accepting $950m of TARP funding in 2009 (see 'Lincoln Financial Accepts TARP Money', published by hartfordbusiness.com, 15 June 2009); and the AMBAC Financial Group, which missed an interest payment on its debt and filed for Chapter 11 bankruptcy protection on 8 November 2010 (see 'Ambac Financial Group Files bankruptcy to Restructure Bond Debt', published by Bloomberg on 9 November 2010).

4.7.6 Group structure and size has no impact on risk appetite and risk-taking behaviour

The AIG example suggests that this thinking error (if that is what it is) '*cuts both ways*'. At first, AIGFP was risk averse and cautious because it wanted (and needed) to protect AIG's AAA rating. A triple-A rated insurer was unusual but AIG had been triple-A rated for many years, which gave it a significant competitive advantage. So AIGFP often turned away potential CDS contract opportunities rather than take a risk that *might* put the triple-A rating at risk.

As AIGFP became more profitable and its proportionate contribution to group profits grew, the pressure to protect the triple-A rating seemed to fall (or vanish) to be replaced by pressure to increase profit margins, if necessary by taking on more risk, so that group profits and group dividends would continue to grow long after growth would otherwise have petered out.

Eventually, AIGFP realised that its underwriting standards had fallen too far, so it stopped accepting new CDS risks. However, without the kind of external pressure that existed at first (and might still have existed if 'Hank' Greenberg had still been the group's CEO), it seems not to have realised that the answer to the '*we have taken too much risk*' problem was to stop taking new risks, *and* de-risk what you already have.

This may suggest that group structure and group size first prevented AIGFP from taking too much risk; then encouraged it to take too much risk; and then '*hung it out to dry*'. If that is right, it also suggests, as a minimum, that a corporate entity's place in a group can affect its risk taking behaviour for good, and ill.

4.7.7 AIG is a one-off and a victim of extreme market circumstances, which do not justify the changes being made in its name

This assertion is at least superficially attractive. Whilst not entirely unforeseen or unforeseeable, the crisis is now thought to have been the most severe market and main street event since the great depression of the 1930s. We should not, therefore, be surprised that it brought an insurance group to the brink of collapse. We ought not to think that the fact that this happened means that sweeping *insurance* regulatory changes are necessary or desirable, if we are to avoid another AIG.

However, the truth is that, whilst AIG may have been brought to the brink of collapse by extreme market events, there is little or nothing about its near collapse that is genuinely crisis-specific. Rather, earlier failures may suggest that the changes that are being made now should have been made long ago. If that is right, this seems to be a thinking error as well.

4.8 Conclusion

It is at least possible that the thinking errors described in this chapter have two causes: (a) a misunderstanding of '*operational risk*'; and (b) communication by policy makers and insurance regulators that has been so poor that it has failed to engage and persuade insurance market professionals.

The '*operational risk*' misunderstanding also has several causes. The '*operational risk*' debate has taken a '*back seat*' for far too long. When it has been front and centre, it has focused too much on '*the risk of loss arising from inadequate or failed internal processes, personnel or systems*', and not enough on '*the risk of loss arising from ... external events*'.[69] There also seems to be an underlying assumption that the best way to mitigate operational risk is to require insurers to hold more capital. Whilst that might be a good answer to some operational risks (for example, an identifiable and measurable change of law risk), it can hardly be the best answer to them all.

The communications issue seems to arise because policy makers and regulators have discussed systemic risk, and the best ways of addressing it, at international fora that are too remote from the ordinary market professional. The debate has relied on ambiguous terms (for example, '*traditional*' and '*non-traditional*' insurance and insurance business), which have created confusion and allowed the market to dismiss the emerging themes too easily. Finally, of course, the regulatory community has coalesced around a theory and expression of '*systemic risk*', without reaching an overall agreement about its meaning and effect. There is also, at least, a perception that this theory has been developed by bankers for banks, before being adapted by bankers for insurers, all of which tends to undermine its credibility.[70]

These things have allowed thinking errors to emerge and survive unchallenged. They may even have allowed the strongest and most common thinking errors to thrive, because they all have at least a shred of truth embedded within them.

This may seem academic; but if policy makers really want to prevent '*another*' AIG, and they really want to protect consumers from the '*operational risks*' inherent in insurance and insurance businesses, they are more likely to achieve their objectives if operational risk is properly understood and mitigated. They are more likely to achieve that, if insurance market professionals have a better understanding of the regulatory narrative than policy makers have managed to deliver so far. If that is correct, it seems to suggest that a coherent regulatory approach to, and clearer and more consistent regulatory narrative about, systemic risk in insurance is desirable, if not essential. It also seems to suggest that regulators have a lot more work to do before moving on.

69 '*Operational risk*' is '*the risk of loss arising from inadequate or failed internal processes, personnel or systems, or external events*'. See recital 33 of the Directive 2009/138/EC of the European Parliament and of the Council of 25 November 2009 on the taking-up and pursuit of the business of insurance and reinsurance, as amended (Solvency II)).

70 There is clearly some truth in this assertion – for example, the Financial Stability Board is chaired by Mark Carney, a leading central banker; and many of its members and staff are bankers too. This pattern is repeated, for example, in and by the UK's Prudential Regulation Authority, which is a leading contributor to European and broader international thinking in this area. It is led by experienced central bankers, but has very few senior, experienced, insurance professionals whose experience it can call upon as it develops its thinking in these areas. However, this may also be a '*thinking error*'. Perhaps it is just that it makes more sense, from a systemic risk and financial crisis management perspective, to adapt an existing system for a new sector than to start entirely from scratch.

CHAPTER 5

Anticipating new sources of systemic risk in insurance

Daniel Schwarcz and Steven L. Schwarcz

5.1 Introduction

Insurers played a central role in the 2008 global financial crisis. American International Group (AIG)—a holding company principally consisting of insurance businesses—was, by most accounts, a primary culprit in destabilizing the global financial system.[1] AIG's role in the crisis was rivaled to some extent by several financial guarantee (or "monoline") insurers, which offered insurance against the default of various types of bonds but were unable to make good on their promises.[2]

As a result of these and other events, insurance regulation is in a state of flux worldwide. Historically, insurance regulation has centered predominantly on the goal of protecting policyholders by ensuring that insurers have sufficient financial capacity to pay claims. The financial crisis has raised the possibility that insurance regulation should also be attuned to limiting the prospect that insurance-related shocks could systemically threaten the larger financial system and the real economy. But the issue remains intensely controversial. While global sentiment seems to endorse the need for robust regulatory oversight of systemic risk in insurance, the embrace of this newly framed rationale for insurance regulation has been decidedly more lukewarm in the United States.[3]

This chapter suggests that the insurance industry can indeed pose systemic risk to the larger financial system. In doing so, the chapter emphasizes two points. First, it argues that there exist deep, substantial, and—most importantly—ever-changing connections between the insurance industry and the rest of the financial system. The most important such connection, we suggest, arises from the fact that insurers are among the largest investors in the world. Indeed, emerging evidence suggests that insurers were substantially responsible both for inflating the value of mortgage-backed securities prior to the crisis and in disrupting markets in these securities in the midst of the crisis.

---

1 William K. Sjostrom, Jr, "The AIG Bailout", 66 Wash. & Lee L. Rev. 943 (2009).

2 Robert P. Bartlett, "Inefficiencies in the Information Thicket: A Case Study of Derivative Disclosures during the Financial Crisis", 36 J. Corp. L. 1, 4 (2010).

3 Most of this chapter's observations are not unique to the US insurance industry, and thus should have broad relevance. And although we discuss certain issues primarily in the context of US-based insurance regulation, even those observations should have salience outside the United States given the ongoing convergence of insurance markets and their regulation. The International Insurance Society's 48th Annual Seminar in 2012 focused, for example, on "emerging insurance markets moving toward a more common approach to market structure, methods and regulation." Available at: www.iisonline.org/forum/market-trends/ (last accessed July 17, 2013).

This is hardly the only linkage between insurers and the rest of the financial system. For instance, insurers play a major and underemphasized role in issuing financial guarantees to individuals through various life insurance products, such as guaranteed investment contracts and annuities with various guarantees. These connections are merely illustrative of our larger point: interlinkages between insurers and the rest of the financial system can, and often do, crop up in new and distinctive guises, whose systemic significance is itself always changing, and thus cannot always be easily measured or dismissed in advance.[4]

Second, the chapter suggests that certain segments of the insurance industry are vulnerable to "black swan" events that may initially arise outside of the financial system. This is most clearly true for catastrophe events, which generally involve substantial correlated losses among policyholders within a short period of time. Such events could be particularly destabilizing for large swaths of insurers if carriers' standard efforts to hedge, reinsure, or avoid these risks proved unsuccessful. Yet, we argue that while risk-management strategies in the insurance industry effectively limit common forms of catastrophe risk, they are often poorly constructed to deal with tail-end forms of catastrophe risk, such as a global pandemic.

Importantly, we argue that insurers' interlinkages to the larger financial system and their potential vulnerability to tail-end events are not simply the product of individual "too big to fail" firms, such as AIG. Instead, there exist pervasive correlations among individual insurance companies in their financial strategies, product design, and risk mitigation strategies, among others. These correlations stem from common economic features of insurance, insurance regulatory restrictions that apply to insurers, shared suppositions and strategies that are embedded within the culture of insurance executives and managers, and rational herding behavior among firms. Whatever their source, these correlations mean that the insurance industry and its activities can distort markets in non-obvious ways that substantially contribute to systemic risk. Ultimately, these conclusions suggest the need for a regulatory structure that is adapted to anticipating, measuring, and mitigating existing and newly emerging sources of systemic risk in insurance.

5.2 The traditional narrative

The prevailing view, which predates the financial crisis, is that insurance, or at least traditional insurance, does not create or amplify systemic risk.[5] Although various

4 See Testimony of Daniel Schwarcz, US House of Representatives, Subcommittee on Insurance, Housing and Community Opportunity, regarding "Insurance Oversight and Legislative Proposals," November 16, 2011:

> "The proposed legislation seems to ignore one of the central lessons of the 2008 Global Financial Crisis: that we do not always know what we do not know when it comes to systemic risk .... it ensconces the traditional view that insurance activities pose limited systemic risk and restricts the capacity of federal regulators to learn as they go and adapt to evolving research and knowledge. It does this by effectively exempting insurers from the heightened prudential standards that ought to apply to systemically risky firms, by limiting the tools available to federal agencies to investigate systemic risk within insurance companies, and by undermining the capacity of federal regulators to respond to facts on the ground that reveal the threat of systemic risk."

5 See Scott Harrington, "Capital Adequacy in Insurance and Reinsurance," in CAPITAL ADEQUACY BEYOND BASEL: BANKING, SECURITIES, AND INSURANCE 93 (Hal S. Scott ed., 2005); Richard Herring

definitions of systemic risk exist, all emphasize the risk that an event will trigger a loss of economic value or confidence in a substantial segment of the financial system that is serious enough to have significant adverse effects on the real economy.[6] This definition applies just as well in the insurance context as it does elsewhere.

The view that traditional insurance is not systemically risky is based on several claims. Perhaps the most important is that insurers have only limited interconnections with the larger financial system.[7] The interconnectedness of financial institutions is one of the central criteria by which most regulators and analysts assess systemic risk.[8] Unlike many financial intermediaries, insurers' funding traditionally stems principally from their policyholders, through their payment of premiums. Insurers have not historically depended substantially on other financial institutions to sustain, or even grow, their operations. From this perspective, policyholder premiums are a stable funding source because policyholders generally (though not always) are only free to withdraw monies on the occurrence of contractually specified events, such as property destruction or death. These events do not have any relation to financial risk, it is generally thought, thus insulating insurers from the risk of a sudden funding shortfall stemming from financial panic.

Another basis for the view that traditional insurance is not systemically risky turns on size, which is another major criterion by which regulators and analysts assess systemic risk.[9] Indeed, a major report by the Geneva Association, an industry-sponsored insurance think tank, argues that insurers are not systemically risky primarily because they are "significantly smaller" than banks.[10] Insurers in the United States had about $7.1 trillion of assets on their books in 2011, whereas banks had $12.6 trillion.

The third basis for the view that traditional insurance is not systemically risky turns on "substitutability."[11] Insurance is usually thought of as less uniquely essential to the operation of the economy than other types of financial services, such as banking.

& Til Schuermann, "Capital Regulation for Position Risk in Banks, Securities Firms, and Insurance Companies," in CAPITAL ADEQUACY BEYOND BASEL: BANKING, SECURITIES, AND INSURANCE 23–24 (Hal S. Scott ed., 2005). Robert W. Klein, "The Insurance Industry and Its Regulation: An Overview," in THE FUTURE OF INSURANCE REGULATION IN THE UNITED STATES 28 (Martin F. Grace & Robert W. Klein eds., 2009); Geneva Association, Cross Industry Analysis, 28 G-SIBs vs. 28 Insurers, Comparison of Systemic Risk Indicators (Dec. 11, 2012) (hereinafter the "Geneva Report"); Mary A. Weiss, "Systemic Risk and the U.S. Insurance Sector" 2 (Feb. 23, 2010 unpublished draft). Available at: www.naic.org/documents/cipr_weiss_systemic_risk_100223.pdf.

6 One of us has proposed a more specific definition, which is along the same lines. Steven L. Schwarcz, "Systemic Risk," 97 GEO. L. J. 193, 204 (2008) (defining systemic risk as "the risk that (i) an economic shock such as market or institutional failure triggers (through a panic or otherwise) either (x) the failure of a chain of markets or institutions or (y) a chain of significant losses to financial institutions, (ii) resulting in increases in the cost of capital or decreases in its availability, often evidenced by substantial financial-market price volatility.").

7 See Geneva Report, *supra* n. 5 (arguing that insurers are "much less interconnected" to other financial services than banks).

8 It is one of three primary factors, along with size and substitutability, according to the FSB's criteria. The FSB (2009).

9 See *ibid.*

10 The Geneva Report.

11 Substitutability is another criterion by which regulators and analysts assess systemic risk. See the FSB, *supra* n. 8.

At least in recent years, the prevailing sentiment has come to recognize a narrowly framed exception to this view: "non-traditional" insurance activities, most now acknowledge, can indeed be systemically risky.[12] This label is generally understood to encompass two activities. The first, which corresponds to AIG's failure, is the writing of credit default swaps (CDSs), an insurance-like contract that protects counterparties against credit events.[13] Such CDSs—which have increasingly been used by insurers[14] and, even more, by insurance-company affiliates[15]—are associated with the potential for a domino-effect collapse as a consequence of contractual interconnections.[16] The second, which corresponds to monoline carriers, involves financial guarantee insurers that directly insure against the risk of defaults on bonds, other debt securities, and mortgage loans.[17]

5.3 The insurance industry's potential to generate systemic risk

As the global financial crisis vividly revealed, certain non-traditional forms of insurance, such as derivatives activities and monoline insurance of financial products, can contribute to systemic risk. But that is hardly the whole story. The connections between the insurance industry and the larger financial system are deep, pervasive, and perhaps most importantly, constantly evolving. At the same time, the insurance industry itself is susceptible to tail-end, catastrophic risk. For these reasons, efforts to conclusively define the parameters of potential systemic risks in insurance—which characterize much of the extant academic literature on insurance and systemic risk, as well as many policy discussions on how to regulate systemic risk in insurance—are both dangerous and misguided.[18]

12 See J. David Cummins & Mary A. Weiss, Systemic Risk and the U.S. Insurance Sector 26–27 (2011).

13 In a CDS, one party (the credit or protection seller) agrees, in exchange for the payment to it of a fee by a second party (the credit or protection buyer), to assume the credit risk of certain obligations (the reference obligations) of a specified borrower or other obligor (the reference entity). If a credit event (for example, default or bankruptcy) occurs in respect of that obligor, the credit seller will either: (a) pay the credit buyer an amount calculated by reference to post-default value of the debt obligations, or (b) buy the debt obligations (or other eligible debt obligations of the obligor) for their full face value from the credit buyer. Steven L. Schwarcz, Structured Finance, A Guide To The Principles Of Asset Securitization § 10:3.1, at 10–16 (3d ed. 2002 & Supp. 2006) (hereinafter Schwarcz, Structured Finance).

14 "The top five end-users of credit derivatives are banks and broker-dealers (44%), hedge funds (32%), insurers (17%), pension funds (4%), and mutual funds (3%)." U.S. Gov't Accountability Office, GAO-07-716, Credit Derivatives: Confirmation Backlogs Increased Dealers' Operational Risks, but Were Successfully Addressed after Joint Regulatory Action 3 (2007).

15 See, e.g., Nadege Jassaud & Sebastian Schich, "Credit Default Swaps: Towards Tighter Regulation of the 'Shadow Insurance Sector,'" in The Future of Insurance Regulation and Supervision: A Global Perspective (Patrick M. Liedtke & Jan Monkiewicz, eds. 2011) 171 (observing that insurance-company affiliates are much more likely than insurers to sell protection under CDSs).

16 See Steven L. Schwarcz, "Regulating Complexity in Financial Markets," 87 Washington University Law Review 211, 235 (2009/2010).

17 See *supra* n. 4 and accompanying text.

18 *Cf.* Iman Anabtawi & Steven L. Schwarcz, "Regulating Systemic Risk: Towards an Analytical Framework," 86 Notre Dame L. Rev. 1349, 1354–56 (2011) (arguing that systemic risk can be transmitted and amplified when low-probability adverse events that threaten firm integrity combine with interconnections among firms and markets in a financial system).

5.3.1 Interconnections between insurers and the larger financial system

(a) Insurers as owners of financial assets

Most discussions of systemic risk in insurance overlook or downplay the most important linkage between the insurance sector and the rest of the financial system when it comes to assessing systemic risk.[19] This linkage involves the industry's position as a major owner of financial assets. The business of insurance requires taking in policyholder premiums and, at some later point in time, paying those premiums back to policyholders if an insured event occurs. As a result, insurers—and life insurers, in particular—are among the most important investors in financial securities in the entire financial system. One recent analysis concluded that insurers own approximately one-third of all investment-grade bonds[20] and, collectively, own almost twice as much in foreign, corporate, and municipal bonds than do banks.[21]

Insurers' collective role as primary purchasers of financial securities would not be systemically noteworthy were it not for the fact that their investment decisions—including what types of securities to invest in and when to offload securities from their books—are, in many cases, deeply correlated. There are several explanations for this. First, the business models of many insurers tend to favor certain types of securities. For instance, because life insurers' liabilities are long term, such insurers tend to invest heavily in long-term assets to attempt to limit asset/liability mismatch. Second, insurers generally face a complex array of regulatory rules that impact their investment strategies, including risk-based capital rules, and investment restrictions.[22] Although these rules are designed to ensure that insurers are able to pay their obligations as they come due, they have the side-effect of producing similarities in insurers' investment portfolios and decisions.[23] This is particularly true because these regulations often incorporate the ratings of private rating agencies, even after the Dodd–Frank Wall Street Reform and Consumer Protection Act 2010.[24] Third, insurers carefully safeguard their own financial strength ratings, which are produced by a small handful of rating agencies, many of whom use similar models of financial strength and ability to pay claims.

---

19 But see Viral V. Acharya *et al.*, "On the Financial Regulation of Insurance Companies" (2009). Available at: http://web-docs.stern.nyu.edu/salomon/docs/whitepaper.pdf (arguing that insurance may be more systemically risky than commercial banks; because it is such a large part of investments, insurer downgrades can, and have, caused systemic harm); Robert F. Weber, "Combating the Teleological Drift of Life Insurance Solvency Regulation", 8 BERKELEY BUS. L. J. 35, 53 (2011) (noting that the failure of a life insurer can trigger an asset fire sale, which can, in turn, "contribute to other fire dales in other corners of the market, in which case the effects of an insolvent insurer's sell-off are likely to be unpredictable.").

20 See Paul Schultz, "Corporate Bond Trading Costs: A Peek Behind the Curtain", 56 J. FIN 677, 679 (2001).

21 John Patrick Hunt, "Credit Ratings in Insurance Regulation: The Missing Piece of Financial Reform," 68 WASH. & LEE L. REV. 1667 (2011).

22 See generally Robert Klein, A REGULATOR'S INTRODUCTION TO THE INSURANCE INDUSTRY (2005) 142–44. Although these regulatory rules can, directly or indirectly, drive correlations, this does not make the correlations any less important or real. Because the insurance industry closely impacts consumers (as policyholders), appropriate regulation is necessary. The correlations thus result from the highly regulated nature of the business of insurance.

23 See Charles Whitehead, "Destructive Regulatory Coordination", 96 CORNELL L. REV 323 (2011); Josh Mitts & Ian Aires, Anti-Herding Regulation. Working paper. Available at: http://islandia.law.yale.edu/ayres/Anti-Herding%20Regulation.pdf.

24 See Hunt, *supra* n. 21.

Insurers' coordination of their investment strategies—when combined with their massive collective role as investors—can have potentially destructive consequences from a systemic risk perspective. First, such coordinated investment activity can inflate bubbles in certain securities or sectors related to those securities. Consider here a recent working paper that shows that life insurers were a core purchaser of mortgage-backed securities in the 2000s.[25] The central reason for life insurers' coordinated investments in mortgage-backed securities was that these instruments simultaneously returned a high yield, but were treated as being of limited risk under prevailing risk-based capital rules, not to mention rating agency models of insurers' claims paying abilities. By investing heavily in these instruments, insurers played a central role in fueling the speculative bubble in mortgage-backed securities.[26] Such instruments would never have ballooned as they did if it were not for demand for these securities from investors. Distortions in the markets for mortgage-backed securities are largely understood to have been a central driver of the financial crisis writ large.

Second, insurers' coordinated investment activities can also ignite or exacerbate fire sales for particular assets that have systemic ramifications.[27] For instance, the actual or potential downgrading of the credit rating on a series of bonds can prompt large numbers of insurers to sell the downgraded (or about-to-be downgraded) bonds in a coordinated fashion, in order to avoid adverse regulatory or rating agency consequences.[28] A recent paper in the *Journal of Financial Economics* found compelling evidence of just such a process.[29] Studying insurer behavior between 2001 and 2005, the paper found evidence that insurers facing comparatively large regulatory constraints, because they were already operating close to regulatory restrictions regarding their investment portfolios, were more likely than other insurers to immediately sell bonds that were downgraded from investment-grade status. This process of forced selling by regulatory constrained firms caused the price of downgraded bonds to temporarily fall below their fundamental value.[30]

In certain cases, this type of fire sale caused by coordinated insurer selling of particular asset types can contribute to or trigger systemic risk. Recent evidence suggests that insurers contributed to distortions in mortgage-backed securities in

---

25 Craig Merrill, Taylor D. Nadauld, Philip Strahan, "Final Demand for Structured Securities." Available at: http://ssrn.com/abstract=2380859.

26 Ibid.

27 See Anabtawi & Schwarcz, *supra* n. 18 at 1372–1373 & 1372 n. 92 (observing that fire sales are often key contributors to systemic risk).

28 Cf. *supra* n. 22 (observing that systemic correlations can result from the highly regulated nature of the business of insurance).

29 See Andrew Ellul, Chotibhak Jotikasthira, & Christian T. Lundblad, "Regulatory Pressure and Fire Sales in the Corporate Bond Market", 101 J. FINANCIAL ECON. 596 (2011).

30 There are low cross-holdings between insurers' and US banks' investment portfolios. Cummins & Weiss, *supra* n. 12, at 31–32. To that extent, fire sales of investment securities by insurers would not directly impact the value of investment securities held by banks. It may, nonetheless, indirectly impact that value, such as by depressing larger segments of the securities markets; it might even trigger systemic risk through a market panic. See Anabtawi & Schwarcz, *supra* n. 18, at 1353–56 (explaining how a market economic shock can become systemic). Furthermore, Cummins and Weiss, supra n. 12, observe that European insurers and banks may have high cross-holdings. This suggests not only that the systemic risk of insurer fire sales may be greater in Europe but also that the (arguably) currently low US cross-holdings may fluctuate and become greater.

2008, when many insurers— facing similar regulatory and rating agency pressures—attempted to sell these products at the same time.[31] In doing so, insurers contributed to the sudden illiquidity of these instruments. This, in turn, was substantially responsible for the failure, or near failure, of numerous investment banks, including Lehman Brothers, which was principally driven by the "toxic assets" on their balance sheets that could not be offloaded due to a sudden freeze in the markets for these assets.

A crucial, and largely overlooked, point regarding these interconnections between insurers and the rest of the financial system is that insurers' role in stoking systemic risk through their coordinated investment activities need not involve mass failures or near-failures of numerous insurers. A dominant narrative in the debates regarding insurance and systemic risk argues that insurers other than AIG and the monoline carriers are not systemically risky because remarkably few insurers ultimately failed in connection with the global financial crisis.[32] But, in a way, this very fact is suggestive of why the industry can be systemically risky: despite helping to build the bubble in "toxic securities," insurers seem to have collectively offloaded them at the first sign of trouble. Just like the first people in line during a run on a bank, insurers may have got through the financial crisis relatively unscathed, but that does not mean that they were not instrumental in causing the crisis in the first place.

Although insurers need not fail en masse in order for their role as investors to stoke systemic risk, the converse is not true: substantial failures of a series of insurers could well disrupt the financial system by causing insurers to liquidate their portfolios or suspend their future investments. In many cases, an insurance company's failure can result in an immediate need for the company or its receiver to liquidate much of its portfolio.[33] For instance, an insurance company could be required to quickly liquidate its portfolio if it failed due to a catastrophic event triggering an unmanageable number of claims, due to a failure of a reinsurer, or due to a run on products that permitted policyholders to withdraw funds or take out loans against their policies. If many insurers simultaneously experience this type of distress—which is plausible given correlations in carriers' catastrophe exposures, product features, and reinsurance portfolios—it could trigger, or exacerbate, the types of distortions in capital markets that were witnessed in 2008.

Ultimately, then, there is strong newly emerging evidence that insurers played a major and under-appreciated role in the crisis of 2008 by virtue of their role as investors in mortgage-backed securities. Of course, this evidence—like much about the financial crisis—is still uncertain and requires further research and assessment.

---

31 See Craig B. Merrill, Taylor D. Nadauld, Rene M. Stulz, & Shane Sherlund, "Did Capital Requirements and Fair Value Accounting Spark Fire Sales in Distressed Mortgage-Backed Securities?" NBER Working Paper No. 18270 (Aug. 2012).

32 See, e.g., US Government Accountability Office, *Insurance Markets: Impacts of and Regulatory Response to the 2007–2009 Financial Crisis* *17 (GAO-13-583 June 2013). Available at: www.gao.gov/assets/660/655612.pdf (last accessed June 12, 2014).

33 But see *Insurance Oversight and Legislative Proposals: Testimony before House Financial Services Subcommittee on Insurance Housing and Community Opportunity* *9 (2011) (statement of the National Organization of Life and Health Insurance Guaranty Associations). Available at: www.nolhga.com/pressroom/articles/HFSCnolhgaTestimonyNov15_2011.pdf (last accessed June 12, 2014) (arguing that insurers need less liquidity than banks).

However, the point here is not (just) that insurers did, in fact, contribute to systemic risk in our most recent global financial crisis through their role in stoking demand and triggering fire sales in mortgage-backed securities. Rather, it is that insurers, as massive investors who often act in a coordinated fashion with respect to their investment appetites and decisions, play an important role in the global financial system, and in the potential accumulation of risk in that system.

(b) Other potential linkages between insurers and the financial system insurers' guarantees against financial risk

Insurers' existing—and potential—connections to financial markets are hardly exhausted by their roles as investors. Various additional linkages exist. In some cases, the magnitude of these interconnections is not currently sufficient to raise systemic risks. In other cases, it is hard to know how even to measure the systemic implications of these connections. But both of these statements could almost certainly have been made about insurers' (and their affiliates') participation in credit default swaps ten years ago.

(I) Insurers as guarantors of investment performance

As described above, much has been written acknowledging that insurers or their affiliates can contribute to systemic risk to the extent that they engage in "non-traditional" insurance transactions. This is generally understood to encompass writing credit default swaps and issuing financial guarantee insurance, both of which involve insurers directly insuring against financial risk.

Remarkably, however, the most common and widespread category of financial guarantees that insurers provide is generally left out of this description. A substantial percentage of life insurers' premiums are currently attributable to products that are principally investment-oriented and that guarantee contractually specified investment returns to policyholders. Examples include variable annuities, fixed-indexed annuities, and guaranteed investment contracts. Perhaps the most stark example of this – which illustrates how insurance products can morph into financial guarantee products – is the contingent deferred annuity, wherein a carrier guarantees that an investment vehicle chosen by the policyholder and maintained independently of the insurer (such as a mutual fund) will yield contractually specified payments for the remainder of the policyholders' lifetime.[34]

To be sure, there are a number of important distinctions between this set of commonly offered products and the CDSs and financial guarantee insurance described earlier. However, these distinctions do not clearly establish that these commonly sold financial guarantee products are systemically riskless. An important distinction between these two sets of products, for example, is that the policyholders who

34 See NAIC Contingent Deferred Annuity Subgroup, *Report of the CDA Subgroup to the Life Insurance and Annuities Committee Members* (Feb 22, 2012). See also *Letter from Birny Birnbaum, Executive Director, Center for Economic Justice, to Ted Nickel, Chair, NAIC CDA Subgroup* *2 (Oct 8, 2012). Available online at: www.naic.org/documents/committees_a_contingent_deferred_annuity_wg_cej_recommendations.pdf (last accessed June 12, 2014) (voicing concern that adverse market conditions could result in significant financial loss for CDAs because exhaustion of holders' financial assets would trigger massive simultaneous claims).

would lose out in the event of an insurer's inability to pay are individuals rather than financial entities. But the widespread failure of investment guarantees to individuals could conceivably produce broader consequences: reduced retirement savings could trigger unanticipated mortgage and credit card defaults, a sudden uptick in the need for social services, or labor market distortions as newly retired individuals attempted to re-enter the job market.[35]

(II) Insurance Companies within Complex Financial Services Groups

Insurance companies are increasingly part of financial services conglomerate groups that provide an array of financial services, including banking and broker/dealer services.[36] This creates the prospect that insurance company failures or distress could have serious consequences for non-insurance financial firms within the conglomerate. Risks are much more likely to spread among corporate affiliates than among independent firms operating at arm's length.[37] A related concern is that the holding company or other affiliates might be motivated to take risky actions, effectively supported by (and thus taking advantage of) government-backed guarantees of insurers. Although this concern is commonly cited in banking regulations,[38] it is also a concern in insurance. In the United States, for example, explicit state-guarantee funds, and potentially implicit federal guarantees in the event that state-guarantee funds fail, would seem to create a similar type of moral hazard among affiliates.[39]

---

35 One lesson of the global financial crisis is that the financial distress of individuals can easily morph into financial distress for the financial system. *See*, e.g., National Commission on the Causes of the Financial and Economic Crisis in the United States, "The Financial Crisis Inquiry Report" 213–221 (2011) (describing how the rising default rate of individual homeowners snowballed into a global financial crisis).

36 Aerdt Houben & Mark Teunissen, "The Systemicness of Insurance Companies: Cross-Border Aspects and Policy Implications", in Liedtke & Monkiewicz, (eds) The Future of Insurance Regulation and Supervision, *supra* n. 15, 246, 254–59 (noting that euro area insurers' financial assets have almost doubled in the last decade and that many hedge funds and private equity groups are managing assets owned by insurers). In part, the rationale for the rise in conglomeration is to exploit synergies between financial services and parents' businesses and also to take advantage of economies of scale and scope. Some firms also hope that business diversification would reduce their earnings fluctuations. Gordon F. Boreham, "The Rise of Non-Bank Financial Conglomerates: A Major Trend", Service Industries J. 95 (Oct. 1989).

37 See Richard J. Herring & Anthony M. Santomero, "The Corporate Structure of Financial Conglomerates", 4 J. Fin. Serv. Res. 471, 477–480 (1990).

38 See Herring & Santomero, *supra* n. 37, at 480. US bank regulation attempts to address this concern most directly through s. 23A of the Federal Reserve Act, which restricts transactions, such as lending, between federally insured deposit-taking banks and their nonbank affiliates. See, generally, Saule T. Omarova, "From Gramm-Leach-Bliley to Dodd-Frank: The Unfulfilled Promise of Section 23A of the Federal Reserve Act," 89 N.C. L. Rev. 1683, 1686 (2011).

39 To be sure, insurance regulations attempt to "ring-fence" insurance companies by requiring disclosure and approval of all material affiliated transactions. New state rules also attempt to enhance the power of regulators to demand information about insurers' affiliates and also attempt to enhance group supervision by requiring that an Own Risk and Solvency Assessment Framework be completed at the holding company level. But it is an open question whether these changes will be enough to reverse the clearly inadequate appreciation that state regulators had pre-2008 of risk to insurers posed by their affiliates. Moreover, all of these approaches to ring-fencing are directed to protecting insurers from risks arising from their affiliates. None of them are directed at the opposite threat: the prospect that distress might spread to an insurance affiliate from an insurer. See generally Steven L. Schwartz, "Ring-Fencing," 87 s. cal. l. rev. 69 (2013).

(III) Insurance-linked securities

Insurers increasingly rely on financial markets to take on catastrophe risk. The most prominent example of this is catastrophe bonds, issued by insurers.[40] Catastrophe bonds pay principal and interest to investors after a contractually specified term but, unlike ordinary bonds, the issuer's obligation to repay principal or interest on a catastrophe bond is forgiven if contractually specified catastrophic events occur within the bond's term. This makes catastrophe bonds unusually risky for investors, who are at substantial risk of losing their entire investment if a catastrophe bond is triggered.[41] Investors are nonetheless willing to invest in catastrophe bonds because they assume that their returns provide investment diversification, displaying little or no correlation to the returns of shares and conventional bonds.[42] Thus, the probability of a hurricane hitting a major urban area is not impacted by the prospect of instability in financial markets.

Currently, investment in catastrophe bonds is not significant enough to be systemically risky, amounting to about $7 billion a year. But analysts expect that the size of this market could increase substantially in upcoming years and, in fact, recent years have seen exponential growth in these types of financial instruments.[43]

Catastrophe bonds could also create important linkages between insurance and other financial markets. Most assume that these linkages are limited because financial market and insurance underwriting risks are not correlated. Yet various types of events could conceivably simultaneously trigger instability in both the financial and insurance markets. Consider, for instance, a global pandemic. This could trigger payment on unprecedented numbers of life insurance policies and also create a financial panic by, for instance, triggering mass withdrawals of deposits.

(IV) Insurance as a Prerequisite to Credit

Insurance plays a crucial role in secured lending of all types. When lenders take a security interest or mortgage in collateral, they generally require the borrower to maintain insurance on the property throughout the duration of the loan. On a superficial level, the reason that lenders require such insurance is obvious: they want their collateral protected so that, in the event of default, they can look to that collateral for repayment. An important component of this explanation is that insurers are comparatively well-situated relative to investors to measure and manage the risks associated with the prospect of damage to property. Indeed, this is the core business of property insurers.

If disruptions in property insurance markets suddenly made unavailable property

---

40 There also appears to be growing investor interest in debt securities operating as reinsurance of other insurable risks, including mortality and terrorism. See "EdF's Pylon Makes First European Corporate Cat Bond," 834 Euroweek (2003); "Capital Markets Shield AXA from Extreme Mortality Risk," 978 Euroweek (2006).

41 Daniel Schwarcz, "Regulating Insurance Sales or Selling Insurance Regulation? Against Regulatory Competition in Insurance," 94 Minn. L. Rev. 1707 (2010).

42 See Christopher M. Lewis & Peter O. Davis, "Capital Market Instruments for Financing Catastrophe Risk: New Directions?" 17 J. Ins. Reg. 110, 114 (1998); Angelika Schochlin, "Where's the Cat Going? Some Observations on Catastrophe Bonds" 14 J. Appl. Corp. Fin. 100, 102–03 (2002).

43 Rodd Zolkos, "Catastrophe Bond Market Poised for Record Issuance in 2013," Report, Business Insurance (May 9, 2013).

insurance of various types—such as homeowners, commercial property, auto collision and comprehensive, commercial auto—the result could be substantial disruptions in the credit markets that rely on these forms of property to extend credit.[44]

5.3.2 Vulnerabilities of the insurance system to tail-end events arising outside of the financial system

As noted above, insurers' various existing and potential linkages to the broader financial system have the potential to generate systemic risk even in the absence of widespread instability within the insurance industry itself. Of course, many of the linkages between insurers and the rest of the financial system described above create the prospect of systemic risk only to the extent that the insurance industry itself is subject to the prospect of widespread instability. We suggest below that the insurance industry is indeed subject to such tail-end risk. In doing so, we emphasize tail-end risk that could arise outside of the financial system as an initial matter. Importantly, however, insurers can also be impacted by tail-end risk that could arise from other segments of the financial system itself, including investment risk, inflation risk, and interest rate risk. Because the mechanisms for insurers to be impacted by this risk involve the interconnections between insurers and the remainder of the financial system discussed above, we do not focus on these issues here.

(a) Catastrophe risk

Catastrophe risk arises when individual policyholder losses are correlated, resulting in large numbers of policyholder claims being made within a short period of time. In many cases, insurers actively strive to limit their exposure to catastrophe risk precisely because they face substantial limitations in their ability to raise sufficient funds to pay unexpectedly large numbers of policyholder claims within a short period of time. Some of the most important mechanisms by which they attempt this include excluding catastrophe risk exposure in their insurance policies, diversifying their exposure to catastrophes, and transferring some of their catastrophe risk to reinsurers.

Despite these efforts to manage catastrophe risk, insurers' exposures to such risk can conceivably be quite large. Some insurers, for instance, do surprisingly little to mitigate catastrophe risks that have not occurred in the recent past, consistent with the commonly understood behavioral bias, the availability heuristic. Consider, for example, the risk of a global pandemic on the order of the Flu of 1918, which killed between 20 to 40 million people within a single year. Such an event could result in massive losses to life insurers who would owe immediate payment on their life insurance policies. However, unlike property insurance policies, life insurance policies do not contain coverage exclusions for such a tail-end event.

In other cases, insurers fail to properly limit their exposure because they do not

44 Cummins & Weiss, *supra* n. 12, argue that small insurers would fill in gaps and note that large corporations have many insurance substitutes. But this depends on how large of a disruption there was in the underlying insurance markets.

even consider the possibility of the catastrophe occurring until it does (such as the risk of terrorism, as perceived prior to 9/11). It is obviously difficult, if not impossible, to predict what future catastrophes might occur that the industry has failed to adequately anticipate or guard against.

(b) Reinsurance opacity and interconnectedness

One of the most important ways that insurers attempt to mitigate their exposure to catastrophe risk is by ceding much of that risk to reinsurers, who are comparatively well situated to diversify catastrophe risk around the globe. Both property/casualty and life insurers rely extensively on reinsurance to mitigate their catastrophe risk.[45] For instance, US insurers ceded slightly more than $100 billion in premiums to unaffiliated reinsurers in 2009. This amount roughly approximates the expected recoverable catastrophe cost to reinsurers in a single given year: the potential recovery from reinsurers in the event of a massive catastrophic event or series of such events is obviously much larger. This value of reinsurance is reflected not only in insurers' business operations, but also in their regulatory treatment: insurers are generally able to avoid accounting for policyholder risk through reserves and capital requirements when that risk is transferred to a reinsurer.

At the same time that reinsurance reduces insurer risk, it also introduces new risk due to the prospect that reinsurers will be unable to follow through on their reinsurance obligations. Insurers are forced to bear this risk, because they are legally obligated to pay policyholder losses even if the underlying risks were transferred to reinsurers who failed to make good on their own obligations. Of course, if insurers themselves are unable to pay claims due in part to reinsurer failure, then policyholders will indeed ultimately bear the consequences.

Reinsurer counterparty risk exposes the insurance industry to substantial vulnerabilities that, in many ways, resemble the counterparty risk that investment banks were exposed to as a result of their derivative activities. First, the concentration of the reinsurance industry creates deep and substantial interconnections, such that the failure of one or two major reinsurers could simultaneously impact a substantial segment of the insurance industry at once.[46] The reinsurance industry is extremely concentrated in a few massive firms, such as Swiss Re, Munich Re, and Berkshire Hathaway.[47] In 2009, for instance, five reinsurance groups provided approximately 60% of the world's reinsurance capacity. Concentration in the reinsurance industry,

45 Dwight M. Jaffee & Thomas Russell, "Catastrophe Insurance, Capital Markets, and Uninsurable Risks," 64 J. Risk and Ins. 205, 215 (1997).

46 Cummins & Weiss, *supra* n. 12 ("Reinsurance is the primary source of interconnectedness within the insurance industry."); Viral V. Acharya *et al.*, On the Financial Regulation of Insurance Companies *10 (NYU Stern School of Business Working Paper, 2009). Available at: http://web-docs.stern.nyu.edu/salomon/docs/whitepaper.pdf (last accessed June 12, 2014). ("The reinsurance market increases the interconnectedness of the system exponentially and therefore might increase the systemic risk in the overall market" because of the "bilateral [relationship] in nature and [the lack of] adequate risk controls due to the opacity of bilateral markets").

47 Although regulators have downplayed the risk posed by reinsurers, they admit that "high degrees of market concentration in the reinsurance sector could *everything else being equal* raise sector interconnectedness and limit the degree of substitutability . . . [and thus] potentially raise intra-industry concerns." International Association of Insurance Supervisors, *Reinsurance and Financial Stability* 16 (July 2012) (emphasis in original).

moreover, is only trending upwards due to mergers and acquisitions as well as organic growth.[48]

In addition to generating substantial interconnections within the insurance industry, reinsurer counterparty risk is incredibly opaque—as were the derivative markets that contributed to the financial crisis.[49] As reinsurance is an international business—the largest companies are located in Europe and Bermuda—there is a lack of uniformity about the ways in which these companies are regulated.[50] Not only does this mean that it is hard to know how much regulation directly limits default risk through tools such as reserve and capital requirements, but is also means that it is hard to acquire consistent financial data on different firms. As an important 2006 G-30 report explained, "[t]he risk information published by reinsurers varies significantly across firms in both frequency and scope" resulting in a "widespread perception that publicly available information about both the financial state and the risk profile of reinsurance companies is in many cases inadequate."[51]

Complicating matters further is the fact that reinsurers are subject to a number of deeply complex risks. Because they rely extensively on catastrophe models to price coverage, reinsurers face a substantial amount of model risk.[52] Yet the accuracy of catastrophe models is notoriously difficult to assess.[53] Moreover, as with all models, they rely on historical data to predict future risk, which (as reliance on historical housing data showed) is inherently risky.[54]

All of this makes it very difficult for anyone–including insurers, creditors of reinsurers, credit rating agencies, regulators, and even reinsurers themselves–to accurately gauge reinsurer default risk.

(c) Policyholder runs and guarantee fund structure

The insurance system may also be vulnerable to policyholder runs, a risk that could well increase in the future depending on developments in insurance policy design. In many types of insurance, insureds "only have a right to demand payment on the occurrence of a contractually specified event. This minimizes the risk of a 'run' on an insurer."[55] But this is not true of many life insurance products which often allow

48 Cummins & Weiss, *supra* n. 12, at 26–27.

49 Sojung Carol Park & Xiaoying Xie, *Reinsurance and Systemic Risk: The Impact of Reinsurer Downgrading on Property-Casualty Insurers* *5 (China International Conference on Insurance and Risk Management Paper, 2012). Available at: www.ccirm.org/conference/2012/uploadfiles/A/III-A/1 ParkXie_Reinsurance%20and%20Systemic%20Risk%20The%20Impact%20of%20Reinsurer%20 Downgrading%20on%20Property-Casualty%20Insurers_for_Qinghua2.pdf (last accessed June 12, 2014).

50 M.-L. Rossi & N. Lowe, "Regulating Reinsurance in the Global Market," 27 The Geneva Papers on Risk and Insurance – Issues and Practices 122 (2002).

51 See G-30 Report at 6 G-30, Reinsurance and International Markets (2006)..

52 See, e.g., "Regulating Complexity in Financial Markets," *supra* n. 16, at 217 (discussing model risk).

53 See American Academy of Actuaries Catastrophe Management Work Group, *Catastrophe Exposure and Insurance Industry Catastrophe Management Practices* at *18 (2001).

54 Reinsurers are subject to liquidity risk. G-30 report at 24 G-30, Reinsurance and International Markets (2006).. Additionally, reinsurers face their own form of counterparty risk due to their practice of purchasing reinsurance from other reinsurers (a process known as retrocession). This process can result in "retrocession spirals," wherein the failure of one reinsurer exposes other reinsurers to loss, potentially compromising their ability to pay as well. This possibility was vividly displayed in the 1990s when a chain of Lloyds' syndicates failed as a result of having passed risk back and forth among them.

55 "Regulating Insurance Sales or Selling Insurance Regulation," *supra* n. 41, at 1753.

policyholders to borrow against their policy or cash out their savings.[56] As a result, policyholders who become concerned about their carriers' solvency can demand withdrawals, producing a downward spiral analogous to those found in classical bank runs—in which some bank depositors panic, converging on the bank in a "grab race" to be the first to withdraw their monies.[57]

Although the risk of a run on a life insurer is well understood, it has historically been downplayed because of the substantial fees typically associated with a policyholder deciding to surrender or borrow against a policy.[58] But there is good reason to believe that this barrier to withdrawal is currently changing and will continue to change. Recently, life settlement companies have offered policyholders the option of selling their policies to investors for much larger sums than the surrender value (the opposite side of the insurance-backed securities market, described above). As this industry becomes more and more sophisticated, insurers will increasingly face market pressures to allow policyholders to cash out of their policies at amounts approaching their net present value.

Governments do not generally protect against the risk of insurer runs, as they often do (through deposit insurance or its equivalent) against the risk of bank runs. Even when governments provide some protection against the risk of insurer runs, it may be too limited. In the United States, for example, only states—not the federal government—protect the policyholders of failed insurers; they usually do so through unreliable state-guarantee funds that are not generally pre-funded and, even in the best cases, have limited payouts.

5.4 Conclusion

The analysis above suggests that insurance law and regulation must be attuned to the prospect of systemic risk in insurance. Moreover, lawmakers and regulators must avoid regulatory structures that are premised on narrow understandings of this risk, whether this is linked to "non-traditional" insurance defined only to encompass CDS and financial guarantee insurance, or whether it is focused exclusively on "too big to fail" insurers. Rather, the increasing complexities and interconnections of insurance and finance effectively create a single interconnected system, making it likely that systemic risk will continue to arise in new and distinctive guises. The very nature of insurance regulation needs to adapt in response to these changes.

56 Weber, *supra* n. 19, at 47.

57 See, e.g., Jonathan R. Macey & Geoffrey P. Miller, "Bank Failures, Risk Monitoring, and the Market for Bank Control", 88 Colum. L. Rev. 1153, 1156 (1988) (linking bank runs and depositor collective action problems).

58 See, e.g., Scott Harrington, Beyond Basel *supra* n. 5; Guillaume Plantin & Jean-Charles Rochet, When Insurers Go Bust: An Economic Analysis of the Role and Design of Prudential Regulation 90–93 (2007).

CHAPTER 6

Oversight of systemically relevant insurance practices within the EU: the role of macro-prudential supervision

Miriam Goldby and Anat Keller

6.1 Introduction

This chapter argues that in order to achieve the aims of macro-prudential supervision, it is insufficient to pay enhanced attention to insurance institutions designated as Global Systemically Important Insurers (GSIIs) and that systemic risks that may emanate from practices prevalent in the insurance sector, practices which increase interconnectedness and common exposures, need to be addressed. We argue that in view of the fact that these practices may give rise to the materialisation of systemic risk, even if the entities engaging in them remain solvent, they are more appropriately addressed by macro- rather than micro-prudential oversight. The purpose of this chapter is to assess the extent to which the European Systemic Risk Board (ESRB), a macro-prudential supervisory body set up in the wake of the recent crisis, is equipped to address such risks. The word "practice" has been chosen as it connotes not just "what" is being done (e.g. the decision by an entity to expose itself to a certain type of risk) but "how" it is being done (e.g. how the risk is priced and the extent to which the entity allows itself to be exposed). While a detailed discussion of the interaction among different supervisory bodies goes largely beyond the scope of this chapter, it should be noted that conduct of business supervisors' activities may be essential to an effective response to the "how" of a practice, therefore it is important to flag up the importance of the mechanisms and procedures available for interaction not just between macro-prudential oversight and micro-prudential supervision but also macro-prudential oversight and conduct of business regulation and supervision. This chapter seeks to highlight the role of macro-prudential oversight by focusing on the ESRB (within the European System of Financial Supervision (ESFS))[1] as the prime example of a macro-prudential supervisory body that has cross-border competence.

The first part of this chapter includes a brief analysis of some notable examples of practices within the insurance industry that may have potential systemic relevance. The practices chosen are practices that have been increasing in prevalence in the European Union (EU) in recent years. The second part will attempt to gauge the extent to which the ESRB is positioned and empowered to monitor and respond to such practices.

1 For a general overview of the financial regulation and supervision of insurance in the EU post-crisis, see K Van Hulle 'Regulatory Challenges and Developments in the European Union', Chapter 17 in PM Liedtke and J Monkiewicz, *The Future of Insurance Regulation and Supervision: A Global Perspective* (Palgrave Macmillan, 2011), 294–320.

6.2 The need to monitor practices rather than entities

In the run-up to the recent crisis prudential regulation and supervision tended to focus on the health of individual institutions.[2] Since the 2007–2008 crisis there has been more focus on macro-prudential supervision,[3] an approach which acknowledges that regulation and supervision targeted at addressing institutional fragility are insufficient, and that a more comprehensive monitoring of developments in areas of relevance to the financial sector and the real economy is required.

In Chapter 5 of this book, Daniel and Steven Schwarcz discuss a number of features of insurance business that might constitute potential sources of stress, eventually leading up to failures and fire sales that may have grave systemic consequences.[4] In this chapter we argue that certain practices of EU insurers, both as institutional investors and as issuers of financial products, mean that these vulnerabilities apply also across the EU. These practices mean that systemic impact can originate from the activities of the insurance industry as a whole even if individual companies within it remain financially solvent.[5] While there is a tendency in the literature to distinguish between traditional and non-traditional insurance business, and while the non-systemic nature of the former has been consistently emphasised,[6] the approach we take in this chapter is that in view of the continuing evolution in the way insurance companies do business,[7] these distinctions are unhelpful in designing effective macro-prudential policy that goes beyond the monitoring of individual institutions. Indeed the International Association of Insurance Supervisors (IAIS) has noted that 'the demarcation between traditional and non-traditional lines of [insurance] business (or products) can be blurry'.[8] In a paper published in 2011, Baluch and others found as follows:

2 *Macroprudential Policy and Surveillance in Insurance*, International Association of Insurance Supervisors (IAIS), 18 July 2013. Available at: www.iaisweb.org/view/element_href.cfm?src=1/19149.pdf (accessed 31 July 2014), [7]: 'The traditional approach to financial stability analysis concentrates on the identification of vulnerabilities prior to stress from individual failures, with a firm-specific focus.'

3 See, generally, G Galati and R Moessner 'Macroprudential Policy – A Literature Review', BIS Working Paper No. 337, Bank of International Settlements, Monetary and Economic Department, February 2011. Available at: www.bis.org/publ/work337.pdf (accessed 31 July 2014).

4 See also, D Schwarcz and SL Schwarcz 'Regulating Systemic Risk in Insurance' (2014) 81 *The University of Chicago Law Review*, 1569.

5 Indeed, the International Association of Insurance Supervisors (IAIS) has acknowledged that 'a collection of solvent firms subject to individual distress is viewed as not posing a threat to financial stability. However, the financial crisis has demonstrated that the actions of individual firms may be optimal at the level of the firm but suboptimal from a macroprudential standpoint and, thus, individual firm solvency is not, on its own, adequate to protect against the risk of financial instability'. The IAIS (n. 2), [14]. See also *Why Insurers Differ from Banks*, Insurance Europe, October 2014. Available at: www.insuranceeurope.eu/uploads/Modules/Publications/why_insurers_differ_from_banks.pdf (accessed 7 April 2015), 36–37.

6 See in particular *Systemic Risk in Insurance – An analysis of insurance and financial stability: Special Report of the Geneva Association Systemic Risk Working Group*, Geneva Association, March 2010. Available at: www.genevaassociation.org/media/99228/ga2010-systemic_risk_in_insurance.pdf (accessed 4 August 2014), especially 63; JD Cummins and MA Weiss 'Systemic Risk and the US insurance sector', 27 July 2011. Available at: http://ssrn.com/abstract=1725512 (accessed 4 August 2014).

7 See P Jenkins, 'Insurers may be at the centre of the next big crisis', *Financial Times*, 26 December 2013. Available at: www.ft.com (accessed 25 July 2014).

8 *Insurance and Financial Stability*, International Association of Insurance Supervisors (IAIS), November 2011. Available at: www.iaisweb.org/__temp/Insurance_and_financial_stability.pdf (accessed 4 August 2014), [30].

> Both banks and insurers have diversified from their traditional set of core activities and have become participants in each other's markets (e.g. insurers in the equity, fund and bond market and banks in insurance-linked securities). The result of this diversification is twofold. First, a not insignificant systemic link between banks and insurers has been created. Second, such diversification has changed the business models for both insurers and banks to the point where a return to the traditional (idiosyncratic) models may not be a straightforward task.[9]

Therefore, in this part we will argue in favour of what we shall term "practices oversight" which would require supervisors to monitor closely, on an ongoing basis, existing and emerging practices prevalent among insurers, both as issuers of financial products and as institutional investors and to consider carefully what the resulting systemic impact might be. In the next part we then argue that practices oversight should be viewed as macro-prudential in nature and we will assess whether the macro-prudential powers with which European supervisors have been equipped following recent reforms are appropriate to the performance of this function.

6.2.1 Insurers as institutional investors

In Europe, as in the US, insurers are the largest institutional investors.[10] This means that the industry's decisions to buy, sell or otherwise use assets of a certain type can have significant implications for the purposes of financial stability if two features are present: first, the existence of widespread trends in decision making (e.g. the tendency of a large number of insurers to invest in the same assets), giving rise to common exposure[11] and second, the ability of these investment decisions to intensify the interconnectedness between the insurance industry and the rest of the financial market.[12]

---

9 F Baluch, S Mutenga and C Parsons, 'Insurance, Systemic Risk and the Financial Crisis' (2011) 36 *The Geneva Papers*, 126, 152.

10 See *Funding the Future: Insurers' Role as Institutional Investors* (Oliver Wyman and Insurance Europe, June 2013) (hereinafter OWIE Study 2013). Available at: www.oliverwyman.com/insights.html (accessed 25 July 2014), 12.

11 See C Borio, M Drehmann and K Tsatsaronis, 'Stress-testing macro stress testing: does it live up to expectations?' BIS Working Paper No. 369, Bank of International Settlements (BIS), January 2012. Available at: www.bis.org/publ/work369.htm (accessed 31 July 2014), 17: 'Common exposures of institutions, on both their asset and liability sides, together with undiscriminating responses by investors and counterparties, are the main drivers of the dynamics of financial distress. A financial crisis acts like a tsunami that sweeps away all before it, not like a force that knocks down one domino after another along a specific path.' See also Baluch *et al* (n. 9), 137: '"macro-systemic risk", is one which is not dependent upon a cumulative loss function ... [but where] a single exogenous event leads to simultaneous adverse effect on multiple entities' and the IAIS 2013 (n. 2), [51], 'risk exposures may be viewed as small for a single insurer, but may be large if all other firms have a similar exposure'.

12 See M Billio, M Getmansky, AW Lo and L Pelizzon, 'Econometric Measures of Connectedness and Systemic Risk in the Finance and Insurance Sectors' (2012) 104 *Journal of Financial Economics*, 535. See also Baluch et al (n. 9), 152: 'It is clear from our analysis that the insurance and banking sectors have become increasingly connected over the last decade. Insurers (particularly life insurers) have extensively participated in the capital markets for additional profitability and risk transfer. This has left insurers exposed to systemic contagion via banks. Insurers have also become significant players in the credit protection market, leaving banks exposed to counterparty risk with potential systemic impact. The key question regarding systemic risk in these two sectors is not the one based on absolute levels – that is, which sector possesses the greater systemic risk – rather, there is a need to identify the strength of the systemic link between the sectors as a result of a copula effect between their respective business models.' See also A Houben and M Teunissen, 'The Systemicness of Insurance Companies: Cross-Border Aspects and

A 2013 study by Oliver Wyman and Insurance Europe (OWIE Study 2013) listed three main factors underpinning insurers' investment decision-making processes: first, the particular insurer's profile of liabilities; second, the range of assets available and the associated risk-return profiles; and third, framework conditions, including prudential regulation requirements.[13] Foremost amongst these are capital requirements, which allocate risk weightings to assets depending on their perceived riskiness. In 2011, a study undertaken by Trusted Sources for the City of London Corporation (CLC Study 2011) observed that:

> Some European countries still have quantitative rules in place for insurance companies, but in general there is a move towards fewer restrictions. *This includes the relaxation or lifting of restrictions on investing abroad, in derivatives, in real estate, in mutual funds and in private equity.*[14]

This move should be further facilitated once Solvency II is implemented, as national restrictions will be eliminated.[15]

Thus Solvency II will lift formal restrictions on the types of assets in which insurers are free to invest, formal restrictions that varied from Member State to Member State, bringing about greater harmonisation. Coupled with the imposition of new regulatory requirements, in particular, capital requirements, this should have an impact on the level of homogeneity in insurers' investment decisions across the EU. In 2011, the CLC Study reported that insurers in continental Europe are moving closer to the UK and US model of insurers as institutional investors acting as major participants in the capital markets.[16] Although the mix of assets in which individual companies invest will vary considerably depending on their profile of liabilities and the kind of assets available, 'more than three-quarters of insurers' assets are represented by equities and corporate and government bonds'.[17]

Increased homogeneity in the types of assets held by insurers across the EU may have systemic implications, depending on the riskiness of these assets and the way insurers deal with them in situations of financial stress. In a report published in 2014 the European Insurance and Occupational Pensions Authority (EIOPA) indicated that '[o]ver the last years, the risks stemming from a prolonged period of low interest rates have consistently been ranked as the most important risks faced by the insurance and pension funds sectors'.[18] These risks are particularly pronounced for

---

Policy Implications', Chapter 15 in PM Liedtke and J Monkiewicz, *The Future of Insurance Regulation and Supervision: A Global Perspective* (Palgrave Macmillan, 2011), 246–269.

13 See OWIE Study 2013 (n. 10), 13–18.

14 *Insurance companies and pension funds as institutional investors: global investment patterns*, Report prepared for the City of London Corporation (Trusted Sources, November 2011) (hereinafter CLC Study 2011). Available at: www.cityoflondon.gov.uk/economicresearch (accessed 25 July 2011), 9–10. Emphasis added.

15 OWIE Study 2013 (n. 10), 17.

16 CLC Study 2011 (n. 14), 22.

17 OWIE Study (n. 10), 19. See also *Financial Stability Report* (European Insurance and Occupational Pensions Authority (EIOPA) (14 May 2014), Ref EIOPA-FS-14-044 (hereinafter EIOPA Report 2014). Available at: https://eiopa.europa.eu (accessed 30 July 2014), 12 (large European insurers) and 36 (pension funds).

18 EIOPA Report 2014 (n. 17), 35. See also *European Financial Stability and Integration Report 2012*, Commission Staff Working Document, European Commission, 24 April 2013, Ref. SWD (2013) 156 final (hereinafter EFSIR 2012), 36–37.

life insurers offering guaranteed returns that are higher than the yield they are able to get on their investments.[19] As demonstrated by Becker and Ivashina, insurers as investors have a propensity to "reach for yield", yield on investments being an integral determinant of profitability.[20] In the context of a protracted period of low interest rates, the likelihood that the reach for yield will lead insurers to invest in riskier assets than they would normally do, is intensified, especially if capital requirements are such as to encourage it[21] (i.e. if relevant capital requirements applied favourable risk-weightings to certain types of high-yield assets). This can, in turn, lead to increased common exposures in the sector.

The treatment of securitised assets by Solvency II may be given as an example of how capital requirements can encourage common exposures to high-yield assets, the risk represented by which is not always easy to price accurately. As at June 2013, the 13 European insurers surveyed by the OWIE study were holding €53 billion in securitised assets.[22] Further, the study observed that:

> ... eight of the 13 insurers would like to increase investment in securitisations, but seven of those highlighted Solvency II as a significant potential barrier. This is mainly due to what is considered unnecessarily high capital requirements.[23]

These observations came at a time when measures had started to be taken to enhance credit availability across the EU through increased securitisation activity.[24] To make resultant mortgage-backed and asset-backed securities attractive to the insurance industry, Solvency II capital requirements on securitisations deemed to be of high enough quality were eased.[25] In view of the fact that holding these assets

---

19 EIOPA Report 2014 (n. 17), 8–9.

20 B Becker and V Ivashina, 'Reaching for yield in the bond market' Harvard Business School Working Paper 12-103, 12 March 2013. Available at: www.hbs.edu/faculty/Publication%20Files/12-103_c2425c59-1647-42df-8d1b-7b8ed433fb76.pdf (accessed 30 April 2014). See also EFSIR 2012 (n. 18), 36.

21 See CB Merill, TD Nadauld and PE Strahan, *Final Demand for Structured Finance Securities*, March 2014. Available at: http://papers.ssrn.com/sol3/papers.cfm?abstract_id=2380859 (accessed 30 July 2014), 5.

22 OWIE Study 2013 (n. 10), 25. 'This however represents less than 4% of total outstanding European securitisations and less than 2% in terms of average weight in the asset portfolio.' Insurance Europe, *Insurance Europe response to ECB and Bank of England discussion paper on securitisations*, 4 July 2014, Position Paper ECO-INV-14-104. Available at: www.insuranceeurope.eu (accessed 12 October 2014), 2–3.

23 OWIE Study 2013 (n. 10), 25.

24 C Thompson, 'Europe Asset Backed Deals set for return', *Financial Times*, 24 January 2014. Available at: www.ft.com (accessed 25 July 2014). See also Bank of England and European Central Bank, *The impaired EU securitization market: causes, roadblocks and how to deal with them*, April 2014 (hereinafter BOE and ECB 2014(a)) and Bank of England and European Central Bank, *The case for a better functioning securitisation market in the European Union*, Discussion Paper, May 2014 (hereinafter BOE and ECB 2014(b)), esp. Section 2. Both papers are available at: www.ecb.europa.eu (accessed 13 October 2014).

25 See e.g. C Jones, A Barker and C Thompson, 'EU to ease rules on "toxic sludge" to boost credit', *Financial Times*, 26 March 2014. Available at: www.ft.com (accessed 25 July 2014). However, it has been opined that even the halving of capital charges applicable to highly rated securitisations will not be sufficient to make them attractive: see H Coelho 'Cuts to securitization capital charges too small, say experts' Risk.net, 25 March 2014. Available at: www.risk.net (accessed 25 July 2014); see also, Insurance Europe, 2014 (n. 22), 2; 'While we welcome that Solvency II will now recognise that high quality securitisations can and should be identified, the definition of the high quality "Type A" is unnecessarily restrictive and the calibrations proposed are still far too high.' On the other hand, reportedly insurers

enhances interconnectivity between the insurance sector and the rest of the financial system, this push towards investment in securitised assets may have grave systemic implications should macro-economic or industry-specific factors trigger a rush to offload these assets as happened in 2008[26] (depending of course on the extent of the industry's holdings of these assets).

Investment in securitised assets is not the only trend that may currently be said to be of concern. The EIOPA Report 2014 indicates that '[c]ertain activities such as mortgage loan insurance, agreements on liquidity swaps with banks and direct granting of loans may raise specific concerns.'[27] Liquidity swaps are a type of secured lending whereby the insurer pledges high-credit quality or highly liquid assets and receives in exchange assets which are less liquid, but with a higher yield, usually from a bank. The bank obtains liquid assets which it can use either to meet regulatory requirements (such as capital requirements) or to access central banks' facilities.[28] The systemic significance of these transactions is clear: they increase interconnectedness between banks and insurers.[29] The UK Financial Services Authority (FSA), as it then was,[30] observed an increase in the use of this type of transactions in 2011, a trend that it saw as likely to continue due to significant demand,[31] and indicated that the increased interconnectedness which arose as a result of these transactions could 'create a transmission mechanism by which systemic risk across the financial system may be exacerbated'.[32] While at present EIOPA has observed that 'there is no evidence that the use of liquidity swaps represent a threat to the viability of the European insurance sector overall',[33] it is submitted that practices like these should continue to be closely monitored as, in view of their contribution to interconnectedness, systemic implications may go beyond the viability of individual insurance companies.[34] The FSA warned in 2011 that mark-to-market valuations would need

are still exploring ways to invest in the housing markets, including direct investment in mortgages on which capital charges imposed are much lower, see R Mannix, 'Insurers weight home-loan investment as efficient source of yield', Risk.net, 12 March 2014. Available at: www.risk.net (accessed 25 July 2014).

26 For an account, see S Harrington, 'The Financial Crisis, Systemic Risk, and the Future of Insurance Regulation', (2009) 76 *The Journal of Risk and Insurance*, 785, especially 793–794. Note, however, the view of Cummins and Weiss (n. 6), 17: 'Liquidations of insolvent insurers tend to be orderly and take place over long periods of time. Hence, the probability is very low that an insurer would need to liquidate a large quantity of assets quickly.'

27 EIOPA Report 2014 (n. 17), 24. See also discussion of liquidity swap transactions in Box 4, 24–25.

28 For a more in-depth explanation, see Financial Services Authority, *Guidance consultation: liquidity swaps*, July 2011 (FSA LS Guidance 2011). Available at: www.fsa.gov.uk/pubs/guidance/gc11_18.pdf (accessed 30 July 2014).

29 EIOPA Report 2014 (n. 17), 25. See also EFSIR 2012 (n. 18), 37.

30 As a result of the coming into force of the Financial Services Act 2012, the Financial Services Authority was replaced by two regulators in 2013: the Prudential Regulation Authority and the Financial Conduct Authority.

31 FSA LS Guidance 2011 (n. 28), 1.

32 Ibid. See also securities lending which has similar effects in terms of enhancing interconnectedness. National Association of Insurance Commissioners (NAIC) and the Center for Insurance Policy and Research, *Securities Lending*, last updated 4 April 2014. Available at: www.naic.org/cipr_topics/topic_securities_lending.htm (accessed 30 July 2014). The NAIC observed that: 'aspects of securities lending are an issue of concern, particularly their procyclical nature, their lack of transparency, and the ways they may help to transmit negative market events in one part of the globe to another'.

33 EIOPA Report 2014 (n. 17), 25.

34 See EFSIR 2012 (n. 18), 37.

to be applied to these assets and that applicable solvency and capital requirements would have to continue to be observed.[35] This is significant, as the need to comply with regulatory requirements combined with a sudden drop in the market value of these assets may well trigger a fire sale.[36]

The above are just some of the prevalent practices among insurance companies in the EU that may give rise to systemic implications. They point to the need for close monitoring and continuous assessment of systemic implications. Next we shall consider practices prevalent among insurers as issuers of financial products and assessing the potential systemic implications of these practices.

6.2.2 *Insurers as issuers of financial products*

Investment in similar assets is only one type of co-ordinated practice that may arise among EU insurers. Trends in product issuance may also have systemic implications and should likewise be monitored. Contrary to widespread belief, it is not just the issue of and exposure created by "non-traditional, non-insurance" products such as credit default swaps (CDSs), which can create systemic havoc. Insurance products that are much more commonly issued by insurers can also have systemic significance because they are such as to increase interconnectedness between the insurance sector and rest of the financial system. Catastrophe bonds and payment protection insurance are two prime examples of such products.

(a) Catastrophe bonds

Catastrophe bonds are a type of insurance-linked security (ILS), more specifically an instrument designed to transfer catastrophe risk from the issuer (usually an insurer or a reinsurer) to an investor, usually hedge funds or asset managers. The issue will usually take place through an investment bank and requires the setting up of a special purpose vehicle. The bond is designed to pay out a generous return if the relevant catastrophe does not occur. Were the catastrophe to occur, the principal would be forgiven.[37] This type of product is systemically significant because it creates interlinkages between insurance and the rest of the financial system,[38] and in a persistent low interest rate environment, there has been a high demand for these products.[39] It is noted in the EIOPA Report 2014:

> The ILS market is still a limited and complementary segment of the reinsurance market, but in a slow economic recovery situation continues to gain market share. Despite the fact that available estimates on the ILS market substantially differ in growth projection, the overall trend is assumed to be positive throughout. *It remains to be seen to what extent this*

35 FSA LS Guidance 2011 (n. 28), 2.

36 See CB Merrill, TD Nadauld, RM Stulz and S Sherlund, 'Did capital requirements and fair value accounting spark fire sales in distressed mortgage-backed securities?', National Bureau of Economic Research, NBER Working Paper Series, Working Paper 18270, August 2012. Available at: www.nber.org/papers/w18270 (accessed 30 July 2014). See also A Ellul, C Jotikasthira and C T Lundbald, 'Regulatory Pressure and Fire Sales in the Corporate Bond Market' (2011) 101 *Journal of Financial Economics*, 596 at 603–605.

37 See Baluch et al. (n. 9), 143.

38 See discussion in D and S Schwarcz, 2014 (n. 4), 1606–1608.

39 EIOPA Report 2014 (n. 17), 29.

excess demand for catastrophic bonds creates a market of risk origination which underprices these risks and passes them on to investors who do not have the means to correctly price these risks and properly include them in their risk management.[40]

These concerns are justified in view of the worrying parallels with the sudden rise in securitisations in response to demand in the last decade.[41]

(b) Payment protection insurance

Other types of insurance products that are liable to have systemic implications, depending on the practices that emerge surrounding them, are those used to protect against the manifestation of credit risk. A case in point is payment protection insurance (PPI).[42] Variations of this type of insurance product appear to be very popular in many EU jurisdictions and various aspects of this particular type of insurance and the way it is sold have been identified as problematic from the point of view of consumer protection by EIOPA.[43] It is submitted, however, that this product can also have implications from the macro-prudential perspective. Making PPI available in a widespread and indiscriminate fashion can create moral hazard, reducing both lenders' and borrowers' risk-averseness.[44] This can be exacerbated by what McConnell and Blacker refer to as "systemsthink", a phenomenon involving a coincidence of groupthink and herding.[45] Indeed there was a very high penetration rate of PPI in certain segments of the consumer credit market in the years that preceded the 2007–2008 crisis[46] which suggests that widespread and indiscriminate availability of this product contributed to the pre-crisis credit boom.[47]

---

40 Ibid. Emphasis added. The cumulative issuance of catastrophe bonds rose from $782 million in 1997 when the market began to 63,665 million in 2014, and continues to rise steadily. See Artemis, Catastrophe Bond & Insurance-Linked Securities Deal Directory. Available at: http://www.artemis.bm/deal_directory/ (accessed 7 April 2015).

41 For a recent comprehensive analysis of this see Working Paper by S Chernenko, S Hanson and A Sunderam, 'The Rise and Fall of Securitisation', May 2014. Available at: http://fisher.osu.edu/departments/finance/faculty/sergey-chernenko/ (accessed 1 December 2014), in particular Section IV.

42 See discussion in Baluch *et al.* (n. 9), 130–131 of how mortgage payment protection insurance, a specialised form of PPI contributed to the house price bubble in the UK in the late 1980s and early 1990s. See also E Ferran, 'Regulatory Lessons from the Payment Protection Insurance Mis-selling Scandal in the UK' (2012) 13 *European Business Organization Law Review*, 247, 251–253 and P McConnell and K Blacker, 'Systemic Operational Risk: the UK Payment Protection Insurance Scandal' (2012) 7 *Journal of Operation Risk*, 79, 88–89.

43 See European Insurance and Occupational Pensions Authority (EIOPA), *EIOPA Opinion on payment protection insurance*, 28 June 2013, Ref: EIOPA-BoS-13/115 (EIOPA 2013(a)); and *Background note on payment protection insurance*, EIOPA, 28 June 2013, Ref: EIOPA-BoS-13/116 (EIOPA 2013(b)), Available at: https://eiopa.europa.eu/publications/eiopa-opinions/index.html (accessed 6 August 2014).

44 See McConnell and Blacker (n. 42), 111–112.

45 Ibid., 112–113. See also discussion of 'incentive bias' in GP Miller and G Rosenfeld 'Intellectual Hazard: How Conceptual Biases in Complex Organizations Contributed to the Crisis of 2008' (2010) 33 *Harvard Journal of Law and Public Policy*, 807, 815–817.

46 Ferran (n. 42), 252–253: '[The percentage of credit sales made with PPI, or penetration rate] on second charge mortgage PPI policies [reached] 83 per cent in 2002 and 2003, but was down to 46 per cent by 2008. The penetration rate on PPI for unsecured personal loans was also relatively high, standing at 62 per cent in 2002, but down to 38 per cent by 2008. Credit card PPI peaked at 39 per cent in 2003, but declined thereafter and was at 21 per cent in 2008. A relevant factor when considering the significance of the relatively high level of penetration in certain segments of the market is that second-charge mortgages and some forms of unsecured loan tend to be taken out by individuals who are struggling financially.'

47 See McConnell and Blacker (n. 42), 88: 'In a July 2004 report PriceWaterhouseCoopers …

It is also worth noting that PPI became popular in the UK in an era where one of the policy objectives was to make credit more widely available.[48] In the present environment where EU Member States are doing all they can to attempt to accelerate growth by increasing credit availability, the popularity of PPI and similar products is once again becoming noticeable.[49] Regulators cannot therefore afford to ignore its propensity to feed into credit bubbles with potentially very serious EU-wide systemic consequences. This is, in fact, a prime example of a systemically relevant insurance practice the adequate monitoring of which requires mechanisms for coordination and cooperation between entities in charge of macro-prudential oversight (to ensure that risk is not being unduly mispriced) and conduct-of-business supervisors (to ensure that the product is being sold fairly and that vulnerable customers are protected).

6.3 The ESRB and the possibility of effective practices oversight

The above discussion demonstrates that, as the IAIS noted in 2013:

> ... from a regulatory perspective, the postulation that insurance entities will not be a source of future systemic risk may be too simplistic and can never be normative. It is based on historical observations and neglects the evolving natures of business models. Thus, the failure to identify, assess, monitor and mitigate critical trends runs the risk of missing systemic risk events in the future.[50]

The IAIS's approach is therefore cautious and in line with the findings of heading 6.2 of this chapter. However, the IAIS is not a macro-prudential supervisor, therefore it is worth asking, to what extent are its recommendations being heeded? This leads, in turn, to two important questions: first, does the ESRB (in conjunction with the micro-prudential EU supervisors,[51] in particular EIOPA) have the powers

reported how, over a period of ten years, UK household debt (both secured and unsecured) had risen to historically high levels as consumers borrowed to raise spending levels relative to incomes. This increase was driven in the main by access to so-called easy credit at a time of low interest rates, thus giving rise to a series of boom years with very little discussion about the consequences if things were to go wrong. But as Hancock and Zahawi (2011) noted, 'the economic culture was ultimately dictated by the Treasury, and it was the Treasury which allowed debt to lose its traditional taint of social unacceptability'. In other words unconstrained debt, and with it PPI on the loans taken out, was seen as an easy, and some would say irresponsible, way to bolster economic consumption and improve the general living standards of the population.'

48 See Association of British Insurers and Council of Mortgage Lenders, *Lenders and Insurers Announce Better Home-Buyer Protection in New Public/Private Partnership with Government*, Press Release, 23 February 1999. See also Ferran (n. 42), 251–252.

49 EIOPA 2013(a) (n. 43), [10]: 'In a few countries, EIOPA has also become aware of some firms developing an alternative new generation of protection products. To the extent they share some of the same characteristics as PPI, these newer products could pose some of the same risks, unless undertakings take particular care with their product design and sales practices to ensure that problems with PPI are not repeated.'

50 *Macroprudential Policy and Surveillance in Insurance*, International Association of Insurance Supervisors (IAIS), 18 July 2013. Available at: http://iaisweb.org/index.cfm?event=getPage&nodeId=25233 (accessed 7 April 2014), [20]. See also P Braumüller and A Warzilek, 'Insurance and Financial Stability', Chapter 4 in PM Liedtke and J Monkiewicz, *The Future of Insurance Regulation and Supervision: A Global Perspective* (Palgrave Macmillan, 2011), 62–74.

51 These are EIOPA, the European Banking Authority (EBA) and the European Securities and Markets Authority (ESMA).

and means to monitor these practices (what has been termed by the IAIS, "macro-prudential surveillance"[52])? Second, should its observations give rise to systemic concerns, does it have the powers and means to take (or trigger the taking of) action (termed "macroprudential policy" by the IAIS[53])? After giving an overview of the ESRB and its functions and powers within the ESFS, the first of these questions will be addressed by exploring three propositions: (a) the ESRB's expertise leans towards the banking sector; (b) macro-prudential instruments are currently geared towards the banking sector; and (c) it is doubtful whether the ESRB receives sufficiently timely and comprehensive data on the insurance sector. The actions which the ESRB itself is empowered to take should its macro-prudential surveillance activity give rise to concerns, will be referred to in the discussion, however a detailed exploration of how it interacts with micro-prudential and conduct-of-business supervisors to develop and implement macro-prudential policy will not be engaged in, as it goes beyond the scope of this chapter.

6.3.1 The ESRB and its power to limit systemic risks in the insurance sector

The ESRB was established on 16 December 2010 and forms part of the ESFS. The ESFS is aimed at ensuring the supervision of the financial system in the EU and bringing together the actors of the financial supervision at both national and EU level to act as a network.[54] At the EU level, this network comprises the ESRB and three supervisory authorities: EBA, EIOPA and ESMA (hereinafter together 'the ESAs') and the Joint Committee of the ESAs. At the national level, the ESFS comprises the competent or supervisory authorities in the Member States as specified in the legislation establishing the ESAs.[55] The ESRB is responsible for the macro-prudential oversight of the financial system within the EU. Its objective is to contribute to the prevention or mitigation of systemic risks to financial stability in the EU.[56] The ESRB Regulation[57] defines systemic risk as a risk of disruption in the financial system with a potential to have serious negative consequences for the internal market and the real economy.[58] For this purpose, the ESRB is tasked with collecting and analysing all the relevant and necessary information and identifying and prioritising systemic risks.[59] Where such systemic risks are deemed to be significant, the ESRB has the power to issue warnings and/or recommendations for remedial action and, where appropriate, make those warnings and/or recommendations

52 The IAIS (n. 50), [12].

53 Ibid. at [13].

54 Council Regulation (EU) 1092/2010 of 24 November 2010 on European Union Macro-prudential Oversight of the Financial System and Establishing a European Systemic Risk Board [2010] OJ L331/1 (hereinafter: 'the ESRB Regulation'), preamble para. 14. See also Council Regulation (EU) No. 1096/2010 of 17 November 2010 conferring specific tasks upon the European Central Bank concerning the functioning of the European Systemic Risk Board.

55 ESRB Regulation, arts 1–3, the EBA Regulation, the EIOPA Regulation and ESMA Regulation, art. 2(2)(f), respectively.

56 ESRB Regulation, art. 3.

57 See n. 54.

58 ESRB Regulation, art. 2(c).

59 A Keller, 'Collecting Data: How will the ESRB Overcome the First Hurdle Towards Effective Macro-prudential Supervision' (2013), 24(4) *European Business Law Review*, 487.

public.[60] The warnings and recommendations can be addressed to the Union as a whole or to one or more of the Member States, to one or more of the ESAs or to one or more of the national supervisory authorities.[61]

The warnings and recommendations are non-binding and are subject to the 'act or explain' mechanism set out in article 17 of the ESRB Regulation. The ESAs are required to ensure timely follow-up of warnings or recommendations addressed by the ESRB to the ESA or to a national supervisory authority, using their supervisory and regulatory powers.[62] Furthermore, the compliance with the recommendations is monitored by the ESRB based on reports from the addressee/s detailing the action undertaken and in case of inaction, providing for adequate justification.[63]

It is widely acknowledged that systemic risks do not have borders and may originate from any type of financial institution, intermediary, market, infrastructure and instrument. Hence, the ESRB's mandate and powers are wide enough to include monitoring and remedying systemic risks stemming from the insurance sector. Indeed, the ESRB has recently noted in its annual report that it expanded the scope of its analytical activities beyond banking to include the insurance sector. In particular, it looked at the impact of the low yield environment on the insurance sector and the more immediate implications of Solvency II.[64] Its mandate and powers mean that, in theory, the ESRB is ideally placed to undertake practices oversight in the EU. However, the effectiveness of the ESRB's mandate and powers in ensuring financial stability in the EU is dependent on the spectrum of its expertise and tools. It is argued here that these may be geared towards the banking sector, thereby limiting the necessary system-wide perspective of the ESRB's analysis and monitoring. In this article we explore the argument that a 'banking bias' exists in the ESRB's policy decisions[65] and suggest that involving EIOPA in designing macro-prudential tools and in considering possible policy decisions will enable the ESRB to gain access to relevant expertise and assess the implications and effectiveness of these tools in the insurance sector. In addition, improving the way the ESRB draws upon independent expertise, through the Advisory Technical Committee (ATC) and the Advisory Scientific Committee (ASC) may promote more balanced and informed policy decisions.

(a) Proposition 1: The ESRB's expertise leans towards the banking sector

It has been argued that the ESRB's expertise and, accordingly, its supervisory focus may lean towards the banking sector due to the dominant involvement of central

60 ESRB Regulation, art. 3.

61 Ibid. art. 16.

62 For instance, EIOPA Regulation, art. 36(5).

63 M Goldby and A Keller, 'The Commission's Proposal for a New European Systemic Risk Board: An Evaluation' (2010), 4(1) *Law and Financial Markets Review*, 48.

64 The ESRB 2013 Annual Report, July 2014. Available at: www.esrb.europa.eu/pub/pdf/ar/2013/esrbar2013en.pdf?7756e7d1fb0511c8963b23aa4331a81c (accessed 8 October 2014). On p. 25 this notes that 'a key risk for the life insurance sector is the "double hit" risk, whereby insurers run the risk of a "hit" on both the assets side and the liabilities side of their balance sheets'.

65 Report from the Commission to the European Parliament and the Council on the Mission and Organisation of the European Systemic Risk Board, COM (2014) 508 published on 8 August 2014. Available at: http://ec.europa.eu/economy_finance/articles/governance/pdf/2014-08-08_esrb_review_en.pdf.

banks in its governance and structure.[66] First, out of the 38 voting members of the ESRB General Board a large majority (30) represent central banks.[67] Eight out of the 14 members of the Steering Committee, which prepares the General Board's meetings and monitors the progress of the ESRB's ongoing work, also come from the banking field, with seven of them (currently) being central bank representatives.[68] Second, the European Central Bank (ECB) is tasked with ensuring the provision of a Secretariat providing the ESRB with analytical, statistical, logistical and administrative support.[69] Third, it has been suggested in a recent report of the European Commission on the Mission and Organisation of the ESRB that the composition of the ATC is primarily banking--oriented.[70] The ATC is composed of, *inter alia*, representatives of central banks and national supervisory authorities that are most likely to be from national central banks. The ESRB Regulation permits rotation of the representative of the national supervisory authorities in the ATC depending on the item discussed, hence allowing involvement of representatives from the insurance sector. However, the rotation is at the discretion of each Member State, which is free to agree on a common representative.[71]

Given the existing expertise of central banks in the field of financial stability and the proximity of macro-prudential policy to the monetary policy function, their involvement in the ESRB's governance is essential. Nevertheless, it may be that their dominance in the governance of the ESRB and its supporting committees encourages a "groupthink" culture and does not sufficiently ensure that expertise

66 W Buiter, 'The Proposed European Systemic Risk Board is Overweight Central Bankers', 28 October 2009. Available at: http://blogs.ft.com/maverecon/2009/10/the-proposed-european-systemic-risk-board-is-overweight-central-bankers/#axzz2rRdZO84J; Insurance Europe Response to the European Commission's consultation on the Review of the European System of Financial Supervision, 31 July 2013. Available at: www.insuranceeurope.eu/uploads/Modules/Publications/insurance-europe-response-ec-consultation-esas-review.pdf; German Insurance Association' Response to the European Commission's consultation on the Review of the European System of Financial Supervision, 31 July 2013. Available at: http://ec.europa.eu/internal_market/consultations/2013/esfs/docs/contributions/registered-organisations/german-insurance-association_en.pdf.

67 ESRB Regulation, art. 6. In practical terms this means that central banks can reach the simple majority required for the General Board to act, as well as the qualified majority of two thirds that is required to adopt a recommendation or to make a warning or recommendation public. ESRB Regulation, art. 10.

68 See ESRB Regulation, arts 11 and 4(3). The European Parliament, in its Review on the European System of Financial Supervision, Part 2: The Work of the European Systemic Risk Board – The ESFS's Macro-prudential Pillar, October 2013 recommended adjusting the composition of the Steering Committee by giving greater representation to non-central bank representatives (Recommendation C and Table 4). The review concluded that '… the discussion of risks within the General Board and the ATC has been geared too much towards the banking sector, beyond the natural importance of banking as a source of systemic risk …' (para. 4.3.1). Available at: www.europarl.europa.eu/studies.

69 ESRB Regulation, art. 2.

70 Many respondents praised the ATC for delivering regular input to the General Board agenda. See para. 3.2.2 of the Report from the Commission to the European Parliament and the Council on the Mission and Organisation of the European Systemic Risk Board, COM (2014) 508 published on 8 August 2014. Available at: http://ec.europa.eu/economy_finance/articles/governance/pdf/2014-08-08_esrb_review_en.pdf.

In addition, central banks have a clear say in the process of nominating members of the ASC. See Decision of the ESRB of 20 January 2011 on the Procedures and Requirements for the Selection, Appointment and Replacement of the Members of the Advisory Scientific Committee of the European Systemic Risk Board (ESRB/2011/2).

71 ESRB Regulation, art. 13.

and experience of financial sectors, other than banking, are integrated into its policy decisions.[72] The need for macro-prudential supervision to be flexible and innovative necessitates departure from constrained banking-oriented mode of thinking and movement towards reinvigorated dynamic thinking that is open to other sectors of the financial system.[73]

To allow the ESRB to fulfil its mandate it is important for it to be able to draw upon essential expertise from all sectors of the financial system. The structure and governance of the ESRB and it being an integral part of the supervisory system in the EU provides a solid starting point for inclusion of the essential sector-specific expertise. The ESRB Regulation provides for detailed mechanisms to ensure that timely and comprehensive exchange of information between the various actors of the ESFS is taking place and in particular, between the ESRB and EIOPA.[74] Furthermore, the structure of the ESFS is based on cross-membership between its actors allowing for utilisation of expertise, improved information flow and cooperation. As such, the chairpersons of the ESAs are members of the ESRB Steering Committee, which is responsible for the preparation of the ESRB General Board Meetings. The ESAs' chairpersons are also members of the ATC, which provides advice and assistance on the work of the ESRB.[75] Finally, the ESRB has access to high level of expertise and knowledge from the insurance field through the independent experts in the ASC of the ESRB.[76]

(b) Proposition 2: Macro-prudential instruments are currently geared towards the banking sector

It is suggested here that the macro-prudential toolkit of the ESRB (mirroring the macro-prudential toolkit of the Member States' national supervisory authorities) is geared towards the banking sector and its emerging risks. Macro-prudential tools were initially designed and intended to be used in a banking context. Applying them to insurance entities may, therefore, be inappropriate or ineffective

72 Similarly, the Financial Stability Board has warned in its Peer Review of the UK that the Financial Policy Committee must guard against "groupthink". Available at: http://www.financialstabilityboard.org/wp-content/uploads/r_130910.pdf (accessed 18 September 2014). The term "groupthink" was coined by W H Whyte in March 1952 in *Fortune* magazine as 'a rationalized conformity – an open, articulate philosophy which holds that group values are not only expedient but right and good as well.'

73 The need to avoid groupthink was highlighted by two independent reviews by the Bank of England: D Stockton, 'Review of the Monetary Policy Committee's Forecasting Capability', October 2012 and B Winters, 'Review of the Bank of England's Framework for Providing Liquidity to the Banking System', October 2012.

74 ESRB Regulation, art. 15. See also; Agreement between the ESAs and the ESRB on the Establishment at the ESRB Secretariat of Specific Confidentiality Procedures in order to Safeguard Information Regarding Individual Financial Institutions and Information from which Individual Financial Institutions can be Identified, 25 November 2011. This defines specific confidentiality procedures in order to safeguard information regarding individual financial institutions, provided from each ESA to the ESRB. See also letter from EIOPA to the ECB, 'Exchange of Statistical Information between the EIOPA and the ECB', 3 March 2011.

75 ESRB Regulation, arts 11 and 13 respectively.

76 ESRB Regulation, art 12(1); The nominees of the ASC are not members of the ESAs and are chosen on the basis of their general competence and diverse experience in academic fields or other sectors. The ASC has, so far, produced five reports, none of which relates to the insurance sector.

in mitigating systemic risks emerging from this sector.[77] The insurance sector in the UK has voiced similar criticism regarding the Financial Policy Committee[78] claiming that:[79]

> … we wish to raise our concern that the FPC's statement envisages the application of what may be inappropriate measures to the insurance sector, without any apparent consideration of the fundamental differences between banking and insurance, particularly non-life insurance. This reinforces our longstanding concerns about the absence of insurance expertise within the FPC.

Thus, the presence of more insurance-specific expertise within macro-prudential supervisors such as the ESRB would ensure that an appropriate range of macro-prudential tools are developed, a range designed to address efficiently and sensitively systemic problems emerging from financial sectors other than banking, sectors which may not function in precisely the same way.

Acknowledging the inherent risk in macro-prudential toolkit being banking oriented, the ESRB should consider, when issuing warnings or recommendations, whether a particular tool could have application in the insurance sector and assess its impact on this sector. Ideally, the ESRB should develop tailor-made macro-prudential tools to reflect the specific needs of the insurance sector and its emerging risks.[80] This need is reflected in the Insurance Core Principles issued by the IAIS.[81] Principle 24 explicitly calls for the development and application of macro-prudential tools to limit systemic risk resulting from, or increased by, activities in the insurance sector.[82] In the same vein, the ESRB has confirmed that ultimately macro-prudential policy will require a richer set of instruments to better prevent and mitigate financial stability risks stemming from sectors other than banking, including insurance.[83] Accordingly, in its *Recommendation on Intermediate Objectives and Instruments of Macro-prudential Policy* from 4 April 2013, the ESRB assigned separate and differentiated intermediate objectives of macro-prudential policy to the insurance sector. Regrettably, it has failed to clarify that an adjusted list of macro-prudential instruments should be added in due course.[84]

It is also worth noting that in light of our first proposition, it is questionable whether the ESRB is positioning itself to make good use of available technical expertise for the development and application of an insurance-focused toolkit.[85]

77 Written Evidence submitted by the Association of British Insurers (hereinafter 'ABI') to the Treasury Committee on 'Macro-prudential tools', June 2012, p. 10. Available at: www.parliament.uk/documents/commons-committees/treasury/MPT-Ev-ALL.pdf (accessed 8 October 2014).

78 The independent Financial Policy Committee at the Bank of England is the macro-prudential supervisor in the UK. See the Financial Services Act 2012 which came into force on 1 April 2013 inserting, *inter alia*, Part 1A to the Bank of England Act 1998.

79 Ibid., p. 58.

80 ABI Written evidence, n. 77, p.11.

81 The IAIS Insurance Core Principles, October 2011, ICP 24.1: '… The supervisor also develops and applies appropriate tools that take into account the nature, scale and complexity of insurers …'

82 Revised October 2013, see ICP 24.

83 ESRB Flagship Report on Macro-prudential Policy in the Banking Sector, March 2014. Available at: www.esrb.europa.eu/pub/pdf/other/140303_flagship_report.pdf (accessed 8 October 2014).

84 Recommendation of the ESRB of 4 April 2013 on Intermediate Objectives and Instruments of Macro-prudential Policy ESRB/2013/1. Available at: www.esrb.europa.eu/pub/pdf/recommendations/2013/ESRB_2013_1.en.pdf (accessed 8 October 2014).

85 The IAIS, 'Macro-prudential Policy and Surveillance in Insurance', 18 July 2013, p. 23.

(c) Proposition 3: It is doubtful whether the ESRB receives sufficiently timely and comprehensive data on the Insurance sector

In order to produce high-quality macro-prudential analysis and monitor systemic risks effectively, the ESRB needs to draw upon comprehensive, timely and accurate data on the insurance sector. Regular data collection is a two-way process: drawing upon top-down as well as bottom-up analysis. A top-down analysis focuses on aggregate macro-financial data and is performed in order to monitor vulnerabilities and assess conditions in specific sectors with possible implications for system-wide risks. The source of the top-down analysis is available data from the ECB and other international institutions.[86] In contrast, bottom-up analysis relies on micro-level or firm-specific data that is then aggregated to produce sectoral or system-wide assessments.

EIOPA and the Member States' national supervisors are the main source of micro-data for the ESRB's bottom-up analysis. It is based on the EIOPA dashboard that is designed to signal potential risks and vulnerabilities to the European insurance sector and assess the resilience of this sector.[87] The risk dashboard is making use of data being reported quarterly by 32 large European insurance groups;[88] however, the introduction of the reporting requirement in Solvency II will further enhance the data availability.[89]

The regular exchange of information between the ESRB and EIOPA is done on an annual basis as indicated in the decision of the ESRB on 21 September 2011 on the Provision and Collection of Information for the Macro-prudential Oversight of the Financial System within the Union.[90] This is to be contrasted with the shorter time span of the EBA quarterly reporting to the ESRB.[91]

EIOPA is also actively involved in developing comprehensive data on the insurance sector via conducting stress tests of insurance firms exploring resilience of the EU insurance sector to a number of shock scenarios, such as the solvency impact of a prolonged period of low yields.[92] The usefulness of stress tests is often

86 Such as data on euro area insurance corporations and pension funds (ICPFs) available on the ECB's website.

87 The mechanical process of the risk assessment is complemented by transparent expert judgment that may adjust, where necessary, the initial risk scores providing a forward-looking assessment of the expected evolution of risks; See Keller (n. 59), 481 535.

88 See EIOPA Risk Dashboard – A Background Note, March 2014, p. 4.

89 It will increase the volume and complexity of data at the same time: according to PWC, the typical quarterly reporting will include 75,000 data points, see Demystifying Pillar 3: Getting Implementation on Track, available at http://www.pwc.co.uk/financialservices/regulation/solvency-ii/publications/demystifying-pillar-3-getting-implementation-on-track.jhtml (accessed 8 October 2014).

90 ESRB Decision 2011/6 on the Provision and Collection of Information for the Macro-prudential Oversight of the Financial System within the Union of 21 September 2011, section B2.

91 On other challenges in the ESRB important task of data collection, see A Keller (n. 59).

92 The ESRB's letter to EIOPA endorsing its stress tests in April 2014 specifically points out the close cooperation between EIOPA and the ESRB on exchange of information. Further targeted efforts of gathering data include the collection of information on exposures of insurance companies to sovereign debt and banking – see Commission Staff Working Document, SWD(2014) 261 from 8 August 2014 accompanying the Report from the European Commission to the European Parliament and Council on the Operation of the European Supervisory Authorities (ESAs) and the European System of Financial Supervision (ESFS), COM (2014) 509, p. 14. Available at: http://ec.europa.eu/internal_market/finances/docs/committees/140808-esfs-swd_en.pdf (accessed 8 October 2014).

questioned.[93] One of the issues identified in the EIOPA 2011 survey was that the tests are often performed on the asset side of the insurer's balance sheet while the liability side, which is associated with critical insurance-specific risks, is neglected.[94]

In addition to the regular exchange of information, the ESRB can request from the ESAs disclosure of institution-specific information on an ad hoc basis following a just and proportionate request. Accordingly, the EIOPA and the ESRB have signed an agreement setting out the principles and measures for exchanging such sensitive information while ensuring its confidentiality.[95] However, ad hoc data collection on practices in the insurance sector may still be lagging behind. Recently the ESRB has produced a paper on securities financing transactions following data collection from a sample of European banks and agent lenders. The ESRB's acknowledgment that future data collections may comprise a wider set of addressees, such as insurance companies, does not negate the current information gap in this sector.[96]

Finally, it is important to acknowledge that statistical data has its own limitations in predicting systemic risks.[97] Therefore, continuous dialogue with a wide spectrum of market participants is a requisite for the ESRB macro-prudential surveillance in the insurance sector and will allow it to keep track of financial innovations and to maintain this sector under its radar.

6.3.2 How to rebalance the focus of the ESRB beyond banking risks?

The banking sector was the principal source of systemic risk in the 2007–2008 global financial crisis. It is not surprising, therefore, that the dominance of the banking sector is also apparent in the governance of the macro-prudential supervisor in the EU and in the orientation of the macro-prudential tools. It is suggested that mechanisms to rebalance the focus of the ESRB beyond the banking sector should be put in place.

First, given EIOPA's strong understanding of the impact of macro-prudential tools on insurance entities and policyholders it is advisable to involve it closely in the development of macro-prudential tools and policy decisions. The ESRB Regulation

93 On banking stress tests, see Borio et al. (n. 11) criticising macro stress tests; B Bernanke (2013) 'Stress Testing Banks: What Have We Learned?' Available at: www.federalreserve.gov/newsevents/speech/bernanke20130408a.pdf (accessed 2 January 2015).

94 The IAIS, 'Macro-prudential Policy and Surveillance in Insurance', 18 July 2013, p. 22; EIOPA, 'Financial Stability Report 2011' Second Half-year Report (Frankfurt/M). Available at: https://eiopa.europa.eu/fileadmin/tx_dam/files/publications/reports/FSC-Report-Autumn-2011/EIOPA_Financial_Stability_Report_2011.pdf (accessed 8 October 2014).

95 Agreement between the EBA, EIOPA, ESMA and the ESRB on the Establishment at the ESRB Secretariat of Specific Confidentiality Procedures in order to Safeguard Information regarding Individual Financial Institutions and Information from which Individual Financial Institutions can be Identified 25 November 2011. There is also a letter addressed from EIOPA to the ECB on 3 March 2011 on the Exchange of Statistical Information between the EIOPA and the ECB confirming cooperation between EIOPA and the ECB on exchange of statistical data. Both documents are available at: https://eiopa.europa.eu/disclosure/data-exchange/index.html (accessed 8 October 2014).

96 ESRB Occasional Papers Series No. 6, Securities Financing Transactions and the (re)use of Collateral in Europe, An Analysis of the first Data Collection Conducted by the ESRB from a sample of European Banks and Agent Lenders, 6 September 2014.

97 IMF, 'Macroprudential Policy: an Organising Framework', 14 March, 2011. Available at: www.imf.org/external/np/pp/eng/2011/031411.pdf (accessed 8 October 2014).

sets out a general obligation on the ESRB to cooperate with the participants of the ESFS, including EIOPA. A similar obligation is found in the EIOPA Regulations.[98] This cooperation is currently taking place through regular and ad hoc exchanges of information and the design and analysis of stress tests.[99] However, specific and detailed mechanisms which encourage a regular input from insurance experts in the ATC and the ASC would promote more informed policy decisions by the ESRB in the insurance sector.

Second, a varied membership would assist in facilitating balanced expert input to the ESRB policy decisions. Therefore, the ATC membership could be rebalanced by amending the ESRB Regulation to include a mandatory requirement for an insurance national supervisory representative where the item discussed relates to this sector. Adjusting the composition of the ASC by increasing representation of non-central banks could be another step toward inclusiveness of the insurance sector in the ESRB policy decision making.[100]

6.4 Conclusion

The requirement for supervision to be comprehensive is particularly essential when its aim is to prevent or mitigate systemic risks in the financial market due to the interconnectedness of its players and products. Therefore, the first hurdle for effective macro-prudential supervision in the EU is ensuring that all sectors and practices are monitored comprehensively by the ESRB. The tendency to focus on the banking sector is natural. The banking sector was the most dominant participant in the 2007–2008 global financial crisis. However, this tendency to lean towards the banking sector and overlooking (even for the time being) the activities of other important sectors might prove to be the ESRB's Achilles heel. In this chapter we argue in favour of "practices oversight" which would require macro-prudential supervisors to monitor existing and emerging practices prevalent among insurers which have the potential to be systemically relevant. We also suggest ways to rebalance the ESRB's current focus on banking risks, through mechanisms that will ensure close and frequent consultation with experts from the insurance sectors.

98 Article 1(4) of the ESRB Regulation and art. 2(3) of the EIOPA Regulation.

99 According to EIOPA's mandate, the design of the stress test shall be done in cooperation with the ESRB (reg. 23(1) of the EIOPA Regulation). The adverse market scenarios in the 2014 stress tests reflect the ESRB assessment of the prevailing systemic risks to the financial system. See EIOPA Insurance Stress Test 2014 published on 28 November 2014, section B 12.

100 See n. 68.

CHAPTER 7

Stealth federal regulation of insurance in the United States

Patricia A. McCoy†

7.1 Introduction

In the United States, the federal government dominates financial services regulation with the singular exception of insurance regulation, which traditionally has been reserved to the states. This state-based system has long been criticised by some as too costly for insurers and consumers due to the lack of a uniform national standard. Nevertheless, so far the touted inefficiencies in state-based insurance have never been enough for any of the repeated attempts to shift insurance regulation wholesale to the federal government to succeed.[1]

In part, the continued dominance of state insurance regulation rests on state regulators' relative success in managing two risks: market conduct and solvency.[2] After the 2008 financial crisis, however, systemic risk emerged as a new topic of concern in insurance. This development altered the calculus of the allocation of authority for insurance regulation between the states and the federal government. Since 2008, concerns about cost savings to industry and a single set of national rules for efficiency's sake have moved to the back burner in the ongoing debate over the proper role of the federal government in the oversight of insurance. Instead, systemic risk and global cooperation have become the new *leitmotifs* of that debate.

Suffice it to say, insurers and state insurance regulators have been ill-prepared for this change. In landmark reform legislation in 2010, the U.S. Congress bestowed jurisdiction on the federal government to regulate systemic risk in insurance, to the consternation of the insurance industry and state insurance commissioners.

† This chapter appears with the gracious permission of the U.C. Irvine Law Review, which commissioned an earlier version of this work for the U.S. audience.

The chapter was made possible through generous research support from the University of Connecticut School of Law and Boston College Law School and benefited from comments by Shauhin Talesh and the other participants in the September 19, 2014 insurance law symposium at the University of California at Irvine School of Law. Karen Breda provided invaluable reference librarian assistance. The author also thanks Brian Atchinson, John Cogan, Kathleen Engel, Andromachi Georgosouli, Bill Goddard, Miriam Goldby, Peter Kochenburger, Rosa Lastra, Tom Leonardi, Brendan Maher, Philip Rawlings, Jim Rebitzer, Dan Schwarcz, Steve Schwarcz, Tom Sullivan and Terri Vaughan for their insights into the extent and nature of systemic risk in insurance and the ensuing debate over federal regulation. None of those individuals are responsible, for the views expressed in this chapter, which are mine alone.

1 For an account of that history, see Federal Insurance Office, U.S. Department of the Treasury, *How to Modernize and Improve the System of Insurance Regulation in the United States* 1 (Dec. 2013) [hereinafter cited as the "FIO Modernization Report"].

2 See FIO Modernization Report, *supra* n. 1, at 13.

Both groups oppose systemic risk oversight of insurers by the federal government based on three principal arguments. One is that insurance companies do not pose systemic risk because they do not have mismatches between short-term liabilities and long-term assets that could make them vulnerable to runs. The second is that the meltdown of the global insurer American International Group (AIG) was not caused by insurance, but rather by derivatives trading in an overseas non-insurance affiliate. Finally, these constituencies argue that insurance companies survived 2008 relatively intact thanks to the effectiveness of state insurance regulation.

These arguments, however, have not kept pace with the evolution in theories of systemic risk since 2008. The experience with runs in the shadow banking sector in 2008 highlighted the potential for runs in certain insurance products, particularly in the life insurance industry. The role of insurers as financiers of short-term liabilities has implications for the creation of systemic risk elsewhere in the financial system. In the wake of AIG, the hazards posed by weak group oversight of insurance groups to financial stability have also received attention.

As this suggests, in the United States, the federal government's evolving approach to systemic risk in insurance is a microcosm of the larger debate over sources of systemic risk. In this article, I examine two theories of systemic risk that have surfaced in decisions by the Financial Stability Oversight Council (FSOC or the Council)[3] designating systemically important insurers and consider the broader implications of those decisions for the future federal regulation of insurance.

One of FSOC's theories derives from a classic theory of bank runs, in which a mismatch between short-term liabilities and long-term assets exposes financial institutions to a spike in demand for immediate withdrawals in cash. In the insurance context, FSOC has invoked that theory three times to date based on the cash surrender features in certain life insurance and annuity products. The Council has also pointed to systemic risk created by runs on other products offered by non-insurance affiliates in insurance groups. Finally, FSOC has cited concerns about runs in other parts of the financial system to justify its focus on the role of large insurance companies as suppliers of short-term credit to other vulnerable counterparties.

In addition, FSOC has announced a second, more aggressive theory of systemic risk that focuses on the potential adverse macroeconomic repercussions from loss of coverage by a dominant insurer, whether that withdrawal of coverage is voluntary or due to the insurer's insolvency (and regardless of the cause of any insolvency). Despite the novel nature of this theory, it has not been well-explained in FSOC's formulations to date. Nevertheless, this fuzzy rationale has had real-world consequences because FSOC has relied on it so far in designating at least one insurance company as systemically risky.

Taken together, these theories point to a growing federal role in the U.S. regulation of insurance. To the extent that life insurance and certain annuity policies grant early redemption rights at policyholders' initiative, the life insurance industry faces a

3 The Dodd-Frank Wall Street Reform and Consumer Protection Act in 2010 created FSOC and charged that body, among other things, with designating nonbank financial services providers that "could pose a threat to the financial stability of the United States" as systemically important financial institutions (SIFIs) that are subject to enhanced prudential regulation by the Federal Reserve Board. Pub. L. No. 111-203, § 113(a)(1), 124 Stat. 1376 (2010).

real but uncertain risk of runs that will continue to attract FSOC's scrutiny. In addition, insurance companies engage in other discrete activities that have been found to be systemically risky, including securities lending, derivatives trading, and sponsorship of money market mutual funds. These activities are certain to be subject to heightened federal oversight and may subject insurance companies, regardless of their size, to federal regulation of those activities in years to come.

As a corollary, the fact that these same systemically risky activities can be conducted in non-insurance subsidiaries of insurance groups – as AIG made clear – has propelled effective consolidated group supervision to the forefront of policy discussions. The global reach of internationally active insurance groups and pronouncements on group oversight by international regulatory bodies highlights the fact that only the federal government has the potential jurisdiction and treaty-making authority to conduct group supervision effectively. Finally, the solvency concerns that underpin both of FSOC's theories of systemic risk are likely to pave the way for much more intrusive federal involvement in risk-based capital standards and other types of solvency regulation, first for internationally active insurance groups and eventually for the entire insurance industry.

In short, systemic risk regulation by the federal government, both singly and in tandem with international bodies, is a game-changer. It is likely to transform the locus of U.S. insurance regulation both in ways that are predictable and others that are not. Yet the larger implications of this change for continued state dominance in insurance regulation are not well recognized. To that extent, federal oversight of systemic risk in insurance has the stealth potential to affect the insurance industry by imposing certain federal regulatory standards industrywide.

7.2 A brief historical overview

Historically, the states have held the predominant role in U.S. insurance regulation. This arrangement stands in stark distinction to the regulation of banking and securities in the United States, which both gravitated inexorably toward federal regulatory domination in the twentieth century. In this brief historical overview, I discuss the states' central role in U.S. insurance regulation and the limited federal intervention in that realm through 2009.

7.2.1 Through 1945

In the early decades of the republic, the states made the first forays into U.S. insurance regulation. New Hampshire appointed the first insurance commissioner in 1851 and other states quickly followed suit.[4] Less than twenty years later, the Supreme Court issued a seminal ruling which barred federal intervention in insurance via the Commerce Clause of the U.S. Constitution. In that 1868 decision in *Paul v. Virginia*,[5] the Supreme Court ruled that the business of insurance did not constitute interstate commerce for purposes of the Commerce Clause. One of the

4 FIO Modernization Report, *supra* n. 1, at 11.
5 75 U.S. 168 (1868).

consequences of that decision was that Congress lacked the power to regulate insurance at the federal level, at least under the Commerce Clause, thereby clothing the states with primacy in insurance regulation. A few short years after *Paul* was handed down, the New York superintendent of insurance, George W. Miller, convened the inaugural meeting of what is known today as the National Association of Insurance Commissioners (NAIC), a voluntary organization consisting of the insurance commissioners of all fifty states, the District of Columbia, and the American territories.[6]

In 1944, the Supreme Court reversed its decision in *Paul* and ruled that insurance could, in fact, constitute interstate commerce, giving Congress the constitutional power to regulate insurance transactions crossing state lines.[7] Quickly, the states rallied in opposition to that decision. In response, in 1945, Congress enacted the reverse preemption provision in the McCarran-Ferguson Act,[8] which provides that no federal law may invalidate, impair, or supersede state laws governing the business of insurance unless the federal law specifically relates to the business of insurance.[9] With the passage of McCarran-Ferguson, the states' commanding role in the regulation of insurance was further entrenched and federal attempts to oversee insurance faced even higher barriers to success.

7.2.2 Post-McCarran-Ferguson through 2009

Federal oversight of traditional insurance activities and products within the United States is limited today and it was even more limited before the 2008 financial crisis and the passage of the Dodd-Frank Wall Street Reform and Consumer Protection Act[10] (the Dodd-Frank Act or Dodd-Frank) in 2010. Before Dodd-Frank, federal oversight of insurance fell into three discrete categories. First, federal regulators and courts deemed some traditional insurance products to also constitute "banking" or "securities," thus triggering the application of federal banking or securities laws on top of (or sometimes to the exclusion of) state insurance laws.[11] Second, a major federal statute enacted in 1974 titled the Employee Retirement Income Security Act

6 FIO Modernization Report, *supra* n. 1, at 11; Susan Randall, *Insurance Regulation in the United States: Regulatory Federalism and the National Association of Insurance Commissioners*, 26 FLA. ST. L. REV. 625 (1996).

7 *United States v. South-Eastern Underwriters Ass'n*, 322 U.S. 33 (1944).

8 Pub. L. No. 79-15, 59 Stat. 33 (1945), codified at 15 U.S.C. §§ 1011–1015.

9 15 U.S.C. § 1012(b).

10 Pub. L. No. 111-203, 124 Stat. 1376 (2010).

11 For instance, in 1959, the Supreme Court held that variable annuities, which had long been regulated as insurance by the states, also constitute securities for purposes of the federal securities laws. *Securities and Exchange Comm'n v. Variable Annuity Life Insurance Co.*, 359 U.S. 65 (1959). Variable life insurance is similarly federally regulated as a security. Later, in 1995, the Supreme Court held that national banks could sell fixed and variable annuities as agents. *Nationsbank of North Carolina, N.A. v. Variable Annuity Life Insurance Co.*, 513 U.S. 251, 254–55 (1995). Meanwhile, the federal regulator for national banks, the Comptroller of the Currency, permits national banks and their subsidiaries to underwrite credit insurance, municipal bond insurance, and single-interest insurance (which insures banks against loss or damage to personal property that serves as bank collateral) based on the determination that such insurance is a banking product that is incidental to the business of banking. 12 C.F.R. pt. 37; OCC Interpretive Letter No. 338, 1985 OCC Ltr. LEXIS 23 (May 2, 1985); OCC Letter No. 283, 1984 OCC Ltr. LEXIS 37 (March 16, 1984); Gramm-Leach-Bliley Act, Pub. L. No. 106-102, § 302(b), 113 Stat. 1338, 1407 (1999).

(ERISA)[12] subjected employee benefits – including pension, health insurance, and disability benefits offered to employees through the workplace – to strict fiduciary standards under federal law. As a result, insurance companies that serve as underwriters or plan administrators of health insurance, disability insurance, or pension benefits offered by covered employers must comply with ERISA. Finally, the federal government instituted a number of social insurance programs,[13] the most important being Social Security retirement and disability benefits,[14] Medicare health benefits for the elderly,[15] Medicaid health benefits for the poor,[16] unemployment insurance,[17] and some catastrophe insurance (most notably, flood insurance,[18] nuclear liability insurance under the Price-Anderson Act,[19] and terrorism risk insurance[20]).

Outside the realm of traditional insurance products, private insurance companies may intersect with federal regulation in other ways, depending on their activities. Insurance companies that act as securities broker-dealers have to comply with the broker-dealer registration and oversight provisions of the Securities Exchange Act of 1934.[21] Insurers that serve as investment advisers have to observe the Investment Advisers Act of 1940,[22] while those that sponsor mutual funds or private funds must obey the Investment Company Act of 1940.[23] After the Gramm-Leach-Bliley Act of 1999[24] allowed insurance underwriters to become affiliates of depository

---

12 Pub. L. No. 93-406, 88 Stat. 829 (1974), codified in part at 29 U.S.C. ch. 18.

13 Another major social insurance program in the United States – workers compensation for private-sector employees who are injured on the job – is administered by individual states. See Legal Information Institute, Workers Compensation, available at: www.law.cornell.edu/wex/workers_compensation (last viewed Dec. 10, 2014).

14 See Social Security Administration, Home Page, available at: www.ssa.gov (describing benefits) (last viewed Dec. 10, 2014).

15 See Medicare.gov (describing benefits) (last viewed Dec. 10, 2014).

16 See Medicaid.gov (describing benefits) (last viewed Dec. 10, 2014).

17 Unemployment insurance is offered jointly by the federal government and the states. See U.S. Department of Labor, Unemployment Insurance (UI), available at: www.dol.gov/dol/topic/unemployment-insurance/(last viewed Dec. 10, 2014).

18 See Federal Emergency Management Agency, National Flood Insurance Program, available at: www.fema.gov/national-flood-insurance-program (describing program) (last viewed Dec. 10, 2014).

19 Pub. L. No. 85-256, 71 Stat. 576 (1957), codified at 42 U.S.C. § 2012(i). See U.S. Department of Energy, Office of the General Counsel, Price-Anderson Act, available at: http://energy.gov/gc/price-anderson-act (last viewed Dec. 10, 2014); National Association of Insurance Commissioners and the Center for Insurance Policy and Research, Nuclear Liability Insurance (Price-Anderson Act), available at: www.naic.org/cipr_topics/topic_nuclear_liability_insurance.htm (describing coverage) (last viewed Dec. 10, 2014).

20 See U.S. Department of the Treasury, Terrorism Risk Insurance Program, available at: www.treasury.gov/resource-center/fin-mkts/Pages/program.aspx (describing program) (last viewed Dec. 10, 2014); National Association of Insurance Commissioners and Center for Insurance Policy and Research, Terrorism Risk Insurance Act (TRIA), available at: www.naic.org/cipr_topics/topic_tria.htm (describing program) (last viewed Dec. 10, 2014). In late 2014, Congress adjourned without extending the Terrorism Risk Insurance Act, which was scheduled to expire at year-end 2014. In January 2015, however, Congress extended that legislation in the Terrorism Risk Insurance Program Reauthorizing Act of 2015, Pub. L. No. 114-1, 114th Cong., 1st Sess. (2015).

21 Pub. L. No. 73–291, 48 Stat. 881 (1934), §§ 3(a)(4)(a), 3(a)(5)(a), 3(a)(18), 8, 9(a), 10(b), 11, 15, codified as amended at 15 U.S.C. §§ 78c(a)(4)(a), (a)(5)(a), (a)(18), 78h, 78*i*, 78j(b), 78k, 78*o*. See *generally* U.S. Securities and Exchange Commission, Guide to Broker-Dealer Registration, available at: www.sec.gov/divisions/marketreg/bdguide.htm#I (last viewed Dec. 10, 2014).

22 Pub. L. No. 76-768, 54 Stat. 847 (1940), codified as amended at 15 U.S.C. §§ 80b-1 et seq.

23 Pub. L. No. 76-768, 54 Stat. 789 (1940), codified as amended at 15 U.S.C. §§ 80a-1 et seq.

24 Pub. L. No. 106-102, 113 Stat. 1338 (1999).

institutions under the common control of a financial holding company, affected insurance companies became subject to consolidated holding company oversight by the Federal Reserve. Insurance company affiliates of financial holding companies must also observe the limits on interaffiliate transactions under sections 23A and 23B of the Federal Reserve Act.[25]

7.3 The changing dimensions of the debate

As the last section discussed, federal forays into insurance regulation have been limited to certain sectors, with health insurance, variable annuities, and pensions being the most important examples. The landmark passage of the Affordable Care Act[26] and its health insurance mandate in 2010 further expanded the federal presence in health insurance. The federal role in social insurance has also grown. All of these sectors are those in which private insurers' exit from parts or all of those markets or other market failures compelled the federal government to step in.

Apart from these limited federal incursions, the states succeeded brilliantly in fending off federal encroachment in insurance regulation through 2010. For over a century, there have been campaigns from time to time to insert the federal government into the general regulation of insurance. These campaigns have argued for federal oversight based on traditional arguments involving efficiency, solvency, and consumer protection. Otherwise, none of these traditional rationales ever gained sufficient political traction to trump the states' predominant role in insurance regulation.

With the financial crisis of 2008 and the ensuing federal response, the terms of the debate changed in a radical and powerful way. For the first time following the crisis, calls for greater federal oversight of insurance were framed in terms of the potential systemic risk that insurance company activities posed to the financial stability of the United States and the world. The public furor over the federal government's massive bailout of AIG in 2008[27] and the revelations about bonuses to AIG executives in March 2009[28] added urgency to those calls. Following the bailout, many considered it self-evident that the federal government had to oversee the entire financial system, including insurance companies, in order to contain systemic risk.

7.3.1 The traditional dimensions of the debate over state vs. federal regulation

Historically, two of the rationales for a greater federal role in insurance were lax corporate governance by insurers and inadequate solvency regulation by state insurance commissioners. For example, in the early twentieth century, some of the proposals for general federal regulation of insurance were a response to corrupt insurance

---

25 12 U.S.C. §§ 371c, 371c-1.

26 Patient Protection and Affordable Care Act, Pub. L. No. 111-148, 124 Stat. 896 (2010).

27 Federal Reserve Board, *Press Release: Federal Reserve Board, with full support of the Treasury Department, authorizes the Federal Reserve Bank of New York to lend up to $85 billion to the American International Group (AIG)* (Sept. 16, 2008), available at: www.federalreserve.gov.

28 See, e.g., Edmund L. Andrews & Peter Baker, *A.I.G. Planning Huge Bonuses After $170 Billion Bailout*, N.Y. TIMES, Mar. 14, 2009.

company practices and insolvencies. In 1904, a series of insurance company scandals involving stock market manipulation, covert campaign contributions, and officer misappropriation of policyholder funds caused President Theodore Roosevelt to advocate federal regulation of insurance in his annual address to Congress.[29] Sixty years later, in the 1960s, a spate of auto insurer insolvencies, combined with a lack of state guaranty funds to assist injured policyholders, led to renewed calls for an optional federal insurance company charter and a federal guaranty fund.[30] Another string of insurance company insolvencies in the 1980s and 1990s prompted Congress to explore the need for federal solvency regulation of insurers.[31]

Although scandals and insolvencies frequently served as the impetus for efforts to federalize insurance regulation, commonly those proposals invoked the need for efficiency and national uniformity as well. In his 1904 address to Congress, for instance, President Theodore Roosevelt advocated federal intervention on grounds that insurance was "national and not local in its application."[32] The following year, Senator John Dryden of New Jersey sought to implement Roosevelt's proposal by introducing a bill to create a new federal Bureau of Insurance in the Department of Commerce and Labor, based in part on the need to reduce "a vast amount of needless clerical labor to meet the requirements of some fifty different States and Territories and consequent decrease in expense rate."[33]

In these early instances, efficiency and uniformity provided supplemental rationales for legislation that was primarily meant to redress scandals. However, by the end of the twentieth century, national uniformity became the main justification in its own right for proposals for federal oversight. For example, a single national standard was the rationale for a provision in the Gramm-Leach-Bliley Act in 1999 mandating a new federal agency for national insurance agent licensing requirements unless a majority of the states and U.S. territories met a 2002 statutory deadline for agreeing to reciprocal licensing of insurance brokers and agents.[34] Similarly, efficiency concerns, including the cost of state insurance regulation,[35] slow delivery of new insurance products to market, state price regulation, and duplicative and inconsistent state rules, animated repeated proposals in the early 2000s to create national insurance standards and an optional federal charter for insurance companies.[36]

While concerns over consumer protection received lip service during recent debates, the real justification for the proposed federal reforms was reducing regulatory red tape for national and international insurers. Advocates for a greater federal

---

29 Kenneth J. Meier, *The Political Economy of Regulation: The case of insurance* 57–58 (1988); Theodore Roosevelt's Annual Message to Congress for 1904.

30 See FIO Modernization Report, *supra* n. 1, at 15.

31 *Ibid.* at 15–16.

32 Theodore Roosevelt's Annual Message to Congress for 1904.

33 *Bill for Government Control of Insurance; to be introduced in the Senate by John F. Dryden*, N.Y. TIMES, Feb. 27, 1905, p. 5.

34 Pub. L. No. 106-102, § 321, 113 Stat. 1338 (1999). This agency was referred to as the National Association of Registered Agents and Brokers or NARAB.

35 The Federal Insurance Office has asserted, for instance, that per dollar of premium, the costs of state-based regulation are 6.8 times greater for an insurer doing business in the United States than for one operating in the United Kingdom. FIO Modernization Report, *supra* n. 1, at 5.

36 See, e.g., FIO Modernization Report, *supra* n. 1, at 16–17.

role argued, for instance, that national uniformity would give consumers access to innovative new insurance products regardless of where they lived; would reduce opportunities for industry capture of regulators; would help eliminate arbitrage and a possible race to the bottom in insurance standards; and would improve consumer protection for policyholders and beneficiaries more generally.[37] Nevertheless, deregulation was the predominant theme of the debate, with a stress on the cost savings to insurers from streamlining regulation nationally and internationally.[38] Despite the expressions of solicitude for consumers, there was little actual discussion of how to avoid opportunities for industry capture or arbitrage at the federal level or how to set a single federal standard to better protect insurance industry consumers.

Notwithstanding these repeated efforts to inject the federal government into the general regulation of insurance for the sake of better corporate governance, efficiency, and solvency, the states were able to beat back those efforts and preserve their preeminent role in insurance oversight. They succeeded in defeating a greater federal role through two main strategies: accommodation and rebuttal.

In the first strategy, *accommodation*, the states often adopted piecemeal reforms that were designed to harmonize regulation and reduce duplication – with the prospect of more to come – sufficient to convince undecided members of Congress to preserve the status quo. For instance, in response to proposals to create a federal guaranty fund following the auto insurer failures of the 1960s, the NAIC preempted those proposals by adopting two model state guaranty fund acts – one for property and casualty insurance and the other for life and health insurance – in 1969 and 1970 respectively.[39] Numerous states enacted these model laws[40] and all 88 states offer state guaranty funds today.[41]

Later, after federal scrutiny of more insurance company insolvencies in the 1980s and 1990s, the states, acting through the NAIC, adopted new risk-based capital requirements for personal lines insurers and later developed uniform statutory accounting principles for the industry. In addition, the states formulated a new peer review process called the Financial Standards and Accreditation Program that was designed to make insurance rules more consistent across the states.[42] Meanwhile, in 2002, the states defused Gramm-Leach-Bliley's threat to impose national insurance agent licensing requirements by certifying that thirty-five states and territories had agreed to reciprocity in producer licensing, thereby meeting the law's requirements to avoid federal action by the statutory deadline.[43] More recently, the NAIC has

37 *Ibid.* at 1, 5.

38 *Ibid.* at 5, 17; *Department of the Treasury, Blueprint for a Modernized Financial Regulatory Structure* (Mar. 31, 2008), available at: www.treasury.gov.

39 See, e.g., FIO Modernization Report, *supra* n. 1, at 15.

40 *Ibid.*

41 See, e.g., National Conference of Insurance Guaranty Funds, *State Guaranty Fund Web Sites* ("All 50 states and the District of Columbia are served by property and casualty guaranty funds"), available at: www.ncigf.org (last viewed Aug. 8, 2014); National Organization of Life and Health Insurance Guaranty Associations, *What is NOLHGA?* ("The National Organization of Life and Health Insurance Guaranty Associations (NOLHGA) is a voluntary association made up of the life and health insurance guaranty associations of all 50 states and the District of Columbia"), available at: www.nolhga.com (last viewed Aug. 8, 2014).

42 See, e.g., FIO Modernization Report, *supra* n. 1, at 16.

43 *Ibid.*

coordinated multistate market conduct examinations of insurers and boosted the analytical power of these examinations by introducing a new uniform data collection system in 2011 to centralize market conduct data for use by insurance regulators in all fifty states.[44]

The other strategy used by states to fight attempts at federal intervention was *rebuttal*, which was designed in part to appeal to supporters of decentralized government. States argued, for instance, that divergent state insurance regulations provided laboratories of experimentation to aid in determining the right level of regulation. States also asserted that they were more responsive to local conditions and consumer complaints than federal regulators would ever be. In a similar vein, states pointed to tough, pro-consumer insurance commissioners as evidence that industry capture of the states was not as easy it seemed.

These rebuttal arguments took on new life during the aftermath of the financial crisis of 2008. Insurance companies did not suffer the same broad threat to solvency as commercial and investment banks during the crisis and state insurance regulators succeeded in keeping AIG's insurance subsidiaries afloat that fall. Similarly, the financial crisis brought new appreciation for the role of states as laboratories of experimentation. In contrast to insurance, banking regulation had achieved increasing national uniformity through federal preemption of state anti-predatory lending laws during the years leading up to the crisis, only to blow up when federal regulators refused to replace tougher, preempted state standards for subprime mortgage loans with meaningful regulatory controls of their own.[45] Later, it became apparent that many states had been tougher protectors of residential mortgage borrowers than the federal government. Along with that realization came new acknowledgment of the value of multiple gatekeepers, and calls to reduce duplicative state regulation lost some of their firepower.

Other traditional arguments for federal involvement in insurance also took a beating. The financial crisis cast doubt on the wisdom of financial innovations solely for innovation's sake. Similarly, the corruption at the U.S. Office of Thrift Supervision (OTS), its capitulation to industry interests during the housing bubble, and its demise[46] belied claims that state insurance regulators would be easier to capture than a single federal regulator. Finally, the ruinous race to the bottom in mortgage lending standards that was fueled by the optional federal charters for commercial banks and thrifts and the opportunities for arbitrage they provided[47] knocked the wind out of the sail for proposals for an optional federal charter in insurance.

44 See NAIC and Center for Insurance Policy and Research, *The Market Conduct Analysis Framework*, CIPR Newsletter (Oct. 2012), available at: www.naic.org/cipr_newsletter_archive/vol5_market_conduct_framework.pdf (last viewed Dec. 11, 2014).

45 See Kathleen C. Engel & Patricia A. McCoy, The Subprime Virus: Reckless Credit, Regulatory Failure, and Next Steps 157–66 (Oxford University Press, 2011); Patricia A. McCoy & Elizabeth Renuart, *The Legal Infrastructure of Subprime and Nontraditional Mortgage Lending*, in Borrowing to Live: Consumer and Mortgage Credit Revisited 110 (Nicolas P. Retsinas & Eric S. Belsky eds., Joint Center for Housing Studies of Harvard University and Brookings Institution Press, 2008).

46 For the history of OTS during this period, see Engel & McCoy, *supra* n. 45, at 158–60, 174–84, 221–23.

47 See Engel & McCoy, *supra* n. 45, at 157–63; Patricia A. McCoy, *Federal Preemption, Regulatory Failure and the Race to the Bottom in US Mortgage Lending Standards*, in The Panic of 2008 (Lawrence Mitchell & Arthur E. Wilmarth, Jr., eds., Edward Elgar Press, 2010).

In sum, until 2008, the debate over state versus federal regulation of insurance was framed in terms of corporate governance, solvency, and efficiency (with lip service to consumer protection). Those justifications were never enough to cause the states to lose their primacy in insurance regulation and those arguments lost even more of their punch after the financial crisis. Ironically, however, with the onslaught of that crisis, the terms of the debate over the respective roles of Washington, D.C., and the states in insurance regulation dramatically changed, to the detriment of state insurance regulation.

7.3.2 The new terms of the debate

In the aftermath of 2008, U.S. policymakers first trained their focus on the banking, securities, and derivatives sectors. But eventually they raised questions about the insurance industry's role – or lack thereof – as well. The main impetus for that scrutiny was the federal government's bailout of AIG. The distress of financial guaranty insurers and private mortgage insurers and their importance to the housing sector also sparked attention. With these events, the terms of the debate over state versus federal regulation of insurance changed dramatically to encompass new concerns about systemic risk.

During their post-crisis examination of insurance, the Obama Administration and individual members of Congress flagged certain activities of insurance companies and groups as systemically risky. Eventually those concerns led to the creation of the Federal Insurance Office (FIO) and the provisions on systemically important insurers in the Dodd-Frank Wall Street Reform and Consumer Protection Act in 2010.

(a) The insurance-related events of 2008

Apart from one narrow segment of the insurance industry – financial guaranty insurers and private mortgage insurers – traditional insurance underwriters mostly sat on the sidelines during the 2008 financial crisis. Unlike many commercial banks and investment banks, insurance companies remained solvent throughout that period with relatively few exceptions.[48] None of the core products at issue during the crisis – subprime mortgages, residential mortgage-backed securities (RMBS), or collateralized debt obligations (CDOs) – had been issued by traditional insurers. Similarly, no accounts of runs like the ones that capsized the investment banks Bear Stearns and Lehman Brothers, depository institutions such as Washington Mutual and Wachovia, or even money market funds like the Reserve Primary Fund[49] appeared in the trade press coverage of insurance underwriters during that period. With one exception, insurance seemed to remain the sleepy and unglamorous outpost of financial services that it had always been in recent years.

---

48 Government Accountability Office, Insurance Markets: Impacts of and Regulatory Response to the 2007–2009 Financial Crisis 9 (GAO-13-583, June 2013). Life insurers were more likely to experience financial distress during this period than general property and casualty insurers. Even so, most life insurers survived the crisis intact. See *ibid.*; Daniel Schwarcz & Steven L. Schwarcz, *Regulating Systemic Risk in Insurance*, 81 U. Chi. L. Rev. 1443–2123, (2014).

49 For a description of those runs, see Engel & McCoy, *supra* n. 45, at 87–90, 94, 102–121.

Regrettably for the insurance industry, that exception was the precedent-shattering case of AIG. The tale of AIG assumed a life of its own, with far-reaching consequences for insurance and its regulation. While AIG was in some ways an anomaly, its near-failure was so terrifying and its federal bailout so costly that the federal government could not relinquish continued regulation of that group. In turn, the spotlight on AIG and a few other cases of insurance company bailouts by federal authorities prompted closer analysis of other possible sources of systemic risk from insurance.

(b) AIG

Every industry hit by a financial crisis has its poster child. In the insurance industry in 2008, that poster child was the world's largest international insurance group, AIG.[50]

(I) AIG's credit default swap activities

During the early 2000s, AIG embarked on its road to ruin by selling hundreds of billions of dollars in over-the-counter credit default swaps (CDSs) on subprime mortgage CDOs through its non-insurance subsidiary in London known as AIG Financial Products (AIG-FP). Those swaps had a functional resemblance to insurance because they promised payments to the buyers of that protection based upon the occurrence of specified events of default. Nevertheless, in the United States, those swaps were exempt from insurance regulation (and regulation of virtually any other type) and did not require an insurable interest.[51]

While AIG-FP stopped selling new CDS in 2005, it remained liable for over half a trillion dollars in swap protection at the end of 2007.[52] Given the enormity of that liability, AIG's over-the-counter swaps presented systemic risk because a default by a protection seller of that size could trigger a chain reaction of other counterparty insolvencies and defaults.[53]

Unfortunately for AIG, it had managed its CDSs obligations too cockily, setting itself up for a fall. AIG-FP had seriously underestimated the chance that the CDOs it had guaranteed would default and consequently had underpriced the swap protection that it had sold.[54] AIG also grossly misjudged two other risks: market risk, which was the risk that AIG's swaps might drop in value, forcing the firm to take major write-downs and losses to capital, and counterparty risk, the risk that AIG's swap buyers would demand more cash security than expected from AIG to back its

---

50 See FIO Modernization Report, *supra* n. 1, at 18.

51 Commodity Futures Modernization Act of 2000, Pub. L. No. 106-554, titles I-II, 114 Stat. 2763 (2000), previously codified at 7 U.S.C. §§ 1a(13), 2(c)–(h), 27a–27f; 15 U.S.C. §§ 77q, 78c(a)(55), 78i(a), 78j(b), 78*o*(c)(1), 78p(b), 78t(d); New York Ins. L. § 6901(j–1); Re: Credit Default Option Facility (N.Y. Dept. of Ins. Gen. Counsel June 16, 2000). For further discussion, see Eric R. Dinallo, Former Superintendent of the New York State Insurance Department, "Hearing to Review the Role of Credit Derivatives in the U.S. Economy," Testimony before the U.S. House of Representatives, Committee on Agriculture, Nov. 20, 2008; Engel & McCoy, *supra* n. 45, at 220–221.

52 American International Group, Inc., Form 10-Q (2d Quarter 2008).

53 For a full description of this dynamic, see Engel & McCoy, *supra* n. 45, at 105–07, 221–23.

54 "American International Group Investor Meeting – Final," FD (Fair Disclosure) Wire (Dec. 5, 2007).

guarantees. The latter miscalculation proved ruinously costly because the company had invested its proceeds from CDSs in highly illiquid assets that later proved tough to sell when the company needed to raise cash collateral for the swaps.[55]

Initially, when AIG sold its swaps, it was able to do so with no reserves or collateral because the company had a stellar AAA credit rating. Confident that there would be no serious collateral calls,[56] AIG's CDS managers also failed to pay attention to capital adequacy.[57] As a result, AIG-FP only had about $2.1 billion in capital in December 2007 and most of that was of dubious quality.

(II) AIG's securities lending business

AIG's CDS business was located outside of its insurance company subsidiaries. However, that was not true for its securities lending service, which was another systemically risky activity conducted by AIG. In that line of business, AIG's insurance subsidiaries lent their securities to short sellers in return for cash collateral through a non-insurance affiliate named AIG Securities Lending Corporation.[58]

Originally, state insurance regulators had set conservative parameters on the reinvestment of the cash collateral when they approved the practice because the borrowers of AIG's securities were entitled to return those securities and demand back their cash at any time. However, in order to grow its securities lending business, AIG started overstepping those limits by asking for less-than-full collateral and reinvesting the cash collateral it received in illiquid RMBS.[59] Those decisions came back to haunt AIG after the credit rating agencies successively slashed the ratings on those RMBS as the subprime crisis deepened in 2007 and 2008. When AIG's securities lending counterparties appeared to return their securities and demand their cash back, AIG had increasing difficulty repaying them, given its inability to sell off the RMBS it had invested their cash in for anywhere near full price.[60] Compounding this problem, the average term of the RMBS AIG had invested in was substantially longer than the average length of AIG's securities loans, which ranged from overnight to 60 days.[61] Because AIG's insurance subsidi-

55 Brady Dennis & Robert O'Harrow, *A Crack in the System*, Washington Post, Dec. 30, 2008; Vikas Bajaj & Mark Landler, *Mortgage Losses Echo in Europe and on Wall St.*, N.Y. Times, August 10, 2007; Gretchen Morgenson, *Behind Biggest Insurer's Crisis, a Blind Eye to a Web of Risk*, N.Y. Times, Sept. 28, 2008.

56 Brady Dennis, *E-Mails Inside AIG Reveal Executives Struggling with Growing Crisis*, Washington Post, Dec. 30, 2009; Dennis & O'Harrow, *supra* n. 55; Jonathan D. Glater, *With Shares Battered, A.I.G. Ousts Its Leader*, N.Y. Times, June 16, 2008; Morgenson, *supra* n. 55; Eric R. Dinallo, Former Superintendent of the New York State Insurance Department, "Hearing on the Causes and Effects of the AIG Bailout," Testimony before the U.S. House of Representatives, Committee on Oversight and Government Reform, preliminary transcript at 68 and 143, October 7, 2008, available at: http://oversight-archive.waxman.house.gov/documents/20081010162126.pdf (last viewed Dec. 12, 2014).

57 "American International Group Investor Meeting – Final," FD (Fair Disclosure) Wire (Dec. 5, 2007).

58 See Congressional Oversight Panel June Oversight Report: The AIG Rescue, Its Impact on Markets, and the Government's Exit Strategy 42–43 (June 10, 2010); Schwarcz & Schwarcz, *supra* n. 48.

59 Congressional Oversight Panel June Oversight Report *supra* n. 58, at 43–44, 47.

60 *Ibid*; *Spring break: A practice which underpins swathes of the financial system faced turmoil*, The Economist (May 22, 2013).

61 See FIO Modernization Report, *supra* n. 1, at 19.

aries were heavily involved in the group's securities lending activities,[62] they were directly exposed to runs on cash due to those activities.

(III) AIG's collapse and federal bailout

Things began to deteriorate in late 2007, when the credit rating agencies issued a series of downgrades on AIG's credit obligations, thereby depressing AIG's stock value and forcing it to post more collateral. As more downgrades ensued, AIG had to write down its CDS portfolio and the company struggled to meet mounting cash collateral calls to cover its CDS and securities lending obligations.[63]

The day of reckoning came on Monday, September 15, 2008 – the day that Lehman Brothers filed for bankruptcy – when Standard & Poor's and Moody's cut AIG's long-term rating three more notches. The downgrades meant that AIG suddenly had to raise as much as $75 billion in cash to cover its CDS obligations. Although the New York insurance commissioner had just given AIG permission to pull $20 billion in cash out of its insurance subsidiaries in exchange for illiquid assets worth the same amount, that was just a drop in the bucket compared to the total $75 billion that was coming due. Without sufficient time to raise the rest of the cash by dumping tens of billions of dollars in assets into a falling market, AIG rapidly careened toward bankruptcy.[64]

Meanwhile, the Lehman Brothers bankruptcy had sent global markets into a panic and federal officials could not stomach a repeat of that fiasco. Consequently, on Tuesday, September 16, Treasury Secretary Henry Paulson and Federal Reserve Chairman Ben Bernanke grimly capitulated and agreed to an $85 billion federal bailout of AIG. To finance the rescue, the Federal Reserve opened its discount window for the first time ever to an insurance company, citing the "unusual and exigent circumstances" clause of former Section 13(3) of the Federal Reserve Act.[65]

In exchange for that financial lifeline, the federal government took a majority 79.9 percent equity stake in AIG.[66] Once Uncle Sam became AIG's controlling shareholder, it pumped even more money into the company in the form of more loans and commercial paper support to salvage its investment. By the end of 2009, total federal aid to AIG had ballooned to $182 billion:[67] the biggest federal financial bailout of all time.[68]

When Bernanke and Paulson forged the rescue package for AIG, their main aim was to avert contagion. They were concerned about AIG's commanding role as the one of largest sellers of CDS protection on corporate bonds, mortgage-backed securities, and CDOs worldwide. AIG owed a total of $441 billion in swap obliga-

---

62 See, e.g., Congressional Oversight Panel June Oversight Report, *supra* n. 58, at 46; *Spring break, supra* n. 60; FIO Modernization Report, *supra* n. 1, at 18–19.

63 Congressional Oversight Panel June Oversight Report, *supra* n. 58, at 37–40.

64 *Ibid.*, at 59–68.

65 Congressional Oversight Panel June Oversight Report, *supra* n. 58, at 68–71; former 12 U.S.C. §343(3) (2008).

66 Congressional oversight panel June oversigh report, *supra* n. 58, at 71.

67 Government Accountability Office, *Troubled Asset Relief Program: Status of Government Assistance Provided to AIG* (GAO-10-151, Nov. 2009).

68 AIG eventually paid back the loans in full and the federal government sold its equity stake. See Javier E. David, *AIG Makes Final Repayment to Government for Bailout,* CNBC.com, March 1, 2013.

tions, including $20 billion to Goldman Sachs alone. If AIG had gone bankrupt and defaulted on its swaps, investment banks and depository institutions that had bought that swap protection immediately would have to take write-downs, eating into their already thin capital and forcing them to sell more stock just when investors were fleeing equities.[69]

Bernanke and Paulson were also concerned about runs on other financial institutions if AIG filed for bankruptcy. In a briefing to members of Congress on the night of the bailout, both men warned that an AIG bankruptcy filing could lead to a massive run on mutual funds because AIG was one of the ten biggest stock holdings in 401(k) plans. Similarly, AIG's debt would immediately go into default if AIG went bankrupt, thereby exposing the numerous banks and mutual funds who owned that debt to the risk of runs.[70]

On the surface, the AIG debacle did not appear to involve traditional insurance. All of AIG-FP's activities took place outside of AIG's insurance subsidiaries. Furthermore, all its insurance operations remained solvent, thanks to the vigilance of state insurance regulators.

Nevertheless, the risky securities lending activities of AIG's insurers cast doubt on that account. On closer examination, the AIG episode raised troubling questions about insurance regulation and its ability to oversee complex, internationally active insurance groups. In at least one respect, insurance regulators had manufactured that problem themselves. In a classic case of arbitrage, AIG's decision to push its disastrous CDS activities into an unregulated subsidiary was made possible, in part, by the decision by the New York Superintendent of Insurance declining to define CDS as insurance in 2000.[71] This regulatory gap was not confined to the states: the federal government was complicit as well, having made the rash decision in 2000 to exempt CDSs from federal regulation.[72] The point is, however, that the state insurance authorities passed up the opportunity to regulate a systemically risky product that easily could have been defined as insurance. Had they done so, all CDSs would have had to have an insurable interest, which would have eliminated trillions of dollars in speculative bets on other entities' investments in debt known as naked CDSs.

Equally importantly, the AIG chapter shone light on the fact that no state insurance regulator had the authority to oversee AIG's holding company, AIG-FP, or AIG Securities Lending Corporation to determine whether undue risk in those operations threatened the insurance subsidiaries over which they did have purview. Insurance regulation was siloed: state insurance regulators had preeminent oversight of AIG's insurance subsidiaries, but no real authority over its non-insurance

69 Edmund L. Andrews, Michael J. de la Merced & Mary Williams Walsh, *Fed's $85 Billion Loan Rescues Insurer,* N.Y. Times, Sept. 17, 2008; Congressional Oversight Panel June Oversight Report, *supra* n. 58, at 69, 75, 130–33; Gretchen Morgenson, *Behind Biggest Insurer's Crisis, a Blind Eye to a Web of Risk,* N.Y. Times, Sept. 28, 2008.

70 Eric Dash & Andrew Ross Sorkin, *Throwing a Lifeline to a Troubled Giant,* N.Y. Times, Sept. 18, 2008.

71 Re: Credit Default Option Facility (NY Dept. of Ins. Gen. Counsel June 16, 2000). See generally Arthur Kimball-Stanley, *Insurance and Credit Default Swaps: Should Like Things Be Treated Alike?* 15 Conn. Ins. L.J. 241, 247, 252 (2008).

72 See *supra* n. 51 and accompanying text.

affiliates. Accordingly, they did not detect the illegal expansion of AIG's securities lending business and were clueless about its CDS activities. Complicating the states' lack of jurisdiction, AIG-FP was located in London, which state commissioners were powerless to reach. As it happened, AIG *did* have a consolidated federal supervisor by virtue of AIG's ownership of an insured savings and loan institution: the hapless former OTS. As events proved, OTS was not up to the job[73] and Congress eventually abolished the agency in the Dodd-Frank Act.[74]

Despite OTS' miserable performance in supervising AIG, state insurance regulators were no more capable of that task for different reasons. No state law gave them jurisdiction to directly regulate the parent holding companies of insurance groups. Similarly, insurance commissioners lacked the authority to oversee the non-insurance subsidiaries of insurance conglomerates, something that was doubly a problem in the case of foreign subsidiaries.

This lack of state statutory authority had two important consequences. First, to the extent that parent companies and non-insurance affiliates of insurance companies posed systemic risk to the financial stability of the nation, only the federal government could regulate that risk, not the states. Second, the states' lack of effective parent company oversight revealed the limits on the states' own ability to prevent excessive risk-taking in other parts of complex insurance groups. Without mandatory capital requirements for holding companies, state insurance regulators could not ensure that those holding companies served as a source of strength for their insurance subsidiaries.[75] In the case of AIG, the CDS activities of AIG-FP put crushing demands on AIG's parent company for capital support, thereby siphoning off capital that otherwise would have been available to backstop the insurance operations. The availability of that parental support was crucial because AIG's insurance companies had also suffered losses from their own risky securities lending activities. To make matters worse, AIG's holding company then begged state insurance commissioners in September 2008 for permission to upstream cash *from* the insurance subsidiaries to help AIG-FP to meet its collateral calls. The New York insurance commissioner acceded to that pressure and agreed to a $20 billion upstream commitment in exchange for illiquid assets of uncertain value.[76] In this way, AIG's non-insurance activities directly put policyholder reserves at risk.

The bailout of AIG also unleashed the most potent rationale for federal intervention of all. For AIG was the first time that the federal government bore the negative externalities from an insurance group's failure. Moreover, the AIG debacle was

73 For a full account of the myriad failings in OTS' oversight of AIG and how it came to acquire jurisdiction over AIG-FP despite AIG-FP's location in the European Union, see Engel & McCoy, *supra* n. 45, at 221–23.

74 Pub. L. No. 111-203, § 313, 124 Stat. 1547 (2010).

75 This problem persists. The Financial Stability Board reported that "no action has been taken" in the United States (outside of depository institution holding companies and insurance company SIFIs) "to apply insurance capital requirements to the consolidated insurance group. This means that no adjustments are made by states to address any intra-group creation of capital caused by multiple gearing." Financial Stability Board, *Peer Review of the United States – Review Report* 37 (Aug. 27, 2013), available at: www.financialstabilityboard.org/2013/08/r_130827/ (last viewed Dec. 18, 2014) [hereinafter cited as *Peer Review*].

76 Events overtook this decision, however, and ultimately the $20 billion payment was never made. Congressional Oversight Panel, June Oversight Report, *supra* n. 58, at 49–50.

no small event: AIG's rescue was the largest federal bailout of a private enterprise in U.S. history.[77] The political outrage that ensued matched the enormity of the rescue[78] and reflected serious substantive concerns. Moral hazard by industry was certain to result from the impression – which the Federal Reserve's actions confirmed – that AIG was too big to fail. Similarly, the Federal Reserve suffered a serious blow to its legitimacy after making its unprecedented decision to give AIG access to the discount window.

(c) Trouble Asset Relief Program payments to other insurance companies

During the fall of 2008, AIG was not the only insurance company recipient of the federal government's largesse. Over $4 billion of Washington's $700 billion Troubled Asset Relief Program (TARP) went to bail out two other troubled insurers, The Hartford Financial Services Group, Inc., and Lincoln National Corporation. The Allstate Corporation, Ameriprise Financial, Inc., Principal Financial Group, and Prudential Financial applied for and received preliminary approval for TARP funds, but eventually turned them down.[79] Several other insurance companies also applied for TARP funds (including MetLife), but later withdrew their applications or were denied.[80]

The TARP rescues of The Hartford and Lincoln National shed light on other insurance company activities that could spell systemic risk necessitating bailouts. Both companies were life insurers that suffered sharp capital declines after the

77 See Michael Powell & Mary Williams Walsh, *A.I.G. to Pay $725 Million in Ohio Case,* N.Y. Times, July 16, 2010.

78 Public rage boiled over when the press reported in March 2009 that AIG had recently awarded $165 million in bonuses to executives at AIG-FP, notwithstanding the bailout. See Engel & McCoy, *supra* n. 45, at 141.

79 See *Allstate Comments on U.S. Treasury Capital Purchase Program,* BusinessWire, May 15, 2009, available at: www.businesswire.com/news/home/20090515005547/en/Allstate-Comments-U.S.-Treasury-Capital-Purchase-Program#.VI3iqrM5BZU (last viewed Dec. 16, 2014); Arthur D. Postal, *Allstate Says Thanks, but No Thanks to Offer of Federal TARP Rescue Money,* PropertyCasualty360°, May 25, 2009, available at: www.propertycasualty360.com/2009/05/25/allstate-says-thanks-but-no-thanks-to-offer-of-federal-tarp-rescue-money (last viewed Dec. 16, 2014); Principal Financial Group, *Principal Financial Group Declines Funding from U.S. Treasury Capital Purchase Program,* Press Release, June 11, 2009, available at: http://investors.principal.com/investor-relations/news-releases/press-release-details/2009/Principal-Financial-Group-Declines-Funding-from-US-Treasury-Capital-Purchase-Program/default.aspx (last viewed Dec. 16, 2014); Prudential Financial, Inc., *Statement by Prudential Financial, Inc.,* June 1, 2009, available at: www.investor.prudential.com/phoenix.zhtml?c=129695&p=RssLanding&cat=news&id=1294196 (last viewed Dec. 16, 2014).

80 Those insurance companies included Genworth Financial, Jackson National, MetLife, Protective Life Corp., and The Phoenix Companies. See Arthur D. Postal, *Some Insurers Qualify for TARP, but 'Nothing is Imminent,'* LifeHealth Pro, Apr. 20, 2009, available at: www.lifehealthpro.com/2009/04/20/some-insurers-qualify-for-tarp-but-nothing-is-immi (last viewed Dec. 16, 2014); MetLife, *MetLife Issues Statement on U.S. Treasury's Supervisory Capital Assessment Program,* May 7, 2009, available at: www.metlife.com/about/press-room/us-press-releases/2009/index.html?compID=13277 (last viewed Dec. 16, 2014).

Later, in its decision designating MetLife as a systemically important insurer, FSOC recounted other ways in which MetLife had tapped the federal safety net during the financial crisis. During 2008 and 2009, for instance, MetLife's bank received 19 Term Auction Facility loans totaling $18.9 billion through the Federal Reserve. In 2009, MetLife also obtained $397 million through the Temporary Liquidity Guarantee Program offered by the Federal Deposit Insurance Corporation. The insurer borrowed another $1.6 billion through the Federal Reserve's Commercial Paper Funding Facility. FSOC, Basis of the Financial Stability Oversight Council's Final Determination Regarding MetLife, Inc. 14–15 (Dec. 18, 2014), available at: www.treasury.gov (last viewed Dec. 19, 2014).

market nosedive in the fall of 2008 saddled them with hefty investment losses and multiplied their liabilities on guaranteed benefits under their variable life insurance and annuity products.[81] In turn, the TARP applications filed by these and other insurance companies sensitized the Treasury Department to the counterparty exposure and fragility of some life insurers to market volatility.

(d) Financial guaranty insurers

Another segment of the insurance industry – financial guaranty insurers – was hard hit but did not receive federal bailouts during the financial crisis. Those insurers, also known as "bond insurers," provide a layer of insurance against default on bonds. Traditionally this insurance was limited to municipal bonds. However, with the explosion of private-label mortgage securitization in the late 1990s, financial guaranty insurers began to sell insurance to investors against defaults on RMBS and CDOs as well.[82] In 2008, there were nine main U.S. bond insurers and they guaranteed over $2 trillion in mortgage-related securities in the years leading up to the crisis. During the housing bubble, the bond insurers also issued CDSs on RMBS and invested in RMBS and CDOs, including securities they had guaranteed themselves.

In recognition of the potentially ruinous exposure posed by financial guaranties, state insurance regulators traditionally limited financial guaranty insurers to a monoline structure which prohibited those companies from offering other types of insurance.[83] In other ways during the run-up to 2008, however, state regulators were overly sanguine about the risks these companies were taking. In particular, they allowed the financial guaranty insurers to operate with relatively little capital (in some cases zero) because of the historically low default rates on municipal bonds and residential mortgages.[84]

This thin capital buffer left financial guaranty insurers ill-prepared for what was to come. Starting in early 2007, financial guaranty insurers were hit with a mounting number of claims as defaults spiked on home mortgages and RMBS and CDOs.[85] By 2008, bond insurers were reeling from losses. This is apparent from the sharp increase in the industry's combined ratios from 2006 to 2008. The combined ratio is the percentage of premiums that an insurer pays out in claims and expenses. A ratio under 100 percent means profitability; a ratio over 100 percent raises profitability concerns. In 2006, the financial guaranty insurance industry's average combined ratio was 10 percent. By 2008, the same ratio was 484 percent. Only one

---

81 See, e.g., The Hartford Financial Services Group, Inc., Form 10-K, at 22–24, 65, 67, 156–58, 165, 181–82, 191 (2008); Lincoln National Group, Form 10-K, at 49–50 (2008).

82 See, e.g., FIO Modernization Report, *supra* n. 1, at 19–20, 30.

83 Ibid., at 30.

84 *Ibid.*, at 29–30.

85 For the same reason, the private mortgage insurance industry was buffeted with losses. Private mortgage insurers guarantee repayment of individual home mortgages if the borrowers default. Typically, these insurers focus on higher-risk mortgages (typically where the loan-to-value ratio exceeds 80 percent). See Basel Committee on Banking Supervision, Joint Forum, *Mortgage Insurance: market structure, underwriting cycle and policy implications, Consultative document* 2–3 (Feb. 2013), available at: www.bis.org (last viewed Dec. 14, 2014); Federal Insurance Office, U.S. Department of the Treasury, *Annual Report on the Insurance Industry* 34 (June 2013), available at: www.treasury.gov (last viewed Dec. 14, 2014).

Table 7.1: Bond insurer health as of May 2012

Bond insurer	*S&P rating as of May 2012*	*Writing new business?*
Berkshire Hathaway	AA+	No
Assured Guaranty	AA-	Yes
MBIA/National	BBB	No
Radian	B+	In runoff
Ambac	Not rated	Seized by the State of Wisconsin in 2010
Syncora	Not rated	In runoff
ACA	Not rated	In runoff
FGIC	Not rated	Seized by New York State in 2011
CFIG	Not rated	In runoff

bond insurer – Warren Buffett's company, Berkshire Hathaway – had a combined ratio of less than 100 percent at the end of 2008.

Soon the rating agencies responded with downgrades. By the end of 2008, all of the U.S. bond insurers except Berkshire Hathaway had lost their AAA ratings; Berkshire lost it later on. By May of 2012, eight of the nine bond insurers were no longer writing new business and more than half had been seized or were in runoff (*see* Table 7.1).

These credit rating downgrades were disastrous to the financial guaranty industry's viability. In the structured finance business, the bond insurers were essentially lending out their AAA credit ratings to issuers for a fee – their financial survival hinged on their AAA ratings. If the ratings dropped below AAA, it would harm their ability to write new business and bring in new premiums.

That is exactly what happened. By 2011, the market for insured municipal bonds shrank from 50 percent of new issues pre-crisis to only 5 percent. The contraction of this market made it temporarily difficult for some municipalities to raise money by selling bonds.[86] Meanwhile, the private-label market for structured mortgage finance collapsed and has not come back in any significant way. As of 2013, only two U.S. bond insurers – Assured Guaranty and a new entrant, Build America – were actively providing financial guarantees.[87] While some observers express optimism about the industry,[88] its near-term future prospects remain uncertain.

The events of 2008 showed how financial guaranty insurance could spawn systemic risk in multiple ways. First, the downgrades of the bond insurers led to downgrades on the securities that they guaranteed. This affected both mortgage-related securities and municipal bonds. Institutional investors such as commercial banks and insurance companies that were limited by law to owning investment-grade

86 See, e.g., FIO Modernization Report, *supra* n. 1, at 19.

87 See Federal Insurance Office, U.S. Department of the Treasury, *Annual Report on the Insurance Industry* 35 (June 2013), available at: www.treasury.gov (last viewed Dec. 14, 2014); Jeffrey Stern, *Do Capital Markets Need Financial Guaranty Insurers?* 1–2 (Oct. 6, 2014), available at: www.pillsburylaw.com/siteFiles/Publications/Law360_Stern_Oct62014.pdf (last viewed Dec. 14, 2014).

88 See Fitch Ratings, *Monolines Can Add Value Even with 'A' Category Ratings* (Aug. 15, 2014); Jeffrey Stern, *Do Capital Markets Need Financial Guaranty Insurers?* (Oct. 6, 2014), available at: www.pillsburylaw.com/siteFiles/Publications/Law360_Stern_Oct62014.pdf (last viewed Dec. 14, 2014).

holdings often had to sell bonds that had been downgraded to junk, which put downward pressure on prices. Similarly, financial institutions that bought swap protection from the bond insurers had to mark those swaps to market, sustaining losses and eroding their capital. Making matters worse, some bond insurers and private mortgage insurers refused to pay claims, sometimes because regulators ordered them to do so.

Financial guaranty insurance was just one of the sources of systemic risk in the insurance sector. AIG's CDS activities and securities lending by its insurance company subsidiaries both proved vulnerable to runs. In the life insurance sector, costly guaranteed minimum benefits on variable life and annuity products caused some of the nation's largest life insurers to ask for federal lifelines. Meanwhile, the bond insurance industry was virtually wiped out in 2008 and remains on life support. Together these events fueled calls to regulate insurance for systemic risk.

(e) The federal and international policy response

In the aftermath of 2008, the U.S. government, in tandem with global regulators, moved aggressively to erect a new, overarching system for the regulation of systemic risk. That system was federal in nature, which meant that any financial institution posing systemic risk faced the prospect of federal oversight. The urgent need for systemic risk regulation and the surprising new concerns about systemic risk in insurance that 2008 unearthed opened the door to a new, major federal presence in insurance regulation. Meanwhile, international bodies leaned on the United States to strengthen its systemic risk oversight, which reinforced the federal government's hand in intervening in insurance regulation.

(f) The Dodd-Frank Act

Although the federal government had tinkered with systemic risk on a hit-or-miss basis before 2008, the manifest deficiencies in that oversight compelled Congress to mandate a formal and elaborate federal system for systemic risk regulation in the Dodd-Frank Act in 2010. This system contemplated both the supervision of individual, systemically risky financial institutions and of systemically risky activities more generally. In addition, Dodd-Frank established the new FIO as a beachhead for the new federal role in insurance.

(I) Federal regulation of systemically important insurers

AIG's near demise and its unprecedented federal bailout impelled Congress to enact several provisions in the Dodd-Frank Act to address systemic risk emanating from the insurance sector. Front and center, Congress was distressed that no one regulator – state or federal – had exercised any effective consolidated oversight of AIG for systemic risk. Similarly, Congress was concerned about the lack of any special resolution facility for failing systemically risky nonbank firms akin to the Federal Deposit Insurance Corporation (FDIC) resolution procedures long used for failing banks.[89]

89 In contrast to depository institutions, federal regulators had no good process for putting AIG into an orderly federal receivership. At the time, the federal government could not locate a buyer for the

In response to these and similar concerns, Congress created a new framework for federal oversight of systemic risk in Dodd-Frank. The linchpin of that framework was the creation of the Federal Stability Oversight Council in Title I.[90] Among other things, Congress charged FSOC with deciding whether to designate particular nonbank financial services providers, including insurers, as systemically important financial institutions (SIFIs) for the purpose of added federal regulation.[91] To carry out that oversight, Congress authorized the Federal Reserve Board to supervise and regulate all SIFIs, including bank and nonbank SIFIs alike, using enhanced prudential standards.[92] In addition, in Title II of the 2010 legislation, Congress authorized the federal government to place failing financial institutions, including insurers, into federal receivership in the unusual circumstance where their failure and resolution under otherwise applicable state or federal laws would have serious adverse effects on the financial stability of the United States.[93]

To date, FSOC has designated three large insurance enterprises – AIG, Prudential Financial, Inc., and MetLife – as nonbank SIFIs.[94] As a result, these insurance company SIFIs are subject to examination by the Federal Reserve Board. In addition, they face enhanced federal prudential standards including group-wide minimum leverage and risk-based capital requirements,[95] liquidity requirements, risk management requirements, resolution plan and credit exposure report requirements, concentration limits, a contingent capital requirement, enhanced public disclosures, short-term debt limits, and other prudential standards instituted by the Federal Reserve Board.[96]

---

company, so its only options were to put AIG into bankruptcy or to grant a government bailout. Fresh off the Lehman Brothers bankruptcy, the Federal Reserve was understandably anxious about an AIG bankruptcy and chose the safer route. As a result, the federal government came to control the world's largest insurance company overnight.

90 Dodd-Frank Act, Pub. L. No. 111-203, § 111, 124 Stat. 1547 (2010).

91 *Ibid.*, § 113(a), 124 Stat. 1547 (2010). Nine of FSOC's ten voting members are federal regulators outside of the insurance area. The tenth is an independent member with insurance expertise who is appointed by the President and confirmed by the Senate for a six-year term. In addition, two of FSOC's five non-voting members are from the insurance sector: the Director of the Federal Insurance Office and a state insurance commissioner, picked by his or her peers. *Ibid.* at § 111(b)–(c) 124 Stat. 1547 (2010).

92 *Ibid.* at §§ 114, 115(a)(1), (c), 117(a)–(b), 161(a)–(c), 162(a)–(b), 165 124 Stat. 1547 (2010). Under Dodd-Frank, TARP recipients that were bank holding companies with total consolidated assets of $50 billion or more on January 2, 2010, but that later ceased to be bank holding companies, are also subject to enhanced standards and supervision. *Ibid.* at § 117.

93 *Ibid.* at § 203(c)(4), 124 Stat, 1547 (2010).

94 FSOC, Basis of the Financial Stability Oversight Council's Final Determination Regarding American International Group, Inc. (July 8, 2013), available at: www.treasury.gov (last viewed Aug. 11, 2014) [hereinafter cited as FSOC *AIG*]; FSOC, Basis for the Financial Stability Oversight Council's Final Determination Regarding Prudential Financial Inc. (Sept. 19, 2013), available at www.treasury.gov (last viewed Aug. 11, 2014) [hereinafter cited as FSOC *Prudential Financial*]; FSOC, Basis of the Financial Stability Oversight Council's Final Determination Regarding MetLife, Inc. (Dec. 18, 2014), available at www.treasury.gov (last viewed Dec. 19, 2014) [hereinafter cited as FSOC *Metlife*].

95 In December 2014, Congress passed an amendment to Dodd-Frank which clarified that the Federal Reserve Board will not be required to include insurance subsidiaries when establishing the minimum leverage and risk-based capital requirements on a consolidated basis for depository institution holding companies and nonbank SIFIs. Nothing in the amendment, however, prohibits the Board from establishing capital requirements at the group level. Insurance Capital Standards Clarification Act of 2014, S. 2270, 113th Cong., 2d Sess., § 2(2) (2014), codified at 12 U.S.C. § 5371(c)(1)–(c)(2).

96 Dodd-Frank Act, Pub. L. No. 111-203, §§ 165(b)(1)(A)–(B), 165(c), 124 Stat. 1547 (2010).

(II) The creation of the FIO

Congress did not stop with the designation and federal supervision of systemically risky insurers in the Dodd-Frank Act. In addition, it mandated the creation of a new FIO located within the U.S. Department of the Treasury in Title V of Dodd-Frank.[97] For the most part, however, the FIO's authority is truncated and the Office does not displace the traditional supervisory and regulatory role of the states over insurance.

In lieu of having regulatory responsibilities, the FIO's jurisdiction is mostly restricted to monitoring the insurance industry (including for access to insurance and for regulatory gaps that could contribute to systemic risk), recommending nonbank SIFI designations for individual insurers, assisting the Secretary of the Treasury in administering the Terrorism Insurance Program under the Terrorism Risk Insurance Act of 2002, and consulting with the states on insurance matters of national and international importance.[98] Where the FIO has teeth is in its power to develop federal policy on the prudential aspects of international insurance issues and to assist the Secretary in negotiating international treaties and other agreements regarding the prudential regulation of the business of insurance or reinsurance. As part of that authority, the FIO represents the United States in the International Association of Insurance Supervisors (IAIS) and can issue determinations that provisions of federal treaties preempt state insurance law.[99]

FIO also plays a formal role in the designation and federal oversight of nonbank SIFIs under Titles I and II. The Director of the FIO is a nonvoting member of FSOC for purposes of FSOC decisions on designations and oversight.[100] Furthermore, the Director must give approval, along with two-thirds of the Governors of the Federal Reserve Board, before the Secretary of the Treasury may seek to appoint the FDIC as the federal receiver of an insurance company on grounds of systemic risk.[101]

(III) Across-the-board supervision of systemically risky activities

Often the preoccupation with SIFI designations gives the false impression that systemic risk regulation in the United States outside of commercial banking is limited to the oversight of SIFIs. The federal government, however, also has broad authority to issue industry-wide regulations for financial activities posing systemic risk. This type of regulation allows regulators to address systemic risk emanating from the activities of numerous interconnected market actors, large and small.

There are growing instances of across-the-board systemic risk regulation in the United States. The Dodd-Frank Act mandated extensive new regulation of derivatives trading. Standardized derivatives must now be cleared and executed through central clearinghouses to improve transparency and limit counterparty risk.[102]

97 *Ibid.* at § 502, 124 Stat. 1547 (2010), codified at 31 U.S.C. §§ 313–314.
98 *Ibid.* at § 502(a)(3), 124 Stat. 1547 (2010), codified at 31 U.S.C. § 313(c).
99 *Ibid.* at § 502(a)(3), 124 Stat. 1547 (2010), codified at 31 U.S.C. § 313(c)(1)(E)–(F), (c)(2).
100 *Ibid.* at § 111(b)(2), 124 Stat. 1547 (2010).
101 *Ibid.* at § 203(a)(1)(C), 124 Stat. 1547 (2010).
102 *Ibid.* at §§ 723, 763(a), (c), 124 Stat. 1547 (2010).

Dodd-Frank also imposed margin requirements on swaps to reduce the risk to counterparties and to tamp down leverage.[103] Swap dealers and major swap participants are subject to new minimum capital requirements to safeguard against insolvency.[104] Finally, Dodd-Frank authorized the Securities and Exchange Commission (SEC) and the Commodity Futures Trading Commission to institute new data reporting and recordkeeping requirements for derivatives.[105]

Naturally, the asset-backed securitization industry was another target of reform in Dodd-Frank. Dodd-Frank imposed new requirements on that industry regarding conflicts of interest, mandatory disclosures, representations and warranties by issuers, asset review and evaluation obligations, and the retention of risk by securitizers to ensure that they have "skin in the game."[106]

Other reforms address capital markets trading and investment fund activities. Under the Volcker Rule, Dodd-Frank restricted proprietary trading by bank holding companies.[107] Meanwhile, for the first time ever, investment advisors to hedge funds and private equity funds must register with SEC.[108] In addition, private fund advisors must make periodic filings with the Commission on topics such as assets under management, use of leverage, counterparty credit risk exposure, and trading practices.[109] In 2014, the Commission adopted further reforms to reduce the risk of runs on money market funds in response to pressure from FSOC.[110]

More such regulations can be expected down the road. In Fall 2014, the SEC announced plans to expand mandatory reporting by investment funds to include data on separate accounts, their holdings of derivatives, the liquidity and valuation of their assets, and their securities lending activities.[111] The SEC also said that it planned to review options for improving fund liquidity and for limiting the use of derivatives by retail mutual funds to boost returns through leverage.[112] The Commission also trained attention on a living will requirement for investment advisors and funds and on stress tests to evaluate the ability of funds to meet spikes in redemptions following economic shocks.[113] The Commission announced those

103 *Ibid.* at §§ 731, 764(a), 124 Stat. 1547 (2010).

104 *Ibid.* at §§ 731, 763(a), 124 Stat. 1547 (2010).

105 *Ibid.* at §§ 728, 763(i), 766, 124 Stat. 1547 (2010).

106 *Ibid.* at §§ 621, 941–945, 124 Stat. 1547 (2010).

107 *Ibid.* at § 619, 124 Stat. 1547 (2010).

108 Securities and Exchange Commission, *Rules Implementing Amendments to the Investment Advisers Act of 1940*, 76 Fed. Reg. 42950 (July 19, 2011); Securities and Exchange Commission, *Exemptions for Advisers to Venture Capital Funds, Private Fund Advisers With Less Than $150 Million in Assets Under Management, and Foreign Private Advisers*, 76 Fed. Reg. 39645, 39680 (July 6, 2011).

109 Securities and Exchange Commission, *Reporting by Investment Advisers to Private Funds and Certain Commodity Pool Operators and Commodity Trading Advisors on Form PF*, 76 Fed. Reg. 711287 (Nov. 16, 2011).

110 Securities and Exchange Commission, *Money Market Fund Reform; Amendments to Form PF,* 79 Fed. Reg. 47735 (Aug. 14, 2014).

111 See Andrew Ackerman, *SEC Preps Mutual Fund Rules: Agency Eyes Greater Disclosure of Portfolio Data, Stress Tests for Asset Managers*, WALL ST. J., Sept. 7, 2014; *Enhancing Risk Monitoring and Regulatory Safeguards for the Asset Management Industry,* Remarks by Securities and Exchange Commission Chair Mary Jo White at the New York Times DealBook Opportunities for Tomorrow Conference, Dec. 11, 2014, at 3–4, available at: www.sec.gov (last viewed Dec. 15, 2014).

112 See Andrew Ackerman, *supra* n. 111; Mary Jo White, *supra* n. 111, at 4.

113 *Ibid.*; Mary Jo White *supra* n. 111, at 5; Dodd-Frank Act, Pub. L. No. 111-2013, § 165(i)(2), 124 Stat. 1423 (2010), codified at 12 U.S.C. § 5365.

plans after FSOC changed its focus in July of that year from designating large asset managers as nonbank SIFIs to regulating potentially risky activities in the investment fund and asset management industries.[114]

All of these U.S. initiatives for systemic risk regulation occurred against a backdrop of parallel initiatives by international financial regulatory bodies. In the process, the U.S. reforms underwent global scrutiny, increasing the pressure for a stronger federal presence in insurance regulation in the United States.

(g) International response

In the aftermath of the financial crisis, the G20 leaders asked the Financial Stability Board (the FSB) to address the systemic risk presented by global SIFIs (G-SIFIs). The FSB responded by publishing a systemic risk policy framework and designating a number of large banking groups as global systemically important banks in November 2011.[115] Meanwhile, it delegated the tasks of developing systemic risk policies for insurers and identifying global systemically important insurers (G-SIIs) to the IAIS.[116]

The IAIS identified nine initial G-SIIs in July 2013. The three U.S. insurers on that list were AIG, MetLife, Inc., and Prudential Financial, Inc.[117] That same month, the IAIS unveiled its policy framework for G-SIIs.[118] Among the framework's prescriptions were heightened supervision, orderly resolution facilities, backstop capital requirements, and higher loss absorption capacity for non-traditional insurance and non-insurance activities.[119]

The IAIS' recommendations for enhanced supervision were not just limited to G-SIIs. In addition, the IAIS promulgated its Common Framework for the Supervision of Internationally Active Insurance Groups (nicknamed *ComFrame*) to foster global convergence in the oversight of internationally active insurance conglomerates, regardless of whether they are designated as G-SIIs.[120]

Meanwhile, in 2013, the FSB completed a peer review of insurance regulation in the U.S. that criticized state-based regulation and recommended replacing it with federal regulation.[121] According to the FSB, "[g]iven the drawbacks of the current regulatory set-up, the US authorities should carefully consider and provide recommendations to Congress as to whether migration towards a more federal and streamlined structure may be a more effective means of achieving greater regulatory uniformity."[122] In addition, the FSB was sharply critical of the states' inadequacies

---

114 See Ackerman, *supra,* n. 111.

115 Financial Stability Board, *Global systemically important insurers (G-SIIs) and the policy measures that will apply to them* 1 (July 18, 2013), available at: www.financialstabilityboard.org (last viewed Aug. 30, 2014).

116 *Ibid.*

117 *Ibid.* at 1 & 4, Annex 1 (July 18, 2013). These G-SIIs were identified using the methodology announced in International Ass'n of Insurance Supervisors, *Global Systemically Important Insurers, Initial Assessment Methodology* (July 18, 2013), available at: www.iaisweb.org (last viewed Aug. 31, 2014).

118 International Association of Insurance Supervisors, *Global Systemically Important Insurers: Policy Measures* (July 18, 2013), available at www.iaisweb.org (last viewed Aug. 31, 2014).

119 *Ibid.*

120 *Ibid.*

121 See Financial Stability Board, *Peer Review.*

122 *Ibid.* at 10.

in consolidated oversight of insurance groups and in capital adequacy regulation of insurance groups.[123]

These steps by the FSB and the IAIS have exerted pressure to deepen federal involvement in insurance regulation in a number of ways. The IAIS' decision to designate AIG, MetLife and Prudential as G-SIIs undoubtedly played a part in the companies' U.S. SIFI designations. Global regulators' emphasis on effective group supervision further underscored the holes in the U.S. approach to that issue. Meanwhile, the FSB's push for international harmonization of capital adequacy standards for internationally active insurers could well set a standard that could ripple throughout the insurance industry.

7.4 Why federal intervention in insurance is likely to grow in future years

Before 2008, the insurance industry and state insurance regulators succeeded in staving off unwanted federal regulation of private insurance (apart from health insurance, employee benefits, and certain types of catastrophe insurance) partly because the federal government had not been tapped to bail out the insurance sector. That all changed in Fall 2008, when, in a stark departure from the past, the federal government had to bear part of the negative externalities resulting from systemic risk associated with the insurance sector, most notably in the bailout of AIG and the TARP payments to The Hartford and Lincoln National.

History sheds light on the watershed significance of crossing that line. In a related context before 1989, state bank and thrift regulators had significantly broader authority and discretion in regulating federally insured depository institutions than they do today. During the savings and loan crisis in the 1980s, some state regulators relaxed their prudential safeguards against lax lending and equity investments to such an extreme that over 2,000 thrifts and banks failed.[124] Despite the large number of depository institution failures during that period, only a "relatively small number of failures" were needed to "cause serious strains on the [federal] deposit insurance fund."[125] The losses were so enormous that the federal savings and loan deposit insurance fund failed and the federal deposit insurance fund for banks went into the red, forcing Congress to recapitalize both funds at taxpayer expense.[126] In response to this abdication by the states, Congress stripped the states of power to set minimum prudential standards for banks and thrifts in 1989 and 1991 and consolidated that authority in the federal government.[127]

Similar to the events in banking, the federal bailouts to the insurance industry in 2008 inexorably changed the terms of the debate over federal intervention in

123 *Ibid.*

124 See Federal Deposit Insurance Corporation, I History of the 1980s, at 3 fig. 1.1, 107–09, 122–26, 168–69 & tbl. 4.2, 176–86 (1997), available at: www.fdic.gov (last viewed Sept. 4, 2014).

125 *Ibid.* at 16.

126 *Ibid.* at 4 & n.1, 10, 16, 39, 41, 82, 100 (1997), available at: www.fdic.gov (last viewed Sept. 4, 2014).

127 *Ibid.* at 100–05 (1997), available at: www.fdic.gov (last viewed Sept. 4, 2014). The 1989 legislation was the Financial Institutions Reform, Recovery and Enforcement Act, Pub. L. No. 101-73, 103 Stat. 183 (1989) (FIRREA); the 1991 legislation was the Federal Deposit Insurance Corporation Improvement Act, Pub. L. No. 102–242, 105 Stat. 2236 (1991) (FDICIA).

insurance. The question is not whether the federal government will intervene in insurance; rather, it is to what extent and how. Meanwhile, the recent financial crisis, the enactment of Dodd-Frank, the creation of FSOC and the FIO, and the insurance initiatives of their international regulatory counterparts ignited a new and more expansive discussion about the meaning of the term "systemic risk" and the regulatory consequences flowing from that meaning. As I will discuss in the pages to come, the debate over federal regulation of insurance is playing out against the background of the larger debate over the definition of "systemic risk."

7.4.1 Term mismatch and runs

In its broadest sense, "systemic risk" is the risk that an entire system will experience a series of correlated breakdowns. Historically, systemic risk most often has been conceptualized as the problem of directly linked failures. Under that theory, one financial actor's inability to meet its obligations can directly inflict severe losses on its creditors, which can cause them to default on their own obligations and set off a chain reaction that topples other creditors down the line. This can be set in motion by one large shock to a financial sector or the economy or, less often, by a more limited shock to one institution that destabilizes its counterparties. The lower a financial firm's capital or the higher its indebtedness or leverage, the more it will be vulnerable to systemic risk. Alternatively, systemic risk may also arise where the failure of one financial firm causes creditors or investors to question the solvency of similar firms and withdraw their funds.[128]

These scenarios share one thing in common, which is a balance sheet featuring a maturity mismatch between short-term liabilities and long-term assets that makes a financial firm susceptible to runs. The classic example involves a bank run, in which a bank, faced with a stampede by depositors to withdraw their demand deposits, becomes insolvent because it cannot liquidate its long-term assets at fair market value fast enough to pay off its depositors in full. If the bank's distress spreads to other banks – because depositors elsewhere start to worry that their own banks are insolvent, because those banks are creditors of the original bank that failed, or for some other reason – then the bank run may ripen into systemic risk.[129]

Conventionally, the insurance industry has not been considered vulnerable to runs because of differences in its balance sheet makeup and the maturity of its liabilities.[130] The classic model of insurance is premised on the law of large numbers, in which a large number of uncorrelated risks are distributed along a normal curve. In

128 George G. Kaufman & Kenneth E. Scott, *What Is Systemic Risk, and do Bank Regulators Retard or Contribute to It?*, VII Independent Rev. 371, 371–73, 376, 379–80 (2003); see also Franklin Allen & Douglas Gale, *Financial contagion*, 108 J. Pol. Econ. 1 (2000); Xavier Freixas, Bruno M. Parigi, & Jean-Charles Rochet, *Systemic risk, interbank relations, and liquidity provision by the central bank*, 32 J. Money, Credit & Banking 611 (2000); Steven L. Schwarcz, *Systemic Risk*, 97 Geo. L.J. 193, 204 (2008).

129 See, e.g., Douglas W. Diamond & Philip H. Dybvig, *Bank Runs, Deposit Insurance, and Liquidity*, 91 J. Pol. Econ. 401 (1983); Gary Gorton & Andrew Winton, *Financial Intermediation* 63 (NBER Working Paper 8928 May 2002) ("[t]hese definitions have in common the feature that a panic is a systemic event in which consumers want to hold currency in exchange for their demand deposits"); see *generally ibid.* at 63–68.

130 For an examination of this argument, see Schwarcz & Schwarcz, *supra* n. 48.

addition, policyholders usually cannot demand a payout unless and until there is an occurrence of an insured event. For both reasons, insurance claims should be spaced out over a relatively long period of time, which lengthens the average maturity of an insurance company's liabilities to policyholders. Ideally, that allows an insurer to match its liabilities to the longer-term maturities of its assets. Consequently, insurers are less likely than commercial banks to experience a surge in cash redemptions that would threaten their liquidity and require them to liquidate their assets for less than fair market value.[131] Similarly, traditionally insurers were not highly leveraged because they did not rely heavily on financing through debt or substitutes for debt such as derivatives, repurchase (repo) agreements or securities lending.

While this traditional model of insurance often holds true, recent experience showed that the insurance industry is not completely immune from runs. As the financial crisis revealed, there are pockets of activities in some insurance companies and groups that increase their leverage and expose those firms (or their counterparties) to runs. FSOC relied heavily on these areas of concern in designating insurance companies as SIFIs to date.

(a) Term mismatch in shadow banking

The events of 2008 showed that bank deposits were not the only type of short-term liabilities that were subject to runs. As the post-mortem demonstrated, modern finance had spawned a "shadow banking system" of other forms of short-term debt financing that were also vulnerable to runs. For example, all of the top U.S. investment banks in 2008 depended on short-term (often overnight) lines of credit in the form of repo lending for funding.[132] Bear Stearns and Lehman Brothers cratered when their repo lenders refused to renew their overnight loans. Similarly, in the over-the-counter derivatives market, panic about AIG's ability to meet its credit swap protection obligations led to cash margin calls of crushing proportions. Money market funds also experienced runs, one of which capsized the Reserve Primary Fund in September 2008.[133]

These types of runs can spread systemic risk through one and sometimes two pathways. The first involves counterparty exposures. If a mega-firm reneges on its short-term liabilities, that can bring down the creditors who are owed that money, which in turn could topple their creditors.[134] Generally, this concern about a cascading

131 See International Association of Insurance Supervisors, *Global Systemically Important Insurers, Initial Assessment Methodology* (July 18, 2013), available at: www.iaisweb.org (last viewed Aug. 31, 2014).

132 A repurchase or repo agreement is a functional substitute for a loan in which the financial institution seeking to borrow sells securities for cash pursuant to an agreement to buy back the securities at a set price at a later date. See Tobias Adrian *et al.*, Repo and Securities Lending 2–3 (Fed. Res. Bank of N.Y. Staff Report No. 529, Feb. 2013), available at: www.newyorkfed.org/research/staff_reports/sr529.pdf (last viewed Dec. 30, 2014).

133 Diana B. Henriques, *Money Market Fund Says Customers Could Lose Money*, N.Y. Times (Sept. 17, 2008); Lawrence Schmidt, Allan Timmermann & Russ Wermers, Runs on Money Market Mutual Funds (working paper, Feb. 28, 2014), available at: http://rady.ucsd.edu/docs/faculty/timmermann-money-market-funds.pdf (last viewed Dec. 30, 2014).

134 According to Acemoglu, Ozdaglar & Tahbaz-Salehi, highly interconnected financial systems are safer so long as the size and number of damaging shocks remain small. As shocks increase in quantity and in size, however, financial systems featuring a high degree of interconnectedness among large counterpar-

effect is limited to situations where a company's counterparties are other SIFIs and not retail customers. In contrast, the second pathway – where mass liquidation of assets in order to meet redemptions sends market prices into a tailspin[135] – can harm large financial institutions and retail customers alike.

(I) TERM-MISMATCH PROBLEMS IN THE INSURANCE INDUSTRY

As the events of 2008 showed, runs were not limited to investment banks, money market funds, or derivatives issuers. Closer analysis revealed a number of term-mismatch problems in pockets of the insurance industry creating the potential for runs. FSOC cited several such problems in its decisions to designate AIG, Prudential Financial, Inc., and MetLife as SIFIs.

Specifically, FSOC expressed concern about various funding streams that increased the leverage of all three insurance SIFIs and their vulnerability to runs due to term mismatches. For example, the Council pointed to AIG's, Prudential's, and MetLife's securities lending businesses as one worrisome area of counterparty exposures and asset liquidation.[136] Repo financing at all three insurers posed similar concerns.[137] In addition, the Council singled out the three companies' derivatives holdings, which could "require [them] to either post additional collateral or to raise cash to close out certain funding transactions."[138] These activities presented term-mismatch problems to the extent that AIG, Prudential, or MetLife could be forced to dump substantial amounts of long-term or illiquid investments[139] in order to raise cash to meet collateral class or repayment demands on short-term repo loans, securities loans, or derivatives obligations.

In its *MetLife* decision, FSOC also flagged a new area of concern, involving term-mismatch problems with MetLife's funding agreement-backed notes (FABNs) and related products. FABNs are financing instruments in which investors buy notes from a special purpose vehicle (SPV) organized by a sponsor such as MetLife. In MetLife's case, those notes are backed by an underlying agreement by MetLife to pay interest and principal on amounts that it borrows from the SPV. Some of these FABNs were short-term, which could create liquidity problems for MetLife if the holders of those notes decided not to renew their investments.[140] In its designation opinion, FSOC pointed out that MetLife had one of the highest leverage ratios among its peers, due in part to its reliance on FABNs.[141] FSOC was also worried

ties become increasingly fragile. Daron Acemoglu, Asuman Ozdaglar & Alireza Tahbaz-Salehi, *Systemic Risk and Stability in Financial Networks*, 105(2) AM. ECON. REV. 564–608.

135 Acharya theorizes systemic runs as "the joint failure risk arising from the correlation of returns on asset side of" financial firm balance sheets. Viral V. Acharya, *A Theory of Systemic Risk and Design of Prudential Bank Regulation*, 5 J. FINAN. STABILITY 224, 225 (2009).

136 FSOC, *Prudential Financial* at 2; FSOC, *AIG* at 3, 14; FSOC, *MetLife* at 10–11, 17, 19.

137 FSOC, *Prudential Financial* at 8; FSOC, *AIG* at 3, 7, 14; FSOC, *Metlife* at 19, 21–22.

138 FSOC, *Prudential Financial* at 2–3; see also FSOC, *AIG* at 3, 11–13; FSOC, *MetLife* at 18–19, 29. In *MetLife*, the Council further stated that the company's hedging activities through derivatives increased its "complexity and interconnectedness with other financial markets participants." *Ibid.* at 9.

139 For example, in the *MetLife* decision, FSOC stressed the company's substantial holdings of relatively illiquid assets, including U.S. corporate fixed income securities and U.S. asset-backed securities. See FSOC, *MetLife* at 24.

140 *Ibid.* at 9–10, 21.

141 The Council also pointed to MetLife's outstanding long-term debt, junior subordinated debt,

that up to sixty-five money market mutual funds could "break the buck" if MetLife defaulted on its funding agreement-backed securities owned by those funds, thereby triggering a run on other money market funds.

FSOC also discerned the potential for runs in the redemption rights issued by all three companies on some of their traditional life insurance products. These insurers issued large amounts of life insurance products (including variable annuities) that guaranteed cash redemptions to policyholders who surrendered those policies or took out loans.[142] Similarly, MetLife's guaranteed investment contracts (GICs) gave customers a unilateral right of withdrawal for purposes of loans, benefits, or transfers to other funds within a plan.[143] Three types of contagion might ensue in case of a surge in redemptions, according to FSOC. First, if large financial intermediaries and other companies had significant exposure to institutional products of that nature, they could face counterparty risk or need to write down those assets from book value to market value if the insurer encountered material financial distress. Second, a decision by such large insurers to sell illiquid assets at fire-sale prices in order to meet redemptions could disrupt the broader financial markets. Last, if policyholders at other companies lost confidence in the solvency of their life insurers that could lead to an uptick in early withdrawals at those companies as well.[144] FSOC expressed further concerns about the widespread effect of any losses on MetLife's retail policyholders and customers if it defaulted on the guaranteed features, given MetLife's position as the largest publicly traded U.S. insurance organization and the largest provider of life insurance in the United States and the size of its customer base, which was 100 million strong worldwide.[145]

In voicing that concern, however, the Council did not explain how those losses could activate a recession or systemic risk. Similarly, while FSOC expressed concern about features of AIG's annuity products that "could make them vulnerable to rapid and early withdrawals by policyholders,"[146] it did not describe those features in any detail or quantify the magnitude of those contracts.

(II) Implications for future federal oversight of insurance

FSOC's focus on term-mismatch problems in insurance groups has several possible implications for the future direction of federal insurance regulation. These repercussions include heightened federal scrutiny of leverage and potential runs in insurance, greater federal oversight of insurance groups more generally, and

---

unsecured credit and committed facilities, and Federal Home Loan Bank financing as sources of its leverage. FSOC, *MetLife* at 9, 16, 18–19, 24.

142 FSOC, *AIG* at 2; see also FSOC, *Prudential Financial* at 2, 8; FSOC, *MetLife* at 13–14, 16–18, 20–23. MetLife also issued other types of guarantees on many of its life insurance and annuity products, including minimum interest rate, minimum living benefit, and minimum death benefit features. If MetLife could not honor those guarantees due to financial distress, the affected policyholders could suffer losses. FSOC, *MetLife* at 11, 14, 17.

143 FSOC, *MetLife* at 12, 18.

144 FSOC, *AIG* at 2–3, 6–7; FSOC, *Prudential Financial* at 2–3, 17; FSOC, *MetLife* at 17–25.

145 FSOC, *MetLife* at 7, 18, 20.

146 FSOC, *AIG* at 6.

across-the-board regulation of insurers, no matter their size, who engage in systemically risky activities.

(III) FEDERAL FOCUS ON LEVERAGE AND POTENTIAL FOR RUNS

First, the SIFI deliberations showed that some large insurers are more reliant on short-term debt than was commonly understood. The extent that insurance companies – especially large insurance companies – rely on short-term debt for part of their financing, will catch FSOC's eye. Since most insurance companies' liabilities are financed by premiums and thus are heavily weighted toward long-term obligations to policyholders, this is relatively rare.

There is one instance in which insurance policies can have demand-like features: certain life insurance and annuity policies that are subject to early withdrawal at the initiative of the policyholder. As a general rule, life insurers reserve the right to suspend these sorts of redemptions. Nevertheless, they are likely to hesitate to invoke that right lest it suggest the appearance of insolvency.[147] Given FSOC's concern about the propensity of these types of life insurance and annuity policies to runs in the form of spikes in redemptions, it comes as no surprise that the first three U.S. insurance SIFI designees were giants in the life insurance industry.

These cash-redemption features are unique to the life insurance industry, but other term-mismatch problems flagged by FSOC involve financial activities engaged in by insurance companies more generally. Securities lending and derivatives trading are the most obvious examples; sponsorship of investment funds (including money market funds and mutual funds) is another. To the extent an insurer's securities lending, derivatives trading or fund activities present systemic risk, FSOC may be watching, whether the company specializes in life insurance or in property/casualty coverage.

(IV) CONSOLIDATED INSURANCE GROUP OVERSIGHT

Another far-reaching corollary of the term, mismatch discussion involves the regulatory implications of holding company structure. The vast majority of U.S. insurance companies are owned by holding companies – numbering about 320 groups[148] – many of which combine insurance underwriters with non-insurance affiliates under one roof. The holding company organization of modern insurance groups has federal implications that state regulators cannot fully deflect.

First, to the extent an insurance group owns one or more federally insured depository institutions in the United States, that group is a holding company subject to consolidated supervision by the Federal Reserve Board. The Federal Reserve has oversight of two types of depository institution holding companies: financial holding companies (which own commercial banks) under the Bank Holding Company Act[149] and savings and loan holding companies (which own

147 See, e.g., FSOC, *MetLife* at 23.

148 See Financial Stability Board, *Peer Review*, *supra* note 121.

149 Pub. L. No. 84-511, 70 Stat. 133, as amended (1956), codified at 12 U.S.C. §§ 1841 *et seq*. The Federal Reserve also supervises ordinary bank holding companies under the same Act, but those holding companies cannot own insurance underwriters. *Ibid*.

savings banks) under the Savings and Loan Holding Company Act.[150] Over the past few decades, a number of large insurance underwriters acquired commercial bank or savings institution affiliates. That trend continued during the financial crisis, when several freestanding insurance companies acquired insured depository institutions in order to qualify for TARP funds or access to discount window loans by the Federal Reserve.[151] Together, about twenty-one U.S. depository institution holding companies were primarily engaged in insurance underwriting in mid-2013.[152] Meanwhile, at least eight of the top 104 U.S. depository institution holding companies (with over $10 billion in assets) on June 30, 2014 were primarily engaged in insurance underwriting.[153]

Before the enactment of the Dodd-Frank Act, the Federal Reserve Board had extremely limited authority over insurance subsidiaries of depository institution holding companies. However, after the 2008 debacle, the Board's reach over ordinary insurers who are part of financial holding companies grew significantly. Specifically, in Dodd-Frank, Congress expanded the Federal Reserve's powers to examine consolidated depository institution holding companies, including those owning insurers.[154] The Board gained new powers to examine all of a holding company's subsidiaries, whether they are depository institutions, functionally regulated subsidiaries such as insurers,[155] or some other type of affiliate. Importantly, the Board no longer has to make a threshold showing that an insurance subsidiary poses a risk to a bank or thrift affiliate or is suspected of violating the law before commencing an examination. For the first time, the Board acquired the power to examine functionally regulated subsidiaries engaged in commodities and/or swaps activities. The Board further gained new

150 Pub. L. No. 90-255 (1968), codified at 12 U.S.C. §§ 1467a *et seq.* Holding companies that own both commercial and savings banks are bank holding companies that are regulated under the Bank Holding Company Act. 12 U.S.C. § 1843(i)(1).

151 See, e.g., Charles Davis, *Remaining TARP Hopefuls Still Waiting*, Life Insurance International, May 11, 2009, available at: www.lifeinsuranceinternational.com/news/remaining-tarp-hopefuls-still-waiting-2136812030 (last viewed Dec. 16, 2014); The Hartford Financial Services Group, Inc., Form 10-K, at 25, 187 (2008) (describing The Hartford's acquisition of Federal Trust Bank, a federally insured thrift institution, in order to qualify for TARP funds); Lincoln National Group, Form 10-K, at 51 (2008) (describing Lincoln National's acquisition of Newton County Loan & Savings, the FSB, a federally insured savings bank, in support of its TARP application). In addition, certain other large insurance companies – including Allstate Corp. and National Financial – own federally insured depository institutions.

152 Financial Stability Board, *Peer Review*, *supra* note 121, at 34; see also Federal Reserve Bank of Chicago, *Top Banks and Holding Companies Report as of June 30, 2014*, at 2, available at: www.chicagofed.org/banking/financial-institution-reports/top-banks-bhcs (last viewed Dec. 17, 2014).

153 National Information Center, *Holding Companies with Assets Exceeding $10 Billion as of June 30, 2014*, available at: www.ffiec.gov/nicpubweb/nicweb/Top50Form.aspx (last viewed Dec. 17, 2014). MetLife, the sixth largest U.S. bank holding company in 2012, sold its bank and deregistered as a bank holding company in 2013, probably to avoid designation as a SIFI. See *MetLife, MetLife Sheds Bank Holding Company Status With Approvals from the Federal Reserve and FDIC* (Feb. 14, 2013), available at: http://investor.metlife.com/phoenix.zhtml?c=121171&p=irol-newsArticle&ID=1785289 (last viewed Dec. 17, 2014); see also Dafna Avraham, Patricia Selvaggi, & James Vickery, *A Structural View of U.S. Bank Holding Companies*, FRBNY Economic Policy Review 65, 71 tbl. 1 (July 2012). That strategy did not stop FSOC from naming MetLife as a SIFI in 2014.

154 Dodd-Frank Wall Street Reform and Consumer Protection Act, Pub. L. No. 111-203, § 604(b), (c)(1), (h)(2), 124 Stat. 1547 (2010), codified at 12 U.S.C. §§ 1467a(b)(4)(A), 1844(c)(2), (c)(5)(B)(v).

155 Functionally regulated subsidiaries of depository institution holding companies include insurance underwriters and securities underwriters.

authority to examine holding companies and all of their subsidiaries for potential systemic risk.[156]

These new federal oversight powers are significant because *any* insurer controlled by a depository institution holding company will be subject to federal monitoring and examination under Dodd-Frank, regardless of size. Partly due to this heightened federal presence, after 2010, some insurance groups divested or changed the charters of their insured depository institutions to escape holding company oversight by the Federal Reserve.[157] That strategy backfired in MetLife's case, prompting FSOC to cite the company's divestiture as a justification to re-subject MetLife to consolidated oversight as a SIFI.[158] Insurance groups that have other reasons to retain depository institution subsidiaries – for instance, because those banks or thrifts are integral to their business models or because those groups want access to the Federal Reserve's discount window – will have to live with the Fed's expanded oversight. To the extent a shadow banking activity is located directly within a financial holding company's insurance subsidiary, that activity is apt to garner closer scrutiny by the Fed.

Even when a large insurance group does not own a federally insured bank or thrift and thus is not a depository institution holding company, it may still face the risk of a SIFI designation where term-mismatch problems threaten the stability of the U.S. financial system. In such instances, umbrella supervision of the entire group is warranted for several reasons. One is to monitor any uptick in systemic risk in the group's individual units and to curtail that risk. Another is to police interaffiliate transactions – such as loans or upstreamed dividends – that might be used to finance systemically risky activities while jeopardizing the financial health of the affected affiliates and their customers, including policyholders or depositors. Safeguarding the parent company's ability to serve as a financial source of strength to subsidiaries that are insurance companies or banks is another justification for consolidated oversight. The umbrella supervisor also needs to be able to monitor

156 Today, safety and soundness examinations of holding companies may be conducted for a broad variety of statutory purposes. One of those purposes is to inform the Board of the nature of the operations and financial condition of the holding company and the subsidiary. Another is to gauge financial, operational, and other risks within the holding company system that may pose a threat to the stability of the financial system of the United States or the safety and soundness of the holding company or of any of its depository institution subsidiaries. Finally, safety and soundness examinations are allowed to scrutinize the systems of the holding company for monitoring and controlling the holding company's risks. Dodd-Frank Wall Street Reform and Consumer Protection Act, Pub. L. No. 111-203, § 604(b), (h)(2), 124 Stat. 1547 (2010), codified at 12 U.S.C. §§ 1467a(b)(4)(A)(i), 1844(c)(2)(A)(i).

Under Dodd-Frank, the Federal Reserve Board is also authorized to conduct compliance examinations to monitor the compliance of the holding company and any of its subsidiaries with the Bank Holding Company Act and federal laws that the Board has specific jurisdiction to enforce against the parent or the subsidiary. Dodd-Frank Wall Street Reform and Consumer Protection Act, Pub. L. No. 111-203, § 604(b), (h)(2), 124 Stat. 1547 (2010), codified at 12 U.S.C. §§ 1467a(b)(4)(A)(ii), 1844(c)(2)(A)(ii).

157 See *MetLife, MetLife Sheds Bank Holding Company Status with Approvals from the Federal Reserve and FDIC supra* n. 153; see also Letter from Robert deV. Frierson, Secretary of the Federal Reserve Board, to Mr. Carlos R. Mello, President and Chief Executive Office, Prudential Bank and Trust, the FSB, October 31, 2012 (allowing Prudential Financial, Inc., to deregister as a savings and loan holding company), available at: www.federalreserve.gov (last viewed Dec. 17, 2014).

158 FSOC, *MetLife* at 28 (observing that "MetLife, Inc. has deregistered as a banking holding company and MetLife is not currently subject to consolidated supervision").

and gauge counterparty exposures to the systemically risky activities in question. Finally, the consolidated supervisor must be able to coordinate (as best it can absent a global super-regulator) oversight of the cross-border activities and resolution of large, internationally active insurance groups.

Despite its many past missteps and lapses, the federal government is the only U.S. regulator with the jurisdiction and capacity to carry out umbrella oversight of insurance groups for systemic risk.[159] No state regulator has full regulatory jurisdiction over insurance holding companies or their non-insurance subsidiaries.[160] Instead, under state insurance holding company system regulatory acts, state regulators only directly supervise licensed insurance subsidiaries within insurance groups. Under the system called "windows and walls," state insurance departments use their oversight of regulated insurers to indirectly monitor certain types of activities within the group. State departments have created "windows" into group activities by obtaining or mandating information on the business dealings of parent companies and non-insurer affiliates. This is accomplished through a variety of methods, including reporting by insurers of financial statements for the parent and all affiliates, the institution of an enterprise risk report, assessments of group capital, examination authority over insurers and their affiliates, memoranda of understanding with primary regulators of those other entities, information gleaned from federal securities filings, and participation in supervisory colleges for internationally active groups.[161]

Similarly, state regulators have set up "walls" by requiring review of specific transactions between insurers and their affiliates to prevent holding companies from inappropriately siphoning cash out of their insurance subsidiaries and to protect the ability of those subsidiaries to pay their policyholders' claims. Transactions requiring advance approval include investment purchases, reinsurance agreements, management and cost sharing agreement, tax allocation agreements, some guarantees, intercompany investments, requests for extraordinary dividends, and any other material transactions that could adversely affect policyholder interests. Companies must also meet state requirements in order to acquire insurance companies.[162]

---

159 Schwarcz & Schwarcz make a forceful argument to this respect, *supra*, n. 48. The European Union has struggled with similar questions concerning whether to follow a decentralized network regulatory approach or a centralized lead-agency model in crisis management. For an analysis of the merits of that debate outside of the systemic risk context, see Arjen Boin, Madalina Busuioc & Martijn Groenleer, *Building European Union Capacity to Manage Transboundary Crises: Network or lead-agency model*, 8 REGULATION & GOVERNANCE 418 (2014).

160 FSOC, *MetLife*, at 27.

161 FSOC baldly questioned the effectiveness of supervisory colleges in its *MetLife* opinion:

> While supervisory colleges may allow state insurance regulators to monitor other parts of an insurance organization, and may enhance communications of confidential supervisory concerns across an enterprise, they are not equivalent to the supervisory and regulatory authorities to which a nonbank financial company that the Council determines shall be subject to supervision by the Board of Governors and enhanced prudential standards is subject [*sic*], nor do they have direct supervisory authority over the holding company or its non-insurance subsidiaries.

FSOC, *MetLife* at 27–28.

162 See, e.g., NAIC, Group Supervision (2014), available at: www.naic.org/cipr_topics/topic_group_supervision.htm (last viewed Sept. 4, 2014); NAIC, *The U.S. National State-Based System of Insurance Financial Regulation and the Solvency Modernization Initiative* ¶¶ 69–81 (NAIC White Paper, Aug. 14, 2013), available at: www.naic.org (last viewed Dec. 17, 2014); Kris DeFrain, *Insurance Group*

Despite its touted virtues, this "windows and walls" system has major shortcomings. The most serious drawback is its inward-looking focus. The "windows and walls" approach naturally focuses on the worthy goal of keeping insurance subsidiaries solvent and able to pay claims. But "windows and walls" do not aspire to protect the larger financial system from outsize risks generated in non-insurance parts of an insurance group.[163] The first-order problem posed by AIG-FP's CDS dealings was the imminent threat of a global financial meltdown; AIG-FP's threat to the solvency of AIG's insurance companies, while of very real consequence, paled in comparison to that global threat.

This inward-looking focus of the "windows and walls" approach results from limitations on the direct jurisdiction of state insurance commissioners over the non-insurance affiliates of insurance company subsidiaries.[164] Those restrictions limit the effectiveness of the "windows and walls" system in several ways. First, only twenty-four states had fully or substantially adopted the 2010 revisions to the NAIC Model Insurance Holding Company System Regulatory Act as of November 2013 that strengthened the group oversight authority of state insurance commissioners. Worse, only seven states had promulgated the 2010 revisions to the implementing regulation by that date.[165] As a result, many states are operating under older versions of the law and regulation that further cramp the ability of state insurance departments to keep apprised of group activities outside of regulated insurance subsidiaries.

Second, even in states that have adopted the 2010 revisions, their information-gathering powers are limited. State insurance departments only can require periodic reports by insurance subsidiaries but not by parent companies or non-insurance affiliates (other than enterprise risk reports, which parent companies must file). Furthermore, insurance regulators do not collect comprehensive data for a number of several reasons. The FSB reported, for instance, that "[g]roup-wide consolidated data and the financial statements of affiliates within an insurance group are not systematically collected and data is usually only requested by regulators in those

Supervision, CIPR NEWSLETTER (NAIC & The Center for Insurance Policy and Research, April 2012), available at: www.naic.org (last viewed Dec. 18, 2014); Memorandum from the Group Solvency Issues (EX) Working Group to Director Christina Urias, regarding Report to Solvency Modernization Initiative (EX) Task Force on Suggested "Windows and Walls" Approach for Regulation of United States Based Insurers Operating within Corporate Groups, Feb. 26, 2010, available at: www.naic.org/documents/index_smi_group_solvency_windows_and_walls.pdf (last viewed Dec. 18, 2014).

163 See, e.g., Kris DeFrain, *supra* n. 162, at 1, 3 ("Had it not been for the 'walls' that were established in the United States, it is likely that the funds protecting policyholders in the AIG insurance companies in the United States could have been raided by the AIG holding company, thereby threatening insurance policyholder protection"; "the particular focus of regulation should be on the insurer's financial status"); Financial Stability Board, *Peer Review, supra* note 121 at 32 (insurance group supervision in the United States "lack[s] a systemic focus"); FSOC, *MetLife* at 27.

164 These jurisdictional challenges are even more difficult when an insurance subsidiary is domiciled in one state and the holding company is incorporated in another state. See Duane Morris, *Insurance Regulatory Update – Holding Company Supervision, Designation of Prudential Financial as Being "Too Big to Fail," Principle-Based Reserving and Captives*, Sept. 23, 2013, available at: www.duanemorris.com (last viewed Dec. 17, 2014).

165 See NAIC, *Solvency Modernization Initiative Dashboard* 1–2 (NAIC, Dec. 12, 2013), available at: www.naic.org/documents/smi_dashboard.pdf (last viewed Dec. 18, 2014) (discussing the 2010 revisions to the NAIC's Model Insurance Holding Company System Regulatory Act, No. 440, and the 2010 revisions to the NAIC's Model Insurance Holding Company System Model Regulation, No. 450).

instances where it has been produced for other mandated purposes.[166] According to the FSB, "[t]his constrains the ability of state authorities to effectively supervise all insurance groups and to analyze events that might impact the group as a whole, absent a framework for consolidated regulation and supervision."[167]

Meanwhile, although the 2010 revisions to the model insurance holding company law require insurance subsidiaries to gather information about activities and exposures throughout the group, those subsidiaries must rely on the kindness of their fellow affiliates to obtain that information.[168] Even the Model Act recognizes that this dependence presents problems. Thus, the Model Act acknowledges that insurance subsidiaries may not always be able to obtain "information not in possession of the insurer" that is requested by a state commissioner. In that event, the Model Act states, "the insurer shall provide the [insurance] commissioner a detailed explanation of the reason that the insurer cannot obtain the information and the identity of the holder of the information."[169] If the department concludes that the explanation is "without merit," it may fine the insurer or suspend or revoke its license.[170] The department may also examine the affiliates to obtain the information or subpoena and depose "any person" for purposes of determining compliance. However, the Model Act provides no agency sanctions against any of the insurer's affiliates for withholding requested information.[171] Alarmingly, these restrictions resemble the similar limitations that the Federal Reserve Board labored under unsuccessfully when supervising bank holding companies before 2010 and indicate that the Model Act is not up to the task of properly monitoring enterprise risk in insurance groups.

Third and in a related vein, "windows and walls" also depend on the existence of and cooperation of other primary regulators to share information. Some affiliates, however, are largely unregulated and do not have a primary regulator. Meanwhile, turf wars, red tape, and lack of standardized data may make cooperation harder and slower than expected.

Fourth, under the Model Act, state insurance regulators only have limited authority to take enforcement action against group personnel outside of an insurance subsidiary. Most of the sanctions are directed at registered insurance affiliates or their officers, directors, employees, or agents.[172] Directors and officers "of

166 Financial Stability Board, *Peer Review*, *supra* note 121, at 36.

167 *Ibid.*

168 See NAIC, Insurance Holding Company System Regulatory Act § 4(A)–(B); NAIC, Insurance Holding Company System Model Regulation with Reporting Forms and Instructions §§ 14, 20, Form B. Section 4(F) of the Model Act does require "[a]ny person within an insurance holding company system subject to registration . . . to provide complete and accurate information to any insurer, where the information is reasonably necessary to enable the insurer to comply with the provisions of this Act." As I discuss below, however, the enforcement mechanisms for this duty are weak.

169 NAIC, Insurance Holding Company System Regulatory Act § 6(B)(2).

170 *Ibid.* Elsewhere in the Model Act, Section 11(F) states that "[w]henever it appears to the commissioner that any person has committed a violation of Section 3 of this Act [on registration and disclosure] and which prevents the full understanding of the enterprise risk to the insurer by affiliates or by the insurance holding company system, the violation may serve as an independent basis for disapproving dividends or distributions and for placing the insurer under an order of supervision . . . " Once again, however, these repercussions only apply to the insurer, not to its non-insurance affiliates.

171 NAIC, Insurance Holding Company System Regulatory Act § 6(B)(2), (E). See the discussion below for possible criminal sanctions against individual holding company directors and officers.

172 NAIC, Insurance Holding Company System Regulatory Act § 11.

an insurance holding company system" do face sanctions in two situations. Any holding company system officer or director who "knowingly violates, participates in, or assents to, or who knowingly shall permit any of the officers or agents of the insurer to engage in" illegal transactions or investments shall face monetary civil forfeitures.[173] In addition, any officer, director or employee of an insurance holding company system who "willfully and knowingly subscribes to or makes or causes to be made any false statements or false reports or false filings with the intent to deceive the commissioner" will be subject to criminal prosecution, imprisonment and criminal fines.[174] The *mens rea* requirement of knowing or willful misconduct, however, makes it difficult to muster the proof needed to impose any of these sanctions. Meanwhile, state insurance commissioners have no authority under the Model Act to sanction insurance group parent companies or non-insurer affiliates, either for activities jeopardizing their insurance affiliates or for activities that threaten systemic harm to financial firms other than affiliated insurers. Instead, "state regulators rely on achieving outcomes indirectly via the regulated [insurers] of a holding company."[175]

Finally, nothing in the "windows and walls" system allows state regulators to see the connections and monitor the exposures of counterparties *outside* of an insurance group. Federal regulators were hamstrung during the Bear Stearns, Lehman Brothers, and AIG crises because they lacked similar data on each firm's counterparty exposures with other financial firms. That experience showed that a line of sight into inter-firm exposures is essential for systemic risk oversight to be effective. But state insurance regulators do not remotely have access to that information and even if they did, they do not have the expertise, budget, or staffing to monitor those interconnections successfully. The international dimensions of systemic risk also make it extremely difficult for other nations to reach omnibus agreements with all 88 state insurance regulators.

Consequently, any time the activities of an insurance group threaten the stability of the U.S. financial system – whether those activities are located within an insurer or are restricted to a non-insurance affiliate – the US government must have the ability to monitor the situation from all angles and to act when necessary. The question is not whether the federal government should oversee insurance for possible systemic risk; rather, the question is the appropriate *type* of systemic risk regulation and the relative roles of the federal government and state insurance regulators in conducting that oversight.[176]

Monitoring for systemic risk will likely be the first area where the federal presence will expand over time. Currently, federal law only permits examinations of insurance groups where a group has been designated a SIFI or owns an insured depository institution.[177] But the need to keep tabs on accumulations of systemic risk will

173 *Ibid.*, §11(B).

174 *Ibid.*, §11(E).

175 Financial Stability Board, *Peer Review*, *supra* note 121, at 37; FSOC, *MetLife* at 27.

176 State insurance regulators, for instance, will continue to play an essential role in the microprudential regulation of individual insurance companies, which is a necessary part of systemic oversight.

177 Congress reaffirmed this need when it enacted provisions in Dodd-Frank giving the federal government expanded authority to require additional reporting by certain insurance companies in the wake of the crisis. As a consequence, all financial holding company subsidiaries – including any insurers

create a broader need for federal reporting by insurance conglomerates generally. Anticipating that need, Dodd-Frank gave FSOC the authority to direct the Office of Financial Research (OFR) to collect information from nonbank financial companies (including insurance companies) for the purpose of assessing the extent to which a financial activity or financial market in which the firm participates, or the firm itself, poses a threat to the financial stability of the United States.[178] So far, OFR has flagged data gaps in securities lending by insurance companies (and the associated reinvestment of cash collateral), management of funds in separate accounts maintained by insurers, and the financial condition of captive reinsurers as areas of concern.[179] Potentially, any added federal reporting requirements in these areas for the purpose of systemic risk could apply to insurers across the board, regardless of size.

(V) Across-the-board regulation of systemically risky activities

A final implication of the concern over asset-liability mismatches implicates the debate about how runs can lead to contagion. Contagion resulting from a run can affect a failed institution's short-term creditors and thus is a function of their interconnectedness. Experts debate whether the spread of contagion to a firm's creditors requires more in order to spawn systemic risk. In particular, must the institution and/or its counterparties also be large enough in size before contagion will jeopardize U.S. or global financial stability?

The Dodd-Frank Act straddled this debate without resolving it. On the one hand, Dodd-Frank expressly defined bank SIFIs based on size[180] and instructed FSOC to consider size when designating nonbank SIFIs.[181] Elsewhere, though, Dodd-Frank and FSOC authorized the regulation of shadow banking activities considered to be systemically risky without reference to the counterparties' size. Derivatives trading and money market funds are just two examples. These types of systemic risk from insurance are not just limited to SIFIs. They can be found in many corners of the insurance industry, regardless of a company's size. Already, this has led to across-the-board federal regulation of those underlying activities by all financial services firms engaging in them, including insurers. While this type of across-the-board regulation of discrete activities for systemic risk is in its infancy, as it grows, it will affect many or all insurance companies enmeshed in those activities.

(b) Supply-side dynamics

As the previous section suggests, traditional discussions of systemic risk have focused on the *demand* for financing through systemically risky financial instruments, not on

– must now provide reports and supervisory information that they provide to their primary regulators to the Federal Reserve Board upon request. Dodd-Frank Wall Street Reform and Consumer Protection Act, Pub. L. No. 111-203, § 604(a)(2), 124 Stat. 1547 (2010), codified at 12 U.S.C. § 1844(c)(1)(C); See also *Ibid.* § 604(c)(2) (repealing 12 U.S.C. § 1848a).

178 Dodd-Frank Act, Pub. L. No. 111-203, §§ 112(a)(2)(A), (d)(3)(A), 154(b)(1), 124 Stat. 1394, 1416 (2010), codified at 12 U.S.C. §§ 5322(a)(2)(A), (d)(3)(A), 5344(b)(1).

179 Office of Financial Research, *2014 Annual Report* 107–111 (2014), available at: www.treasury.gov (last viewed Dec. 18, 2014); Office of Financial Research, *2013 Annual Report* 80–83 (2014), available at: www.treasury.gov (last viewed Sept. 4, 2014).

180 Dodd-Frank Act, Pub. L. No. 111-203, §§ 115(a), 121(a), 155(d), 163(b), 165(j), 166(a), 172(a), 210(*o*)(1)(A), 124 Stat. 1394 (2010).

181 *Ibid.* at § 113(a)(2), 124 Stat. 1394 (2010), codified at 12 U.S.C. § 5323(a)(2).

the supply. In all likelihood, that is because the traditional suppliers of short-term credit to commercial banks are depositors and deposits are viewed favorably for their important and essential role in providing liquidity through maturity transformation and the payment system.[182]

In more recent debates over the dynamics of runs, however, analysts have increasingly paid attention to the supply side of risky asset classes.[183] This new line of inquiry stems from concerns about the role played by investors during the run-up to the fall of 2008, when banks, insurance companies, and other regulated institutional investors, in search of yield, became major suppliers of funds for investment-grade RMBS, CDOs, and credit derivatives. In too many cases, these investors took the creditworthiness of those instruments on faith by placing undue reliance on credit agency ratings instead of doing their own due diligence.[184] When the credit rating agencies downgraded those assets *en masse* due to defaults on the underlying mortgages or securities that backed those assets, investors rushed to liquidate those investments, setting off a loss in liquidity and a freefall in prices.[185]

To date, FSOC's main concern has not been with investor demand for those asset classes *per se*, but instead with the effects on financial markets if those assets are rapidly liquidated.[186] When The Hartford and Lincoln National sought and received TARP infusions after suffering massive losses in their investment portfolios, those TARP payments highlighted the role played by those and other insurers in financing some of the asset classes that jeopardized the financial system in 2008. In response, federal regulators trained their sights on the correlated presence of such assets in insurance company portfolios and the potential domino effect if multiple institutional investors, including insurers, sought to sell off those assets at once. One of FSOC's justifications for designating Prudential as a SIFI, for example, was that the "severity of the disruption caused by a forced liquidation of Prudential's assets could be amplified by the fact that the investment portfolios of many large insurance companies are composed of similar assets, which could cause significant reductions in asset values and losses for those firms."[187] FSOC cited similar concerns with respect to MetLife.[188]

Several potential consequences flow from this new attention to the supply side of the equation. For one thing, federal regulators are increasingly likely to increase reporting requirements to help them pinpoint the location of accumulations of specific risky asset classes, regardless of who is funding them, with no special carve-out for insurance companies. To the extent insurers come under scrutiny for their role in financing any of those asset classes, that could affect insurance company investment portfolio decisions and the institutional and regulatory dynamics driving those decisions. There would also be likely implications for the

182 See E. Gerald Corrigan, *Are Banks Special?*, 1982 Annual Report of the Federal Reserve Bank of Minneapolis, available at: www.minneapolisfed.org/pubs/ar/ar1982a.cfm (last viewed Sept. 31, 2014).

183 For an illuminating discussion of this problem, see Schwarcz & Schwarcz, *supra* n. 48.

184 See Engel & McCoy, *supra* n. 45, at 58–61.

185 *Ibid.* at 107–08, 111, 113–14.

186 See, e.g., FSOC, *Prudential Financial* at 6, 8–9.

187 *Ibid.* at 3, 9.

188 FSOC, *MetLife* at 25.

risk weights assigned by the risk-based capital framework and by the internal capital models for insurers.

As this discussion suggests, the new focus on systemic risk arising from asset-liability term mismatches in insurance has numerous implications for the possible expansion of the federal role in insurance regulation. To complicate this picture, FSOC is espousing another theory of systemic risk in insurance that could broaden these implications even further.

7.4.2 Systemic risk due to other causes of macroeconomic distress

The traditional definition of systemic risk in terms of runs is well-ensconced and will always raise grounds for concern. But recent federal pronouncements foreshadow another, significantly broader theory of systemic risk that does not depend on the threat of runs (either at the financial institution in question or at one of its counterparties). Under this latter conception, systemic risk could arise in insurance where major market participants are so dependent on a specific type of insurance coverage that widespread loss of that coverage could have major adverse macroeconomic repercussions. So far this discussion has been limited to broad market dependence on insurance coverage by individual insurers. But if this logic becomes entrenched, it could extend to entire insurance sectors as well.

This theory of systemic risk is considerably broader than the traditional theory in at least two respects. First, some iterations of this broader theory focus on whether an insurance company is unable or unwilling "to provide a critical function or service relied upon by market participants and for which there are no ready substitutes."[189] Under this formulation, FSOC could view certain voluntary decisions by individual insurers – or whole insurance sectors – to exit the market for coverage of a given "critical" risk as posing systemic risk and thus triggering federal oversight.[190] FSOC hinted at this in the written justification for AIG's SIFI designation, where the Council pointed to "the specialized policies underwritten by AIG's excess and surplus lines insurers," which "could be difficult for competitors to rapidly replace should AIG exit the market."[191]

This rationale alludes to a broader issue that is inherent in all of insurance, which is policyholders' inability to procure other coverage once an insured risk materializes. While FSOC's discussion is not exactly coherent on this score, the

189 FSOC, *AIG* at 6.

190 In the health insurance sector, of course, a similar pattern of private market exit led to federal intervention in the form of Medicare, Medicaid, and the Affordable Care Act (with an added overlay of ERISA regulation for health plans provided through workplaces). The same pattern of federal intervention following loss of private coverage can be seen in segments of the market for catastrophic risk, including nuclear accidents, flood damage, and terrorism risk. None of these previous forays into federal intervention in insurance was justified in terms of systemic risk. FSOC's innovation consists of reframing the question by asking whether a decision by private insurers to exit certain insurance markets could result in systemic risk.

191 See FSOC, *AIG* at 8. FSOC pointed out in that regard that "AIG's commercial insurance policies cover many of the largest U.S. corporations, including 98 percent of the Fortune 500." *Ibid.* Although FSOC did not technically rely on this rationale in its *Prudential* and *MetLife* designations, it cited other market exit concerns in classifying both companies as SIFIs. See FSOC, *Prudential Financial* at 10–11; FSOC, *MetLife* at 25–26.

Council's discussion of the millions of retirement product customers served by AIG and MetLife hinted at concerns about the ability of Baby Boomer customers to replace their AIG or MetLife annuities after retirement if either of those companies defaulted on those obligations.[192]

In addition, this theory of systemic risk is broader than the theory based on runs because it defines systemic risk according to the result – mass financial distress to insureds or their third-party beneficiaries following loss of coverage – instead of according to the cause of the loss of coverage. According to this wider view, it is irrelevant whether loss of coverage is due to term mismatches or some other reason resulting in an insurer's insolvency, such as a spike in claims due to correlated risks, other types of actuarial miscalculations or under-reserving, undercapitalization, or portfolio losses. *Any cause* of insurance insolvency that could inflict macroeconomic harm would give rise to systemic risk.

Intimations of this more expansive view of systemic risk can be seen in FSOC's decisions naming all three insurers as SIFIs. In the case of Prudential, FSOC justified its SIFI designation in part because numerous corporations and pension plans depended on coverage by Prudential to meet their pension obligations:[193]

> Corporations, banks, and pension plans have exposures to Prudential through retirement and pension products, corporate- and bank-owned life insurance, and other group insurance products. Many employee benefit retirement plans have large exposures to Prudential through insurance and stable value products. Material financial distress at Prudential could impair the ability of pension plans to meet certain obligations to retirement plan participants.

FSOC raised similar concerns regarding AIG:[194]

> AIG provides group annuities for private pension funds through its life insurance subsidiaries, and its institutional business line offers stable value wrap products. If AIG were to experience material financial distress, the pension plan parties to these wrap contracts could be forced to write down their assets from book to market value, resulting in costs for the pension plan sponsors . . . and [putting] unprecedented strain on the [state guaranty fund] system.

It voiced similar comments in the case of MetLife:[195]

> [M]aterial financial distress at MetLife could force pension plans and other institutional users of these products to write down certain of their assets from book value to market value, which could result in significant costs for the pension plans and potentially also for their institutional sponsors.
>
> . . .
>
> The exposures of MetLife's individual policyholders and institutional customers could cause MetLife's material financial distress to impair those entities and affect financial market functioning and the economy.

192 See FSOC, *AIG* at 6 (describing "AIG's retail policyholders" as "including over 18 million life insurance and retirement product customers in the United States"); FSOC, *MetLife* at 20–21 (emphasizing MetLife's 100 million retail policyholders worldwide).

193 See FSOC, *Prudential Financial* at 2.

194 See FSOC, *AIG* at 6.

195 See FSOC, *MetLife* at 17, 21.

In proceeding down this path, FSOC proposed a sweeping new theory of systemic risk that is not necessarily self-evident when applied to insurance. The pension and annuity liabilities that FSOC identified should have a long tail. Absent any features of those contracts that allow immediate cash redemptions, their payout should be distributed over a long period of time. Due to this curve of anticipated payouts, if AIG, Prudential, or MetLife were to founder, there would be a relatively long time horizon to resolve policyholders' claims as they came due.

Given the breathtakingly novel nature of this second definition of systemic risk, FSOC is therefore obligated to explain exactly *how* loss of these types of coverage by AIG, Prudential, or MetLife could threaten the financial stability of the United States. Unfortunately, there is no explanation of that causal nexus in any of the three insurance SIFI designations. FSOC did not explain why the exposure of the companies' annuity counterparties was so enormous that their partial loss of coverage could actually trigger an economic downturn and, if so, how. Nor did FSOC provide sufficient facts about the companies' market shares or the relative market share and capacity of their pension and annuity product competitors to allow outside observers to determine whether the insurers' inability to write new pension coverage due to insolvency would really trigger the risk of recession.[196]

For these reasons, FSOC's stated justifications for this second, broader theory of systemic risk leave a lot to be desired. There *is* another notable area, however – financial guaranty insurance – where some of the concerns that FSOC identified about the larger consequences of any type of insurer insolvency actually came to pass during the 2008 financial crisis. What brought the bond insurers down was not a classic mismatch between assets and short-term liabilities. Rather, the bond insurers were hit with an avalanche of claims because they had guaranteed a correlated risk (i.e., the risk that RMBS and CDOs would default). That risk was correlated because defaults on the underlying mortgages that served as collateral pushed down housing prices, making other home mortgage defaults more likely[197] and increasing

196 In the retail context, none of the sample metrics identified in FSOC's guidance about how it will make nonbank SIFI designations addresses the causal nexus between market share and the risk of a recession or financial meltdown. See *Financial Stability Oversight Council Guidance for Nonbank Financial Company Determinations*, 12 C.F.R. pt. 1310, app. A.

197 As housing prices fell in response to mounting foreclosures, that pushed up the loan-to value ratios of neighboring properties. Higher loan-to-value ratios are strongly correlated with increased default risk. See, e.g., John Y. Campbell & João F. Cocco, A Model of Mortgage Default 3 (Working Paper Oct. 2011); Yuliya Demyanyk, *Quick Exits of Subprime Mortgages*, 91 Federal Reserve Bank of St. Louis Review 79–93 (2009); Yuliya Demyanyk, Ralph S.J. Koijen & Otto A.C. Van Hemert, Determinants and Consequences of Mortgage Default 13–15 (Working Paper Jan. 2011), http://ssrn.com/abstract=1706844; Ronel Elul, Nicholas S. Souleles, Souphala Chomsisengphet, Dennis Glennon & Robert Hunt, What "Triggers" Mortgage Default?, 6–7 & tbl. 1 (Fed. Res. Bank of Phila. Working Paper No. 10–13, April 2010), http://papers.ssrn.com/sol3/papers.cfm?abstract_id=1596707; C. Foote, Kristopher Gerardi & Paul Willen, Negative Equity and Foreclosures: Theory and Evidence (Fed. Res. Bank of Boston Public Pol'y Discussion Paper No. 08-3, 2008); Julapa A. Jagtiani & William W. Lang, Strategic Default on First and Second Lien Mortgages during the Financial Crisis, 16, 21 (Fed. Res. Bank of Philadelphia Working Paper No. 11-3, 2009), http://ssrn.com/abstract=1724947; Christopher Mayer, Karen Pence & Shane M. Sherlund, *The Rise in Mortgage Defaults*, 23 J. Econ. Perspectives 27, 42–43 (2009); Anthony Pennington-Cross & Giang Ho, *The Termination of Subprime Hybrid and Fixed-Rate Mortgages*, 38 Real Est. Econ. 399, 413–416 (2010); John Quigley & Robert Van Order, *Explicit Tests of Contingent Claims Models of Mortgage Default*, 11 J. Real Est. Fin. & Econ. 99–117 (1995); Shane M. Sherlund, The Past, Present, and Future of Subprime Mortgages, 9–10 & tbl. 5 (Federal

the probability of defaults on the RMBS and CDOs. Similar problems plagued private mortgage insurers, which suffered sharp losses from the subprime and Alt-A residential mortgages they guaranteed in the years leading to the 2008 financial crisis.[198]

While FSOC and FIO have been strangely silent on the subject of financial guaranty insurers, concerns about private insurance of correlated risks have prompted the IAIS, not surprisingly, to identify those insurers as possible candidates for systemic risk oversight.[199] Probably, the FIO and FSOC have been quiet about designating financial guaranty insurers as SIFIs because the industry shrank so drastically and is no longer insuring mortgage-backed securities in any significant amount. In contrast, private mortgage insurers are continuing to insure home mortgages, which may explain why the FIO is calling for federal regulation of private mortgage insurers.[200]

Nevertheless, financial guaranty insurers may come under renewed federal scrutiny if housing finance reforms take flight. Recent Congressional proposals for housing finance reform would designate financial guaranty insurers as the first loss guarantors in any new private-label RMBS system that emerges. If that were to occur, these proposals would place the guarantors under federal safety and soundness supervision.[201] Furthermore, in light of the events of 2008, financial guaranty insurers that began to guarantee RMBS would also likely come under scrutiny for systemic risk oversight, including SIFI designation.

If FSOC continues down this path, its focus on coverage losses that could result in major macroeconomic repercussions, regardless of cause, has major implications for the systemic oversight of insurance. There are many reasons why a broad spectrum of policyholders could suffer loss of coverage. Major individual insurers or entire insurance sectors could voluntarily exit a market for financial reasons. In other circumstances, a dominant insurer's insolvency could lead to widespread, partial loss of coverage, both in the form of inadequate reserves for current and future claims[202] and in lost capacity to write future policies.

Such insolvencies could occur for a host of reasons other than the unlikely event of a run. Insurers may under-reserve due to incorrect actuarial assumptions or competitive underpricing. They may founder due to steep, unexpected losses in their investment portfolios. Or they may be inundated with claims when correlated risks materialize. Financial guaranty insurers, private mortgage insurers, catastrophe insurers, and annuity insurers are especially susceptible to these types of correlated

Res. Bd. Finance & Econ. Discussion Series Working Paper 2008–63, 2008), www.federalreserve.gov/pubs/feds/2008/200863/200863pap.pdf; U.S. Government Accountability Office, *Nonprime Mortgages: Analysis of Loan Performance, Factors Associated with Defaults, and Data Sources*, 22 (GAO-10-805, 2010).

198 See FIO Modernization Report, *supra* n. 1, at 31–32.

199 International Association of Insurance Supervisors, *Global Systemically Important Insurers: Policy Measures* 14–15, 17 (July 18, 2013), available at: www.iaisweb.org (last viewed Aug. 31, 2014).

200 See FIO Modernization Report, *supra* n. 1, at 7, 31–32.

201 See, e.g., Senate Banking Committee, *Summary of Senate Banking Committee Leaders' Bipartisan Housing Finance Reform Draft* 1–3, 7–8 (2014) (summary of the March 2014 Johnson-Crapo bill), available at: www.senate.gov (last viewed Aug. 31, 2014).

202 State guaranty funds may reimburse some of those losses. However, those funds impose liability caps and do not cover certain lines at all. Commercial lines are especially vulnerable to this lack of state guaranty fund coverage.

risk.[203] FSOC's pronouncements to date suggest that the Council is considering these other possible causes of insurance company insolvencies – in addition to any risk of runs – when contemplating SIFI designations. Consequently, the grounds for SIFI designations of insurers may be broader than the narrow focus on runs would suggest and could get the federal government more deeply involved in solvency regulation.

Lastly, this focus on insurance company insolvencies could have major implications for federal involvement in capital adequacy standards for insurers. Dodd-Frank already requires the Federal Reserve Board to set higher capital standards for insurance group SIFIs.[204] This requirement has been highly controversial due to insurance industry fears that the Fed's approach to capital requirements will be too bank-centric and make the affected insurers less competitive.[205] While Congress addressed those concerns in late 2014 by amending Dodd-Frank to relieve the Board from any obligation to impose bank-like capital standards on insurance subsidiaries in nonbank SIFIs, the Board must continue to impose risk-based capital and leverage standards at group level.[206] Meanwhile, FIO and the Fed have been intimately involved in discussions of heightened global capital standards for internationally active insurance groups (regardless whether those groups have been designated SIFIs by FSOC or G-SIIs by the IAIS).[207] These twin developments could eventually produce a two-tier framework of minimum capital regulation in insurance in which larger, globally active insurance groups are subject to higher capital requirements than smaller insurers. The competitive inequalities and incentives for regulatory arbitrage that could result will produce pressure to harmonize the two tiers of standards and give the federal government a larger voice in state capital standards in the process.

7.5 Conclusion

The state-based model of U.S. insurance regulation has been remarkably enduring to date, in part because the traditional rationales for a greater federal role – efficiency, solvency and consumer protection – have not succeeded in displacing state regulation. However, the 2008 financial crisis, the federal government's unprecedented bailouts of segments of the insurance sector, and the need for a coordinated international approach to containing systemic risk changed the terms of the debate over state versus federal regulation, to the detriment of the states. As a result, the federal government is making new inroads into insurance regulation in the areas of international cooperation and systemic risk. As this chapter discusses, FSOC has embraced two different models of systemic risk, including a vague, unconventional and highly expansive second model, in its insurance company SIFI

203 See Schwarcz & Schwarcz, *supra* n. 48.

204 Dodd-Frank Act, Pub. L. No. 111-203, § 165(b)(1)(A), (c), (k), 124 Stat. 1547 (2010).

205 See, e.g., Arthur D. Postal, *Insurers Make Case against 'Bank-Centric' Rules, but Others Urge Caution*, Property Casualty 360°, March 11, 2014.

206 Insurance Capital Standards Clarification Act of 2014, S. 2270, 113th Cong., 2d Sess., § 2(2) (2014), codified at 12 U.S.C. § 5371(c)(1)–(c)(2).

207 International Association of Insurance Supervisors, *Global Systemically Important Insurers, Initial Assessment Methodology* (July 18, 2013), available at: www.iaisweb.org (last viewed Aug. 31, 2014).

designations to date. To the extent that FSOC continues to expound and build on that novel theory of systemic risk, the federal government is likely to become more immersed in solvency standards for the insurance industry generally, particularly for internationally active U.S. insurance groups.

CHAPTER 8

The emerging special recovery and resolution framework of G-SIIs and its effectiveness

Andromachi Georgosouli

8.1 Introduction

Financial institutions notably – but not exclusively – banks provide a wide range of financial infrastructure services. These include the processing of payments and the provision of credit and liquidity. Given their special role for the economy, their disorderly failure tends to give rise to the materialization of systemic risk. This causes major disruption. In the past, the availability of government bailouts addressed the problem of contagion but it engendered moral hazard and encouraged financial firms to take more excessive risks at the taxpayer's expense. Conversely, the application of ordinary insolvency law did little to stop the spread of contagion in the financial system. Recently, a special recovery and resolution regime has been offered as a third and arguably superior solution. This works in two ways. On the one hand, it implements measures that internalize the cost of systemic risk (although the need for public funding is not entirely precluded) while, on the other hand, it seeks to lead the distressed financial institution into recovery or – where this is not possible – into its orderly resolution.

In the past three years, noticeable progress has been made with respect to the development of a special recovery and resolution regime of banks.[1] By contrast, the creation of a special recovery and resolution framework for insurers has been slow. At domestic level, the case for expanding the current resolution regime for banks (and systemically important investment firms) to insurers in adapted form is the subject of vehement debates. Internationally, a resolution framework for globally active and systemically important insurers – known as G-SIIs – has begun to emerge.[2] A recurring theme in these debates is that of the effectiveness of the proposed measures. This chapter examines this issue focusing in particular on the emerging Insurance Resolution Framework (IRF) for G-SIIs. Given the early stages of its evolution, any determination of its effectiveness is bound to be an imprecise science but, nevertheless, forward-looking and of practical importance, to the extent

1 J. Armour 'Making Bank Resolution Credible' *ECGI Law Working Paper 244/2014* (February 2014) (offering an overview of first and second generation of special resolution arrangements of banks in the US and in the EU).

2 At the November 2010 Meeting in Seoul, the G20 leaders endorsed a report by the FSB on reducing the "moral hazard posed by systemically important financial institutions". Initially, the global supervisory community focused on the banking sector and the identification of global systemically important banks but the G20 reiterated the expectation that the IAIS would eventually complete its assessment methodology for identifying G-SIIs in time for the G20 summit in June 2012.

that it identifies certain inherent limitations with policy implications that could possibly set the tone for further legal reform.

In terms of structure, the chapter starts off with an overview of the key features of the envisaged IRF exploring in particular the work of the Financial Stability Board (FSB) and the International Association of Insurance Supervisors (IAIS) in setting the foundations of this framework. Against this backdrop, it makes a tentative assessment of its likely effectiveness. Although the analysis focuses on G-SIIs, some of its findings may be of more general relevance in the sense that they might inform how we think of resolution irrespective of the geographical footprints of the insurance provider in question.

8.2 A first look at the envisaged special recovery and resolution regime of G-SIIs

The IRF of G-SIIs is embryonic. Despite its early state of development, the work of the FSB and the IAIS offer a first glimpse into its key features. Similarly to the recovery and resolution regime for other Systemically Important Financial Institutions (SIFIs), the IRF for G-SIIs has two chief objectives: to ensure that the resolution of a financially troubled G-SII will neither cause systemic disruption nor increase costs for taxpayers and to protect vital economic functions through mechanisms that make it possible for shareholders and unsecured creditors to absorb losses in a manner that respects the hierarchy of claims in liquidation. Unlike the recovery and resolution framework for other SIFIs, policyholder protection is a distinctive aspect of both the recovery and the resolution stages of G-SIIs and it is to be pursued primarily through measures that ensure the continuity of coverage of the risk insured.

The *FSB Key Attributes of Effective Resolution Regimes for Financial Institutions* stand at the epicenter of this international regulatory framework. Together with the enhanced supervision and High Loss Absorbency (HLA) regimes, it constitutes one of the three pillars of policy measures applicable to G-SIIs. The FSB Key Attributes describe the core elements of effective resolution mechanisms for financial institutions irrespective of whether they are nationally or internationally active. They apply to any financial institution whose disorderly failure is or may be systemically significant including their holding companies, non-regulated operational entities within a financial group or within a conglomerate, as long as it can be shown that these are significant to the business of the group or conglomerate in question.[3] According to the FSB, an insurance resolution must possess a wide range of features.[4] It must delineate the scope of application and the mandate and powers of the resolution authority with clarity. It must contain provisions for the set off, netting, collateralization and segregation of clients' assets as well as other safeguards. It must have in place a legal framework setting out the conditions for cross-border cooperation agreements to facilitate, *inter alia,* access to information and information

3 The FSB, *Key Attributes of Effective Resolution Regimes for Financial Institutions* (October 2011) at 5.
4 The FSB *Key Attributes* above at 1.

sharing. Last but not least, it must provide for crisis management groups (CMGs), resolvability assessments and recovery and resolution planning.

In July 2013 and as a response to the FSB Key Attributes, the IAIS published a methodology for identifying G-SIIs known as the IAIS Common Framework and Methodology and a set of policy measures that will apply to them.[5] G-SIIs are defined as insurance-dominated conglomerates, insurance groups and any insurers whose distress or disorderly failure (because of their size, complexity and interconnectedness) would cause significant disruption to the global financial system and economic activity.[6] The earmarking of an insurer as a 'G-SII' carries significant practical implications. These are enhanced supervision, resolution and higher loss absorbency measures. The policy measures that will apply to G-SIIs fall under three complementary categories: (a) requirements with regard to recovery and resolution planning arrangements; (b) requirements establishing an enhanced group-wide supervision framework; and (c) higher loss absorbency requirements entailing, *inter alia,* the maintenance of capital which will be permanently and fully available. For the remainder of this section, the emerging recovery and resolution framework for G-SIIs is discussed with some reference to enhanced group-wide supervision and loss absorbency requirements where appropriate.

G-SIIs will be expected to plan ahead for rainy days and develop, among other things, a recovery and resolution plan (RRP).[7] The recovery plan and the resolution plan serve different purposes and are complementary to each other. Where there is a reasonable prospect of recovery, the recovery plan offers a roadmap of measures to be taken with the view of restoring the viability of the G-SII. It must be drawn on the assumption that public funding will not be available for the resolution of the G-SII and it must be planned in advance paying due regard to the cross-border impact of contagion, simultaneous stress situations both idiosyncratic as well as market-wide. It will include measures that reduce the risk profile of the G-SII, strategic options such as the restructuring of liabilities as well as a credible course of action and processes whereby the G-SII is expected to cope with capital and liquidity shortfalls.[8]

The resolution plan facilitates the effective use of resolution powers to protect systemically important functions. Consequently, its primary objective is that the resolution of the failed insurer will neither cause severe disruption nor expose taxpayers to loss. To this end, it must *inter alia:*

(a) identify financial and economic functions for which continuity is critical;
(b) lay out suitable resolution options to preserve those functions or wind them down in an orderly manner;

5 The IAIS ComFrame and Methodology (designation criteria) apply to Internationally Active Insurance Groups only. Domestic insurance groups fall outside the scope of application despite the fact that these may well be of systemic significance at a local or regional level.

6 The IAIS, *Global Systemically Important Insurers: Policy Measures* (18 July 2013) at 3.

7 Note 3 above, 16.

8 Note 3 above, Annex III at 33.

(c) specify data requirements on the firm's business operations, structures and systemically important functions;
(d) identify potential barriers to effective resolution and actions to mitigate those barriers;
(e) set out actions to protect insured depositors and insurance policyholders; and
(f) describe clear options or principles for the exit from the resolution process.

Senior managers are going to play a key role in drafting credible RRPs and they will assume responsibility for providing the necessary input to the resolution authorities, namely information that is necessary for the preparation and assessment of RRPs. According to the FSB recommendations, firms must, *inter alia,* have in place a robust governance structure and sufficient resources to support the recovery and resolution planning process. This includes clear responsibilities of business units and the appointment of a senior level executive exclusively responsible for ensuring that the firm is and remains in compliance with RRP requirements and that the RRP is integrated into the firm's overall governance processes. In addition, firms must have in place the necessary systems, which will enable them to generate the information that is required for the implementation of the RRP that applies to them.

While G-SIIs will be asked to prepare the recovery plan, the resolution plan will be the responsibility of the competent resolution authorities. Specifically, the resolution authorities will have a broad array of powers and options to resolve a G-SII that is no longer viable. These options can be divided into stabilization and liquidation options. Stabilization options will ensure the continuity of systemically important functions. An example here would be the sale or transfer of shares to a third party through a bridge institution. The liquidation options will provide for the orderly closure and winding down of all or parts of the G-SIIs business in a manner that protects insurance policyholders. The following tools are expected to be in the regulator's disposal:

(a) run-off (namely the power to discontinue the writing of new business by an insurance firm in resolution while continuing to administer existing contractual policy obligations);
(b) portfolio transfer (moving all or part of the insurance business to another insurer without the consent of policyholders);
(c) insurance guarantee schemes (IGSs);
(d) bridge institutions;
(e) consensus-based restructuring of liabilities;
(f) mandatory bail-in; and
(g) compulsory winding down.

A distinctive feature of the envisaged IRF for G-SIIs is that the competent authorities should no longer rely on public ownership or bailout arrangements.[9] Instead, bail-

9 Note 3 above, 12.

ins are expected to play a more prominent role. In this connection, it is important to make a parenthesis and briefly explain what a bail-in is and what its relationship with bailout mechanisms is likely to be under the IRF.

Although there is no generally accepted definition of a bail-in, notionally, bail-in mechanisms come in two forms.[10] They are either consensual or mandatory depending on whether they are initiated voluntarily and on a contractual basis by the parties concerned or whether, alternatively, they come about as a result of the competent regulator exercising its statutory power to mandate a bail-in. Typically this will entail either *ex ante* intervention through which the regulator mandates the insertion of a contractual clause by virtue of which debt is converted into equity when certain conditions apply or some form of *ex post* intervention whereby the regulator modifies existing contractual terms to the same or similar effect (e.g. writing down of debt). The most commonly envisaged restructuring would be a debt-equity swap, but other possibilities exist such as a simple cancellation of equity or debt.[11] Bail-in may be thought appropriate for a range of reasons but it is primarily regarded as a recovery rather than a resolution tool. For example, it may be used for the purposes of restoring the viability of a failing G-SII, or in order to increase its loss-absorbing capacity. Although rare in practice, a contract-based bail-in is not controversial because the parties are assumed to have given their consent. By contrast, a mandatory bail-in is controversial because it is instituted on non-consensual basis and typically as an antidote to the general reluctance of the parties to restructure the liabilities of the failing G-SII voluntarily. This being the case, for the remainder of this chapter my focus will be on mandatory bail-in unless otherwise specified.

Bail-outs are not ruled out but public funding is envisaged to be temporary and a measure of last resort. The FSB recommends that the availability of bail-outs must be subject to strict conditions that minimize the risk of moral hazard. They are likely to be made available only when all other sources of funding are exhausted or cannot achieve the orderly resolution of the insurer in question and on condition that losses to equity holders and residual costs will be allocated as appropriate to unsecured and uninsured creditors and the industry. Some form of external funding may also become available to facilitate a sale or to fund continued operations under temporary control of public authorities until a buyer is eventually found.

10 See notably, J. Zhou, V. Routledge, W. Bossu, M. Dobler, N. Jassaud, and M. Moore, 'Resolving Systemically Important Financial Institutions: Mandatory Recapitalization of Financial Institutions Using 'Bail-Ins'' in C. Enoch, L. Everaert, T. Tressel and J. Zhou (eds), *From Fragmentation to Financial Integration in Europe* (IMF, Washington D.C., 2014), chapter 23 at 433–456 at 437. See also note 3 above, 8–10 (analyzing the objectives that a bail-in may serve).

11 In the UK and by virtue of s. 48B of the Banking Reform Act 2013 amending the Banking Act 2009, the bail-in may involve *inter alia* the cancellation of any liability owed by the institution, conversion of an instrument into a different form and a determination that a contract under which the institution has a liability is to have effect as if a specified right had been exercised under the contract subject to the discretion of the Bank of England. See A. Bainbridge, D. Shearer, J. Atkison, K. Gray and S. Lovegrove, 'Legislative Comment: The Banking Reform Act 2013' (2014) 114(Mar) *Compliance Officer Bulletin* 1–32 at 19.

Similarly to banks, in the case of financially distressed G-SIIs, the continuity of critical functions is considered paramount. Typically 'critical functions' are understood as functions with systemic implications as, for example, payments and the provision of credit and liquidity or in the case of G-SIIs, the continuity of risk coverage either during the recovery of the financially distressed G-SII or during the resolution of the failed G-SII where its recovery is no longer feasible.

Contrary to typical critical functions like payment services, the failure to provide continuous coverage of the risk insured does not always give rise to knock-on effects due to the long-term horizon of traditional insurance contracts.[12] From this it does not follow that the earmarking of the continuity of risk coverage as a critical function is not appropriate. The rationale for the special place of the continuity of coverage of the risk insured in the IRF is rooted to the desideratum of policyholder protection, which in its turn calls for measures that protect the interests of those policyholders for whom the risk insured is yet to be materialized (and probably it will not) as well as for those policyholders for whom the payment of compensation is due as a result of the materialization of the risk insured. The obligation to pay compensation upon the materialization of the risk insured is not connected with the payments system in a similar fashion that the execution of banking payment obligations does. Nevertheless, it is a critical function because it involves payment that affects consumer confidence, namely a key transmitter of contagion when plummeted. Accordingly, it also justifies measures, which will ensure its provision either at the recovery or at the resolution stage of a G-SII.

The FSB recommends a legal framework for cross-border cooperation, which is almost entirely of soft-law nature.[13] This comprises, *inter alia*, CMGs, institution-specific cross-border cooperation agreements and arrangements that facilitate information sharing among the competent authorities subject to confidentiality requirements and other legal constraints (e.g. for the purposes of protecting sensitive data). Drawing on existing regulatory practice, resolution authorities are asked to consider the impact on financial stability in other jurisdictions and they are expected to refrain from discriminating against creditors on the basis of their nationality, the location of their claims or the jurisdiction where these claims are payable. Where a host authority takes discretionary action, it will give prior notification and consult the foreign home authority. Last but not least, it is envisaged that foreign

12 Accordingly, a question to be asked here is whether – in relation to the IRF for G-SIIs – policyholder protection demands that that we take the continuity of the coverage of the risk insured as an aspect of the insurance business that matters in its own right independently of any systemic risk implications. At present neither the FSB nor the IAIS provide further guidance on this issue. On the latest consultation proposals, see, however, the FSB, *Recovery and Resolution Planning for Systemically Important Insurers: Guidance on Identification of Critical Functions and Critical Shared Services – Consultative Document* (16 October 2014). Available at: www.financialstabilityboard.org/2014/10/c_141016/. It is not the aim of this chapter to examine in detail policyholder protection during the recovery and the resolution stages of a G-SII, although some further remarks are made below, where I examine the relevance of IGSs to the successful implementation of the emerging IRF for G-SIIs.

13 Note 3 above at 13–15. Julian Adams (Deputy Head of the PRA and Executive Director of Insurance) 'Global systemically important insurers: issues, policies and challenges after designation' *Bank of England Speech* at the Genneva Association 24 March 2014. Available at: www.bankofengland.co.uk/publications/Documents/speeches/2014/speech717.pdf. See also note 22 below.

resolution measures will be given effect either by way of mutual recognition or by taking measures under the domestic resolution regime that support and are consistent with the resolution measures taken by the foreign home resolution authority.

While the purpose of the Crisis Management Group (CMG) is to facilitate preparedness for and the management and resolution of a cross-border financial crisis, the objective of the institution-specific agreements is to provide certainty in respect of several key issues including the objective and processes for cooperation through the CMG, the roles and responsibilities of the competent authorities, the process of information sharing etc.[14] More generally institution-specific cross-border cooperation agreements must be forward looking in that they must provide a roadmap of how to overcome existing legal and other impediments.[15] International coordination will be further facilitated by the actions of a group-wide supervisor. The latter will have *inter alia* the overall responsibility of overseeing the implementation of a Systemic Risk Management Plan (SRMP) across the group.[16]

On-going resolvability assessments constitute another key feature of the emerging IRF of G-SIIs. This is going to be a three-stage process. One of its chief purposes is to make authorities and the G-SII in question aware of how its future default might affect systemic risk both nationally and globally if no arrangements for its orderly resolution are in place. Apart from this, resolvability assessments will at a minimum involve the identification of factors and conditions that impact on the effective implementation of resolution actions and they are further expected to facilitate the determination of specific actions that are considered necessary for the improvement of the resolvability of G-SIIs.

The supervision of G-SIIs will be built along the lines of the IAIS Insurance Core Principles (ICP) and the Common Framework (ComFrame).[17] The ICP is a set of 26 principles stating the essential elements that must be present in a supervisory regime in order to promote a financially sound insurance sector. The ComFrame draws on and expands upon the ICP but – contrary to ICP – it addresses exclusively issues of group-wide supervision of internationally active insurance groups with the

14 Note 3 above at 14–15.

15 On several occasions, the FSB has described in some detail the recommended allocation of responsibilities between the competent home and host resolution authorities. For instance, with respect to RRPs, the FSB recommends that the home resolution authority should lead the development of the group resolution plan in coordination with all members of the firm's CMG. Host authorities should be given access to RRPs and the information and measures that would have an impact on their jurisdiction. Host resolution authorities may maintain their own resolution plans for the firm's operations in their jurisdictions but this must be consistent with the group plan. Note 3 above at 17–18.

16 Through the drafting of the SRMP, a G-SII will be expected to address the risks identified in the designation decision and explain how it will manage, mitigate and possibly reduce its systemic risk under the oversight of the group wide supervisor. For example, systemic risk may be mitigated through (a) the use of additional capital so as to internalize at least some of the cost of the externalities that arise from such risk taking, (b) the separation of systemically important activities from traditional insurance business and (c) the implementation of HLA measures.

17 Further refinement of the IAIS ComFrame is due as the IAIS has set out to study the impact of the ComFrame's qualitative and quantitative requirements and make adjustments accordingly.

view of establishing an internationally coherent framework for the supervision of large global groups.[18] The IAIS proposes a combination of proactive and reactive measures. For example, the IAIS system of enhanced supervision and HLA are put forward as a set of measures that are proactive in nature, whereas resolution measures are reactive in the sense that they are instrumental to the orderly resolution of a G-SII where its default is no longer avertible.[19]

The designation of G-SIIs marks the end of the first phase of the development of the IRF.[20] There are still many phases to come.[21] The establishment of CMGs for the initial cohort of G-SIIs is expected in July 2014 together with the completion of an SRMP. The IAIS also plans to finalize capital requirements for loss absorbency applicable to G-SIIs with respect to group activities and to develop RRPs and liquidity risk management plans by the end of 2014. The development of a detailed framework of HLA is unlikely to start before the end of 2015 and, once in place, it is unlikely to be implemented before January 2019.

These international initiatives run in parallel with efforts at regional and domestic level to extend the resolution framework for systemic banks to non-banks including insurers. In the US, the Dodd-Frank Act established the Orderly Liquidation Authority (OLA) and it introduced an extended receivership regime for all systemic financial institutions as early as 2010.[22] In the UK, the Banking Act 2009 introduced a Special Resolution Regime (SRR) for deposit-taking institutions (banks).[23] Later, the Financial Services Act 2012 extended the scope of application of the relevant provisions to cover large investment firms, central counterparties and firms in the same group of a failing bank but not insurers.[24] More recently, the Banking Reform Act 2013 introduced further amendments to the existing bank resolution regime including new bail-in powers.[25] In the EU, two of the latest developments are of direct relevance here. The first one is the publication of the European Parliament

---

18 The most recent draft of the ComFrame was issued in 2013 and it is currently going through a 'field testing' stage. It is due to be adopted in 2018 subject to further modifications, with the IAIS Members implementing it thereafter. Internationally active insurance groups are identified in light of two criteria: (a) international activity; and (b) the size of the group based on a rolling three-year average.

19 HLA targets activities that bear the potential of generating aggregate systemic risk. It requires the permanent availability of capital of highest quality to cover losses at all times. HLA is expected to facilitate earlier regulatory intervention and to enhance the resilience of the G-SII.

20 Currently nine global insurers figure in the IAIS list of G-SIIs. These are: Allianz SE, American International Group Inc, Assicurazioni Generali SpA, Aviva plc, AXA SA, MetLife Inc, Ping An Insurance (Group) Company China Ltd, Prudential Financial Inc and Prudential Plc.

21 Note 6 above at 31–32.

22 For a critical analysis see, A. E Wilmarth Jr., 'The Dodd-Frank Act: A Flawed and Inadequate Response to the Too-Big-To-Fail Problem' *89 Oregon Law Review* 951–1057 (2011). Although US systemic insurers are subject to consolidated supervision at a federal level and under the auspices of the Financial Stability Oversight Council, according to Title II (Orderly Liquidation Authority) of the Dodd-Frank Act 2010, their resolution is still governed by State laws. Nevertheless, the FDIC has inter alia the power to issue systemic risk determinations and to replace the competent State level agencies, if they fail to act within 60 days from systemic risk determination.

23 Banking Act 2009, ss 14–32 and ss 33–48.

24 Financial Services Act 2012, s. 101.

25 See generally, A. Bainbridge *et al* above note 11.

Report back in October 2013.[26] The Report calls the Commission to follow the timeframe by the FSB and to take into account the work of the IAIS on this subject in the context of level two Solvency (Omnibus) II, the Financial Conglomerates legislation and the Insurance Mediation Directive. The second one (SRMR) is the adoption of the Bank Recovery and Resolution Directive (BRRD) and the Single Resolution Mechanism Regulation (SRMR) both of which provide the legal backdrop of the Single Resolution Mechanism in the context of the European Banking Union (EBU) for Eurozone countries and non-Eurozone Member-States which nevertheless wish to opt-in.[27] While the BRRD applies to all EU Member States, the SRMR applies only to those Member States that participate in the EBU.[28] Although, insurers fall outside the scope of the BRRD and the SRMR, both legal instruments are expected to shape future developments in the recovery and resolution of insurers at least in terms of legal reform and approach to implementation at regional level.[29]

8.3 Will it work?

Although there is no concrete set of criteria for the determination of the effectiveness of the IRF, the FSB articulation of the resolution objectives for SIFIs suggests that such an evaluative exercise may be carried out by measuring the impact of the envisaged IRF on the creation of those institutional conditions that would, on the one hand, reduce the complexity, and interconnectedness of the financial network to which the insurance sector belongs and, on the other hand, incentivize institutional investors (creditors of G-SIIs) to be mindful of the systemic implications of their failure to act as gatekeepers of a kind of market discipline that punishes moral hazard and rewards sustainable economic growth. The higher it scores, the better it is likely to do in: (a) managing systemic risk; (b) minimizing public expenditure shifting thus the financial burden away from the taxpayers; (c) curbing moral hazard; and (d) delivering policyholder protection during the recovery and the resolution stages of a G-SII.[30]

It is often argued that policyholders cannot generally have their liabilities be paid off on demand or on maturity. Payments to policyholders usually result upon

26 European Parliament, *Report on recovery and resolution framework for non-bank institutions* (2013/2047 (INI)), Committee on Economic and Monetary Affairs, Rapporteur: Kay Swinburne (22 October 2013) at p. 9 (paras 32 and 33).

27 The Bank Recovery and Resolution Directive 2014/59/EU (15 May 2014) and the Single Resolution Regulation (EU) No. 806/2014 (15 July 2014) are complementary and harmonize bank recovery and resolution in the European Banking Union (EBU) and the EU. See, http://ec.europa.eu/finance/general-policy/banking-union/index_en.htm.

28 See, M. Schilling, 'Bank resolution regimes in Europe: Part 1: recovery and resolution planning, early intervention' (2013) 24(6) *European Business Law Review* 751–779 and 'Bank resolution regimes in Europe: Part 2: recovery and resolution planning, early intervention' (2014) 25(1) *European Business law Review*, 67–102.

29 For a general discussion about the rationale for an SRR in the EU see, M. Cihak and E. Nier, 'The Need for Special Resolution Regimes for Financial Institutions – The case of the European Union' (2012) 2 *Harvard Business Law Review* 395 at 405–406.

30 The proposed criteria for assessing the effectiveness of the IRF for G-SIIs generally draw on Cihak and Nier's account with regard to the desirability of special recovery and resolution regimes for systemic financial institutions. Note 29 above at 403.

materialization of the risk insured (e.g. car insurance only pays if the driver has an accident) or if the policyholder cancels the policy typically at an onerous rate. For example, annuities cannot be withdrawn. Similarly, with-profits insurance products can only be cashed in if the policyholder is willing to suffer substantial surrender penalties and loss of guarantees. Although these remarks suggest that a run on an insurer is going to be rather rare and that, if it happens, it will be relatively easier to manage, policyholder runs are a reality at least in some types of insurance – most notably that of life insurance.[31] Furthermore, recently there has been an increasing relaxation of barriers to withdrawals allowing policyholders to cash out their policies without being penalized. Accordingly, there is nothing to stop policyholders from demanding immediate withdrawals especially when concerned with the solvency of their insurance provider engendering thus a downward spiral similar to that associated with textbook bank runs. The remainder of this section takes issue with some potentially troubling features of the emerging IRF and puts forward some tentative suggestions on how certain of them could be addressed.

8.3.1 The methodology of assessment: Are the IAIS designation criteria for G-SIIs credible?

The identification of certain insurers as systemic is the catalyst in bringing them within the remit of the IRF. Currently, the designation of G-SIIs is based on five main criteria: size, global activity, interconnectedness, the degree of engagment in Non-Traditional Non-Insurance (NTNI) activities and substitutability.[32] Size and global activity take 5% to 10% weight in the assessment exercise. Two factors are taken into account in assessing global activity: the revenues derived outside the home country and the number of countries where the G-SII is active. Substitutability is determined in terms of premiums for specific business lines, while interconnectedness is assessed in light of the intra-financial assets and liability, reinsurance, derivatives, large exposures, turnover and Level III assets. NTNI possess features such as leverage liquidity or maturity transformation, shadow banking and credit guarantees all of which are thought to increase the systemic importance of an insurer mainly for two reasons.[33] First, because certain types of NTNI – notably but not exclusively credit default swaps (CDS) and mortgage guarantee products – link insurers with other parts of the financial system that are correlated with the economic cycle and, second, because in the case of NTNI, the longer timeframe of typical insurance liabilities may not be there.[34] Engagement in NTNI and interconnectedness are assigned 45% and 40% respectively as these indicators are taken to be of the greatest systemic importance for insurance.

31 S. Schwarcz and D. Schwarcz, 'Anticipating new sources of systemic risk in insurance' in A. Georgosouli and M. Goldby (eds) *Systemic Risk and the Future of Insurance Regulation* (2015) at Chapter 5.

32 The IAIS, *Global Systemically Important Insurers: Initial Assessment Methodology* (18 July 2013) at 12.

33 Traditionally, insurance business is primarily built on the concept of insurable risk, the accidental and random nature of insured events and the applicability of the law of large numbers.

34 Above note 32 at 12–13.

The reliability of the IAIS methodology of assessment is questionable. The IAIS measures the systemic significance of insurers on the basis of data that draws on a sample of 48 insurers from 13 jurisdictions. Arguably, this data is too narrow to allow for safe judgments about the systemic significance of insurers. Consider, for example, an insurer and a bank with equal systemic importance to the global financial system. The insurer being compared to a smaller peer group could be designated a SIFI, whereas the bank compared to the global financial system may not be.[35]

Further, it is felt that designation indicators focus too much on the size of the insurance firm, not on the potentially systemically risky activities.[36] On this view, size is not a suitable designation factor for insurers. Insurance business is founded on the law of large numbers. As a matter of fact, the size of a traditional insurance portfolio has an inverse correlation to risk. The bigger the insurer, the greater its capacity to pool risks and contribute to the stability of the financial system.[37] As a corollary to size, the global activity indicator is equally problematic.[38] Like size, the increased pooling and diversification associated with global activity has a stabilizing effect on the insurance business because it allows for greater geographical diversification.

The construction of substitutability as a designation criterion is equally troubling.[39] Critics point out that insurance substitutability is construed in a way that conflates non-substitutable and non-insurable items from those that are very expensive to insure. As they explain, immediate substitutability is not required in the insurance sector. Unlike banks, insurers are not typically involved in systemically relevant financial services – notably the payment settlement system and the provision of credit facilities. A breakdown of hours or days in the payment system provoked by the failure of a bank would have immediate and dramatic systemic consequences, whereas a lack of coverage of insurance business lines such as trade credit insurance and marine and aviation would not especially when temporary public financing is available.

Critics of the IAIS assessment methodology also argue that in assessing the risk of interconnectedness it is important to target the *creator* and not the *receiver* of the risk.[40] Insurers are usually receivers of risk and they are in position to absorb it due to their peculiar business model. A further difficulty here is that the indicators selected to measure interconnectedness are largely driven by traditional insurance activities. Again this is problematic not least because it disregards the fact that in the insurance sector there is no equivalent to the mechanism of the inter-bank

---

35 Geneva Association, *The Geneva Association Response to the IAIS G-SII Consultation* at 11.

36 Ibid. at 12–13.

37 Contrast this with banks, where size is an important factor for the assessment of systemic risk. BCBS, *Global systemically important banks: Assessment methodology and the additional loss absorbency requirement* (November 2011) at para. 27. See further, the IAIS, *Global Systemically Important Insurers: Initial Assessment Methodology*, para. 8 stating that "The risk profile of an insurer becomes less risky the more risks are assumed, that is the larger it is and the more diversified its business (the more lines of business it writes)."

38 Above note 35 at 13–14.

39 Ibid. at 19. See further, The Geneva Association, *Systemic Risk in Insurance* (March 2010).

40 Above n. 35 at 14.

market to establish a level of interconnectedness that is comparable to the banking sector.

The above points of criticism are not entirely convincing. Although it is true that the insurance business works according to the law of big numbers, it is equally true that growth in size becomes sub-optimal at some point, especially where perpetual growth is driven by a common perception that public bail-outs will be made available if things go wrong in the future. Similarly, there is some truth in the claim that traditional insurance does not impose the same systemic threat as non-traditional and non-insurance business but the fact remains that insurers can be systemic due to market interconnectedness, low levels of public confidence and a range of other factors which are explained in other parts of this book.[41] Critics are right to stress the conceptual distinction between substitutable, non-insurable items and items that are very expensive to insure and, on this basis, to question the wisdom of the construction of substitutability as a designation criterion. However, they fail to see that an additional parameter for the appraisal of substitutability as a designation criterion is that of the affordability of the substitute insurable product from the point of view of the policyholder. To elaborate, the substitutability of an insurance product is key to ensuring the continuity of risk coverage but so does its affordability. There is a simple reason for this. The insurability of the insurable product is not supposed to be secured by means of some form of temporary public subsidy as this would be at odds with one of the key objectives of the envisaged insurance IRF, which is to ensure that the resolution of a troubled G-SII will not impose financial burdens on taxpayers. It is also naïve to suppose that insurers are not systemic because they are receivers and not creators of systemic risk not least because this position downplays market interconnectedness, complexity and the role of insurers as transmitters of contagion.[42]

This notwithstanding, the IAIS designation criteria are anything but perfect. The IAIS itself has been quite explicit about their inherent limitations. By its own admission, exclusive reliance on its 'indicator-based' approach should be avoided as additional information and explanatory analysis and supervisory judgment may be required.[43] This mutability in the assessment of the systemic significance of certain insurers introduces a level of arbitrariness which, quite understandably, has been a major source of concern for the industry. This problem is particularly acute in the earmarking of certain activities as NTNI. The case of CDS illustrates this quite well. These are currently classified as NTNI by the IAIS, however, on certain occasions insurers use CDS positions for liquidity management rather than speculative purposes.[44]

41 See C. Finney, 'Systemic risk in insurance: Common thinking errors and their resolution (discussing CDSs) and M. Goldby and A. Keller, 'Oversight of systemically relevant insurance practices within the EU: The role of macro-prudential supervision' (arguing that categorizing activities is not necessarily helpful for the purposes of macro-prudential surveillance) in A. Georgosouli and M. Goldby (eds) *Systemic Risk and the Future of Insurance Regulation* (2015) respectively Chapters 4 and 6 in this volume.

42 See above note 31.

43 The IAIS, '*Global Systemically Important Insurers: Initial Assessment Methodology*' (18 July 2013) at 21–22.

44 Arguably, a CDS does not constitute an insurance contract due to lack of insurable interest.

An idea here would be to introduce a third category for activities that pose much lower risk than NTNI and adjust risk weights accordingly in order to signify their semi-traditional nature.[45] Nevertheless, the inclusion of yet one more category of activities for insurers is not a panacea. Some of the shortcomings of this approach are discussed below in the context of resolvability assessments. For the time being, it is sufficient to note that a more detailed and refined classification of activities and risk weights is bound to add complexity and runs the risk of becoming quickly obsolete. There is always a trade-off to be made between, on the one hand, the desiderata of predictability and certainty and, on the other hand, those of flexibility and adaptability. In this particular case, the balance is tipped in favor of flexibility and adaptability to accommodate the timely exercise of administrative discretion under conditions of risk and uncertainty. Given the inherent limitations of any detailed *ex ante* classification of insurer activities, a more promising course of action would be to seek ways in which to circumscribe the practical significance of such a categorization in the first place. For example, regulators would not have to rely too much on this as a tool for the regulation of systemic risk, if an industry-funded compensation scheme were in place to cater for the payment of policyholder claims during the resolution stage of a failed G-SII.[46] This could be further complemented by a set of measures, the purpose of which would be to tackle the monopolistic and oligopolistic tendencies in specific insurance sectors. The latter has the potential of being instrumental to the control of systemic risk because it would put a halt to sub-optimal business concentration and market dominance. Moreover, it would make it easier for policyholders to find similar insurance coverage at comparable rates.[47]

The above points of criticism reflect a widely held skepticism about the merits of the IRF for G-SIIs. This suggests the presence of a more fundamental problem, namely that lack of trust. Taking into account that the industry is expected to play an active role in making the recovery and resolution mechanisms work in practice, this must be addressed as a matter of priority. Building a relationship of trust takes time but a good starting point would be to take advantage of the current attempt of the IAIS to put the methodology of assessment to the test and revise the current designation criteria accordingly.

8.3.2 Resolvability assessments and their inherent limitations

There are several difficulties with the assessment of resolvability in its current form. Chief among them is the distinction between traditional insurance and NTNI activities. As a rule, a G-SII will be deemed resolvable to the extent in which there is an

45 Above note 35 at 17.

46 This course of action is controversial and has its own implementational challenges. In view of this, it is not put forward as a superior alternative but as an option that is worthy of serious consideration. See also discussion below at 145–149.

47 HIH was a group of insurers in Australia with a dominant position in providing indemnity coverage for the building industry. HIH collapsed in 2001. Its impact was local rather than global, however, it demonstrates well the impact that oligopolies and concentration of business have on the economy. See www.aph.gov.au/About_Parliament/Parliamentary_Departments/Parliamentary_Library/Publications_Archive/archive/hihinsurance.

effective separation of traditional insurance and NTNI already in place. The latter is so important that the competent authorities will be vested with the necessary powers to intervene and prescribe the removal of any obstacles to the separation of NTNI where appropriate. Although it is generally understood that the term 'non-traditional' refers to 'business where the promises made by an insurer can only be met through extensive use of market instruments', while the term 'non-insurance' captures the fact that 'insurers may be part of groups offering other financial services', a difficulty here is that the line between traditional and NTNI is not set in stone.[48] The IAIS offers some guidance but this is not mandatory and a lot will depend on the judgment of the competent authority. The penumbra of uncertainty that surrounds the earmarking of NTNI business has been a source of concern for the industry as it undermines the capacity of insurers to manage liquidity and other risk exposures.

An *ex ante* rule-based classification of insurance activities is often offered as a solution to this problem, however, as it was pointed out above in relation to the IAIS designation criteria, the merits of such a response should not be blown out of proportion. It is important to be mindful that here lies the danger of encouraging a culture of complacency and 'box-ticking' by regulators and regulatees alike. Market volatility and uncertainty also call for a degree of discretion and judgment that a rule-based regime will be difficult to accommodate. Of course, in theory, there is nothing to stop the competent authorities from adopting a rule-based classification of insurance activities and revising them regularly so that the classification is kept up to date, but this may not be a realistic option in practice, for example, due to time constraints. Granting the relevant provision the status of non-binding guidance seems to be a more pragmatic approach especially when combined with conversational regulation because it would afford the requisite level of administrative discretion without undermining certainty gravely.

Concerns may also be raised about the reliability of data on the basis of which resolvability assessments are to be made. Qualitative assessments are expected to be part of this assessment exercise.[49] Critics, however, point out that qualitative assessments are arbitrary in the absence of more detailed guidance on what it is actually expected from G-SIIs in terms of their capacity to manage risk exposure. Moreover, qualitative assessments will be made on the basis of data collected by the Own Risk and Solvency Assessment Framework (ORSA).[50] Despite their sophisti-

48 See Julian Adams above note 13. Arguably, the problem emanates from the absence of a universally accepted definition of the insurance contract. Although, there is some truth in this claim, the fact remaims that we can still tell what an insurance contract looks like in a particular context and how it might be different from other contracts, taking into account the wealth of case law and the plethora of statutory descriptions of the main features of a traditional insurance contract as well as of the variety of forms this may take. For a classic description of the insurance contract see, for example, Channell J in *Prudential Insurance Co v Commissioners of Inland Revenue* [1906] 2 KB 658 and commentary in P. Rawlings, J. Lawry and R. Merkin, *Insurance Law: Doctrines and Principles* (Hart Publishing 2011, 3rd edn) at 3–9.

49 Resolvability assessments will be carried out by national authorities with the home country taking the leading role. Above note 3, Annex II (setting out a more detailed account of resolvability assessments applicable to SIFIs).

50 The IAIS Insurance Core Principle 16, which was adopted in 2010, outlines the main ORSA requirements as components of the so-called Enterpise Risk Management for insurers. Ever since, ORSA has gained the status of a global regulatory requirement. For example, various versions of the original ORSA have been adopted respectively in the EU (art. 45 of Solvency II Directive 2009/138/EC (25 November 2009) setting out the principles for the ORSA), the US (NAIC, Risk and Solvency

cation, ORSAs are nothing but a form of self-assessment exercise, which is bound to be riddled with human bias impairing the credibility of information that will eventually be fed back into the resolvability judgments of the competent resolution authorities.[51] A further limitation is that risk assessment frameworks like ORSAs are tailor made to capture risks; not uncertainty, given that the latter is inherently impossible to measure and account for.[52] A comprehensive system of data resource management could improve the quality of information that goes into resolvability assessments especially when combined with a reliable monitoring and follow-up process, the purpose of which would be to ensure that compliance with the appropriate systems and controls is not incidental but fully integrated into the business culture of the G-SII in question.[53]

The assessment of resolvability is understood to be a continuous process. As will be discussed in more detail in a separate section below, the assessment of resolvability involves a convoluted network of coordination between the home country authority, the CMG within the insurance firm and other supervisors and groups of supervisors.[54] An issue of concern here is that coordination will be so time-consuming that it will eventually undermine timeliness of the assessment of resolvability.

8.3.3 The limitations of recovery and resolution plans ('living wills')

Planning ahead of bad times has been a key driver of the envisaged IRF for G-SIIs. To this end, RRPs will be deployed to provide a roadmap of action for the recovery or where this is not possible, the orderly resolution of troubled systemically significant insurers. Essentially, this roadmap of action involves, *inter alia,* a combination of going-concern measures and gone-concern measures. While the former are geared towards the recovery of a troubled G-SII presumably facing temporary financial difficulties, the aim of the latter is to ensure the orderly resolution of the G-SII when its recovery is no longer a realistic option.

In light of the perceived idiosyncratic features of the insurance business model, a question to ask is how much emphasis to place on the recovery side of the RRPs and how much on the resolution side in the case of G-SIIs. Arguably, the long-term nature of insurance liabilities, the different timescales and the long run-off periods of insurance lend support to the view that the focus should be on the recovery rather than on the resolution of the financially distressed insurance firm. Implicit

---

Assessment (RMORSA) Model Act of September 2012) and Australia (APRA, General Insurance Prudential Standards, which took effect in 2013). For a more general discussion of human bias and how it affects the quality of data although in a different context see A. Georgosouli, 'Treating Customers Fairly (TCF): What is so good about it and why it may not work' (2011) 38(3) *Journal of Law and Society* 405–427.

51 This is further discussed below at page 140.

52 F. Knight, *Risk Uncertainty and Profit* (Boston, MA: Hart, Schaffner & Marx; Houghton Mifflin Co., 1921).

53 See also discussion below at page 140. For a more detailed examination see A. Georgosouli, 'Judgement-led regulation: Reflections on data and discretion' (2013) 14 (3/4) *Journal of Banking Regulation* (Special Issue) 209–220 at 214 at page 140.

54 The CMG is expected to draw, *inter alia,* on shared national assessments of the resolvability of subsidiaries by members of the CMG and on the identification of the issues addressed by the firm (or relevant regulatory authorities).

in this argument is the supposition that the orderly resolution of a G-SII pretty much depends on the robustness of the prudential and solvency requirements and supervision that applies to them.[55] However, the same line of reasoning reveals a contradiction in terms as it may equally support the case against subjecting G-SIIs to RRPs in the first place, as long as it points to features of the insurance business that are understood to guard against disorderly default.

In any case, RRPs will be informed by resolvability assessments but, as it was pointed out above, the findings of resolvability assessments cannot be entirely relied upon. Given the complicated organizational structure of G-SIIs, the volume and complexity of the financial transactions that G-SIIs may elect to enter into and market volatility at a global level, it also seems reasonable to wonder whether RRPs can be sufficiently detailed and up to date as new market conditions unfold.[56] A further question to ask is whether the competent resolution authorities and G-SIIs will have the requisite situational awareness to constantly redraft RRPs even in anticipation of surprise, as would befit any attempt to regulate uncertainty. Additional measures will be required to this end, in particular, those that, on the one hand, reward constant alertness, creative thinking and leadership through the right incentive structure and, on the other hand, those that incorporate processes of cognitive challenge into the prevailing bureaucratic culture of the competent regulator (and of the corporate culture of each G-SII to the extent in which some level of sub-delegation of discretion is to be expected). Some examples here include: (a) decision-making on a 'comply or explain' basis, which will be coupled with a veto power to pre-empt protracted debates; and (b) cross-membership in boards.

8.3.4 Mandatory bail-ins for G-SIIs

Bail-ins have the potential to solve a plethora of problems. At least in theory, they stand as an alternative to bail-outs and public spending. They involve neither the finding of an appropriate purchaser nor the transferring of any assets – both of which can potentially bring international coordination to a standstill. Despite their merits, bail-ins raise a range of issues.[57]

A perennial question here concerns the exact point of time to resort to a mandatory bail-in. It is to be expected that the identification of trigger points for the initiation of a bail-in will be based on a combination of qualitative and quantitative assessments (e.g. failure to comply with minimum capital requirements). The qualitative aspect of the bail-in triggers is bound to introduce a degree of uncertainty. The latter is not a trivial matter, as uncertainty tends to increase the cost of capital for the financially distressed G-SII. A rule-based regime would address this

55 See, for instance, the European Parliament, *REPORT on recovery and resolution framework for non-bank institutions* (2013/2047(INI), (Committee on Economic and Monetary Affairs Rapporteur: Kay Swinburne, 22 October 2013) para. 33 at p. 9.

56 Above note 3, Annex III at 34.

57 Thus far the relevant literature focuses on banks. See, notably, E.R. Morrison, 'Is the Bankruptcy Code an Adequate Mechanism for Resolving the Distress of Systemically Important Institutions?' (2010) 82 *Temple Law Review* 449; K. Ayotte and D. A. Skeel Jr 'Banruptcy or Bailouts' (2010) 35 *Journal of Corporation Law* 469.

problem; however, legal certainty is not the only concern that should inform the drafting of the relevant regulatory provisions. Flexibility and adaptability matter as well. Market volatility calls for either regular revisions of rule-based bail-in triggers to keep them up to date, namely an option that may not be realistic in practice, or for *ad hoc* judgments about whether certain vaguely defined principles-based criteria are met to initiate a bail-in. For this reason, a combination of both rules and principles is recommended as this would accommodate the desideratum of a high level of administrative discretion while offering at the same time a more concrete benchmark for the public scrutiny of the regulator's decisions and actions.[58]

Experience with bail-ins in the banking sector also suggests that a bail-in must be activated at an early stage when restoring the viability of the troubled financial institution is a realistic option. Otherwise, its use is likely to cause a bank run because the market would perceive the mandatory bail-in as a sign that the financially distressed bank is soon to become insolvent. In the case of G-SIIs, such a run cannot be ruled out. However, it is less likely to happen. Nevertheless, even in the absence of an event akin to a bank run, the decision to institute a mandatory bail-in is, by its very nature, a serious incident and most probably it will not be taken lightly by the market. Accordingly, it may still shake market confidence aggravating the liquidity shortage of the troubled G-SII. On paper, the 'no creditor worse off' test that is currently implemented for banks and other systemically important investment firms and which is also expected to apply to G-SIIs will ameliorate this problem, by reassuring the creditors (and policyholders) that the bail-in will not make them worse off than they would be in the case of a counterfactual event of insolvency.[59] In practice, the 'no creditor worse off' principle will be difficult to deliver the desired outcome because domestic insolvency laws vary widely from jurisdiction to jurisdiction. Consequently, it is essential to consider introducing other means through which market confidence could be preserved as, for example, the setting of a floor price for debt/equity conversion to reduce the risk of a 'death spiral' in share prices.[60]

At present, there is no clear guidance on the specification of bail-inable insurance liabilities for the purposes of a mandatory bail-in. As long as this remains unsettled, difficulties in raising capital are to be expected. Creditors would generally be reluctant to enter into transactions, when unable to price in the probable cost of a future bail-in. Therefore, some degree of certainty is required at least for the purposes of planning ahead and of efficient risk management. Subordinated and some types of senior unsecured debt seem to be typical candidates of bail-inable liabilities in the case of systemic insurers.[61] By contrast, guaranteed policyholder claims, secured debt and repurchase agreements should be excluded.

58 The FSB stipulates that the competent authorities must define the regulatory thresholds and legal conditions that provide grounds for the initiation of official actions notably thresholds for entry into resolution as well as the scope for the authorities discretion (e.g. the extent to which authorities can refrain from taking actions or avoid acting under certain conditions). Above note 3, Annex III, 38–39.

59 For a discussion of this principle in relation to the Bank Recovery and Resolution Directive see, P. Athanassiou, 'Valuation in resolution and the "no-creditor-worse-off-principle"' (2014) 29(1) *Butterworths Journal of International Banking and Financial Law* 16–20.

60 J. Zhou *et al* above note 10 at 434.

61 In the UK, the Banking Reform Act 2013, and in particular s. 48B(4) sets out a list of liabilities that are excluded from bail-in. These are liabilities representing deposits covered by the Financial

The *ex ante* earmarking of certain liabilities, as bail-inable, is likely to induce insurers to opt for non-bail-inable forms of debt in their attempt to raise debt finance at a minimum cost. A solution to this problem might be to mandate the issuance of a minimum amount of bail-inable liabilities, however, such a solution seems to be ill-conceived. Quite apart from the fact that bail-inable instruments do not secure reliable cash-flows in a similar fashion to corporate bonds, they may not be attractive to insurers (at least in the UK) as instruments that may be used to back annuity books. With hindsight it may be further argued that the perceived scarcity of bail-inable capital is not so much a matter of suboptimal market supply – as this approach implies – as much as a matter of suboptimal demand. Making the issuance of bail-inable capital mandatory would increase the supply of bail-inable liabilities but it would not necessarily ensure that the supply will be matched by demand, let alone keep the cost of raising capital low. In any case, a further issue of concern is the determination of who is allowed to hold bail-inable liabilities for the purposes of mitigating the risk of contagion to other systemically significant financial institutions. There is no straightforward answer to this question. Arguably, institutional investors with long-term horizons in their investment portfolios are good candidates, because they are less likely to serve as conduits of contagion. However, some institutional investors may not be suitable. For example, the wisdom of letting pension funds hold bail-inable liabilities is questionable, to the extent in which this option can be understood to recommend in effect that bail-inable liabilities should be held by the average pensioner, namely an economic and socially vulnerable group of people with little if any sophistication to monitor the investment decisions of pension fund managers and with limited if any capacity of managing the financial burden in the event of a future bail-in.

In view of the problems described above, an alternative to bail-in as a recovery tool might be the inclusion of a contractual clause whereby – instead of debt reduction – the creditors agree on (or have the option to elect) the introduction of some temporary flexibility with regards to the maturity dates of the debt in exceptional and regularly monitored circumstances.[62] To the author's knowledge the desirability of such an arrangement has not been explored in the context of the recovery and resolution of systemically significant insurance firms, however, it merits consideration. In the circumstances, creditors should be allowed (if they so wish) to sacrifice the certainty that comes with fixed maturity dates in order to avail themselves of the less drastic measure of short-term extension of maturities compared to debt reduction especially when such a temporary arrangement could be instrumental to the recovery of the troubled G-SIIs.

Services Compensation Scheme, secured liabilities, liabilities that the insitution has by virtue of holding client assets, liabilities arising from participation in designated settlement systems etc. Differential treatment of some types of senior unsecured debt may be justified in light of their respective systemic or strategic significance. A good example here is unsecured senior debt arising out of clearing and securities settlement obligations. For a discussion in the context of bank resolution see above note 10 at 444.

62 A similar idea labelled as 'reprofiling' has been proposed in the context of sovereign debt restructuring and as an alternative to sovereign debt reduction. IMF, 'The Fund's Lending Framework and sovereign debt – preliminary remarks' (June 2014) at paras 13 and 16 (providing an assessment of costs and benefits).

8.3.5 International regulatory coordination and information sharing

A key feature of the coordination arrangements for G-SIIs is that of CMGs and institution-specific cross-border cooperation agreements between the competent home and host authorities.[63] While the purpose of CMGs is to facilitate the preparatory stage of cross-border resolution as well as the management of the resolution process in the event of a cross-border financial crisis, the purpose of institution-specific agreements is to provide certainty in respect of several key issues including the objective of cooperation through CMGs, the roles and responsibilities of the competent authorities pre- and during crisis, information sharing and the tackling of legal and other impediments.

The role of the CMG is expected to be crucial in the context of cross-border resolution. Part of its mandate will be to monitor, review and report to the FSB and the FSB Peer Review Council on a variety of issues including the progress in coordination and information sharing, the recovery and resolution planning process under institution specific cooperation agreements and their resolvability. Domestic supervisory authorities, central banks, resolution authorities, finance ministries and public authorities responsible for guarantee schemes of both the home and the host countries will be members of the CMG. The multi-membership of CMG raises issues of accountability; it adds complexity and makes the decision-making process time consuming. Moreover, it is not clear how protracted disagreements among CMG members are to be settled in a timely, unbiased and transparent fashion.

To ensure the unbiased judgment of CMG, the parties to the cross-border cooperation agreements will not participate directly in the CMG. Rather they will be represented at the appropriate senior level. However, this institutional configuration on its own may not be enough to guard against bias, granted the natural tendency of those participating in quasi-informal governance schemes to be more sympathetic towards those with whom they share common bureaucratic and national origins.

As it was noted above, the CMG will have the task to monitor progress in cross-border resolution and report back to the FSB and the FSB Peer Review Council. In this connection, a further issue of concern is that negative feedback from the CMG is likely to undermine the credibility of the authorities if made public. Conversely, it is difficult to see how the CMG feedback could serve as a form of constructive criticism if kept confidential.

Moreover, it is left to the discretion of the parties to decide whether institution-specific cooperation agreements will be legally binding or not.[64] Although the expediency of such leniency is well understood, the fact remains that legally binding agreements would add some level of certainty with regard to public disclosure, information sharing and burden sharing, namely issues that are paramount for the success of cross-border resolution. In addition, they would settle problems of coordination and of policy coherence that are liable to crop up as a result of different regulatory cultures and agency conflicts among supervisors. Experience with Memoranda of Understanding so far has shown that these soft law frameworks of

63 Note 3 above at 14–15.
64 Note 3 above at 22.

coordination fall short from preventing turf wars between the competent authorities, because they do not explicitly address the areas where incentive conflicts and other constraints impede the effective exchange of information.[65] In the past, this problem was further exacerbated by the fact that regulators were generally reluctant to take into account cross-border contagion implications in the absence of a legal rule that made this mandatory.[66] The likelihood of unilateral action by local supervisors in the case of a troubled G-SII for the purposes of protecting domestic policyholders is bound to undermine trust and to create tension among the competent authorities of different jurisdictions as well as uncertainty about the legal implications of the cross-border operations of an insurance group.

The successful implementation of insurance-resolution requires an increasing capacity for collecting and processing data (e.g. for the purposes of ongoing resolvability assessments, the reviewing of RRPs etc). However, there may be obstacles to timely access the available data as, for instance, legal constraints (e.g. the duty of confidentiality). A further problem is that the data itself may be unreliable. This is particularly the case, when the competent authorities use self-assessment exercises as a primary source of information for the assessment of the risk management and of solvency of the G-SII in question etc. In any case, a G-SII is unlikely to disclose non-favorable information, especially when there is a little chance that the regulator will ever find out about this. Similarly, people are unlikely to pass on information that is harmful to them or their fellows. Human judgement is also subject to what we call the 'automation' bias – namely, the tendency to disregard information that contradicts information that is generally accepted as correct. Several other factors undermine the quality of data. These include the use of inconsistent management information systems by insurers, which is evident, for example, in the definition and/or interpretation of certain insurance business terms, and accounting discrepancies as, for example, in relation the valuation of some assets, derivatives, insurance contracts and technical provisions. The development of a comprehensive system of data resource management could aid information sharing by improving the timely and effective processing of data; it should be noted, however, that technology is not value neutral.[67] Crucially, it shapes the

65 The problem of regulatory incentive misalignment persists in the context of cross-border bank resolution, despite the progress that has been made in harmonising domestic legislation at least at a regional level as, for example, in the case of the EBU with the adoption of the Single Resolution Regulation and the Banking Recovery and Resolution Directive. In a recent report with respect to banking resolution the IMF notes that "Should a large cross-border bank fail today, it appears unlikely that the pitfalls and misaligned incentives that undermined cooperation in the global financial crisis could be avoided". See IMF, "Cross-border bank resolution: recent developments" (June 2, 2014) at para. 18. A. Enria and J. Vasala, 'Externalities in supervision: The European case' in Kremers, Schoenmaker and Wierts (eds) *Financial Supervision in Europe* (Edward Elgar, 2003) at 60 (considering the matter in the context on EU financial supervision). See further, Committee on the Global Financial System, 'Foreign direct investment in the financial sector of emerging economies', *BIS Working Paper* (2004) (identifying the mismatch of information incentives among regulators as one of the chief causes of ineffective group-wide supervision in the banking sector).

66 S. Stoltz, Banking supervision in integrated financial markets: implications for the EU, CESifo Working Paper Series (Paper number 812, 2002).

67 M. Heidegger, 'The question concerning technology' in *Technology and Values: Essential Readings*, C. Hanks (ed) (2010), 106–108 and K. Bamberger, 'Technologies of Compliance: Risk and regulation in a digital age' (2010) 88 *Texas Law Review* 669–739 at 675–677.

meaning of the goals of those who make use of it – and it may even translate those goals into a course of action that is at odds with the course of action intended by the regulator.'

8.3.6 Policyholder protection and the systemic significance of Insurance Guarantee Schemes (IGSs)

The FSB Key Attributes include policyholder protection among the recommended objectives and functions of the competent resolution authority. They also set the tone of what policyholders are likely to expect in the event of a resolution.[68] In light of the principles that underpin the treatment of creditors and the protection of depositors of non-insurance SIFIs, we can infer that in the case of G-SIIs, the hierarchy of claims and the equal treatment of creditors are to be observed, although deviations may be allowed when are thought to be more suitable for the containment of systemic risk or for the maximization of the benefits of creditors as a whole. In the absence of any specific recommendation to the contrary, portfolio transfers will not be subject to prior policyholder approval and no legal remedies will be afforded to those policyholders who wish to cancel out or otherwise constrain the implementation of measures taken by the resolution authorities.[69]

When insurers in default are unable to fulfill their contractual commitments to policyholders, IGSs (where in place) provide a last resort protection to policyholders and beneficiaries either by securing the continuation of insurance contracts or by paying compensation for losses.[70] This makes IGSs a key tool for the delivery of policyholder protection. In the absence of a harmonisation initiative for the cross-border provision of some form of IGS, the protection of policyholders remains a national matter. This is troubling taking into account that policyholder protection is an integral aspect of the IRF of G-SIIs namely systemically important insurers with global presence.

At present, the availability of an IGS (or similar arrangement) is earmarked rather vaguely as one of the 'specificities of insurance' that any effective IRF must take into account but there is hardly any guidance about the practical implications of this in designing and implementing the IRF that is envisaged for G-SIIs.[71] Although the expediency of the decision to leave out this aspect of policyholder protection can be explained in light of the conspicuous regulatory divergence that underpins the availability of IGS around the globe, the fact remains that the IGS intersects with financial stability and by implication the recovery and resolution of insurers in a pervasive way.[72]

---

68 Note 3 above at pp 6 and 9 respectively. In a similar fashion, the RRP must, *inter alia*, identify action to protect policyholders (see p. 7).

69 Note 3 above at 9.

70 In the EU, last resort protection schemes exist in other sectors of the financial market – in particular, deposit guarantee and investor compensation arrangements under Directive 94/19/EC (Deposit Guarantee Directive of 1994) and Directive 97/9/EC (Investor Compensation Scheme Directive of 1997). Both Directives are currently under review.

71 Nevertheless, authorities responsible for IGSs are expected to be members of the CMGs. Note 3 above at 14.

72 IGS may not be available in particular jurisdictions or – when in place – may differ considerably

Take the example of an insurer that is unable to meet its obligations to policyholders who purchased life insurance to provide themselves with a retirement income. There is no doubt that in the absence of IGS, disappeared retirement savings can fuel such a public outrage that eventually the government has to intervene only this time to 'bail-out' policyholders.[73] Leaving aside the moral hazard repercussions, the public outrage *per se* is indicative of panic and low public confidence.[74] If it persists, a sharp drop in consumer demand cannot be ruled out causing liquidity shortage and making it more difficult for insurers to manage risks and to comply with solvency and capital adequacy requirements. To the extent in which the availability (or otherwise) of IGS bears on the chances of a distressed global insurer eventually becoming insolvent with wider systemic implications, it is recommended that the availability of IGS be explicitly included among the criteria for the assessment of the resolvability of G-SIIs and that the correlation between IGS and insolvency in the insurance sector be clearly reflected in the RRPs of G-SIIs as, for example, by mandating an action plan for overcoming any IGS-related obstacles that may arise in the case of a future resolution.

IGS also intersects with international coordination.[75] If nothing is done to promote some level of convergence, the differences between the existing national IGSs are bound to create uneven level of protection rendering international coordination far more cumbersome. A pervasive difficulty here is that some policyholders may find themselves covered, whereas others may find that they are not or that they are only entitled to a lower level of protection. Under circumstances like these, it will be difficult to reach a consensus on how best to proceed, as national authorities will be under pressure to give priority to the interests of the policyholders of their own jurisdiction. An IRF where a single point of entry is adopted would, of course, align the IGS with the geographic responsibilities of the lead resolution authority, which means that subsidiaries will be covered by the home state IGS of the parent company, but this arrangement might fall short from creating a level playing field between subsidiaries and domestic insurers within the same jurisdiction.

An IGS has the potential of becoming a useful tool for the orderly recovery and resolution of a G-SII. However, it may end up being a major hindrance, if not prop-

in features and level of protection. European Commission *White Paper On Insurance Guarantees Schemes* (Brussels 12.7.2010) at 5.

73 The cases of Equitable Life in the UK and HIH in Australia demonstrate this point quite well. See, *Equitable Life Payments Scheme: achieving a fair allocation and order of payments – Advice to the Government* (21 January 2011) and The HIH Royal Commission, *The Failure of HIH Insurance, Volume 1: A corporate collapse and its lessons*, Canberra 2003.

74 *OECD Report*, 'The impact of the financial crisis on the insurance sector and policy responses' (April 2010) noting that "While the insurance sector may not have the same liquidity challenges as banks, considerations of consumer confidence and protection may still arise and provide grounds for the establishment of a policyholder protection scheme" [Available at http://oecd.org/dataoecd/42/51//45044788.pdf].

75 For instance legal and regulatory divergence is conspicuous among EU member states. For a general discussion of the rate of insurers' insolvency in the EU between 1996 and 2004 see, Oxera 'Insurance Guarantee Schemes in the EU: Comparative analysis of existing schemes, analysis of problems and evaluation of options'. Final report prepared for European Commission DG Internal Market and Services (November 2007).

erly designed from the outset. A question that needs to be asked is what kind of IGS would be appropriate for a global scale IRF?

For a start, the IGS must be consistent with the objectives of the emerging IRF: it must be instrumental to the orderly recovery and resolution of G-SIIs by keeping systemic risk at bay, while at the same time operating in a way that eliminates moral hazard. It is submitted that an *ex ante* funded IGS via a system of levies imposed on the industry would be the best option. In the case of an *ex ante* funded scheme the funds are readily available to compensate claimants.[76] The scheme is also less subject to moral hazard, because insurers that become insolvent will already have contributed to the IGS.[77] In addition, pro-cyclicality is avoided given that insurers are not asked to make contributions under conditions of mounting financial distress and liquidity shortage.

To be sure, all these advantages must be carefully weighed against the costs associated with the set-up and operation of such a scheme.[78] In this regard, it is often argued that an IGS that is funded *ex ante* by way of industry levies increases the cost of insurance for consumers. This objection is not convincing. It is beside the point to exert a polemic against the case for an industry pre-funded IGS just because the cost will roll down to consumers; the latter may actually be willing to bear this additional cost in exchange for greater safety. More generally, the imposition of additional costs to consumers should not always be a matter of concern, as one always needs to ask first whether the market price of the service provided incorporates its actual cost.[79] If not – as, for example, in the case of insurance contracts where the cost of the IGS is not calculated into the price – the consumers pay less than they should have. In any case, the payment of IGS levies is hardly the cause of the problem; more often than not, an insurer's difficulty in meeting its IGS contribution can be suggestive of underlying solvency and liquidity issues. Accordingly, the sooner these are brought under the regulatory radar the better for implementing a credible RRP for the financially distressed insurer.

In those occasions where the risk insured is yet to materialize, an IGS can work as a vehicle for the provision of policyholder protection in two ways.[80] It can secure the continuity of risk coverage by having insurance policies transferred to a solvent insurer or by taking them over directly (portfolio transfer). Alternatively, an IGS may only compensate policyholders or beneficiaries for their losses. So far, the provision of compensation is regarded as a last resort measure, which is to be

76 Oxera above note 75 at 36.

77 Ibid. at 112. Although moral hazard is not exclusively associated with the behaviour of insurers (policyholders and regulators may exhibit this trait too) my focus is on the insurance industry because of its direct involvement in the delivery of the objectives of the emerging IRF.

78 Above note 75 at 116. The provision of caps or overriding limits on annual contributions as part of a scheme whereby contributions reflect the insurer's risk of recovery could waive industry concerns about the imposition of potentially unlimited size contributions. Furthermore, complementary *ex-post* funding arrangements (e.g. reinsurance or external credit facilities) could be introduced to alleviate the risk of funding shortfalls should a large insurer fail.

79 Affordability might be an issue but usually there are ways to deal with this problem. For instance, prices can go down by making the purchase of certain types of insurance mandatory as in the case of car insurance. I wish to thank Emmanuel Voyiakis for bringing this example to my attention.

80 S. Schich and B-H. Kim, 'Guarantee arrangements for financial promises: How widely should the safety net be cast?' (OECD, 2011) Volume 2011, Issue 1 *OECD Journal: Financial Market Trends* at 9.

made available only when all other means for securing the continuity of risk coverage are exhausted. Given the bearing of IGS on financial stability and the costs associated with its provision, it is worth considering whether compensation should become more readily available for some types of insurance and/or for some groups of policyholders. Arguably, compensation seems to be more appropriate in non-life-insurance cases.[81] Ultimately, such a determination must take into account a range of issues including: (a) the short- or long-term nature of the insurance contract in question; (b) the mandatory or voluntary character of the insurance, (c) the nature of the risk for which insurance coverage is sought; (d) the profile of the policyholder; and (e) the accessibility to comparable insurance coverage in the marketplace etc. Moreover, it is suggested that the provision of compensation need not entail equal amounts of compensation for all eligible policyholders. For example, those who suffered losses because they failed to make the gains which they had expected to make or those who were able to take mitigating action but did not should not be treated the same as those policyholders whose financial detriment could be only paralleled to that of depositors of a failed bank or a building society.[82]

8.4 Conclusion

The emerging IRF of G-SIIs draws on the existing resolution framework for banks and other SIFIs. At the same time, it aspires to be responsive to the idiosyncratic features of the insurance industry and to afford an appropriate level of flexibility so that regulatory responses are tailor-made to the circumstances of each particular case. It is based on three pillars: the first one is the identification of those activities that bear the potential of triggering systemic risk in the event of the disorderly failure of the insurer. The second pillar is the designation of certain insurers with global presence as G-SIIs. The third pillar is the adoption of policy measures that are geared towards the recovery of the financially distressed G-SII or – where this is no longer feasible – its orderly resolution. Ongoing resolvability assessments, RRPs, mandatory bail-ins and a soft law framework for coordinating measures for the orderly recovery and resolution of G-SIIs are some of the key elements of this regime, while the provision of run-off powers and policyholder protection are some of the features that separate the IRF from the recovery and resolution regimes applicable to non-insurance SIFIs.

The envisaged IRF is not perfect. This chapter brought attention to some

81 The collapse of a life insurer can result in considerable financial hardship for policyholders, especially for people who have bought life policies to provide for their retirement. Even if policyholders are able to recover part of their savings, they may not succeed in finding similar coverage because their personal situation on the basis of which premiums are calculated, has changed (e.g. in terms of age and health). Accordingly, these policyholders are better off if their contracts are continued rather than immediately terminated in order to receive compensation in cash. If a non-life insurer goes bankrupt, the average loss to policyholders is in general smaller and is usually limited to prepaid premiums. The contracts are short term and most policyholders can easily buy replacement cover from another company.

82 See, for instance, the points made in the Independent Commission on Equitable Life above note 73 at 26–27 (although in the case of Equitable Life, the compensation was funded by taxpayers' money – not the insurance industry – and it was granted on the grounds of maladministration, the nature of which was a repeated failure of a sequence of UK regulators to supervise Equitable Life properly).

difficulties and also made preliminary recommendations of how some of them might be addressed. In particular, it focused on: (a) the IAIS designation criteria; (b) the ongoing resolvability assessments; (c) the limitations of the RRPs; (d) the credibility of mandatory bail-ins for G-SIIs; (e) issues concerning international coordination and information sharing; and (f) IGSs as a tool for the containment of systemic risk triggers in the insurance sector and in that sense as a prerequisite for the effectiveness of the emerging IRF.

Key themes that emerged from the analysis and which will impact on the effectiveness of the IRF include the optimal level of administrative discretion and its bearing on standard setting, the importance of having in place a comprehensive data of resource management at a global level, market competition as a tool for the containment of the impact of an insurer's failure on the economy and the role of culture and cognitive challenge in improving situational awareness under circumstances of uncertainty. The conceptual foundations of the emerging IRF do not constitute a significant breakthrough from the norms that are embedded in the resolution framework of non-insurance SIFIs. This of course is an inconvenient truth as it begs the question of the suitability of the emerging resolution framework for global insurers and whether the recommended reforms are actually in the right direction. In the absence of an alternative frame of reference for thinking about the policy implications of insurance resolution and of the regulation of systemic risk in the insurance sector more generally, the answer to this question will have to be postponed for later. For the time being one thing is certain: The successful implementation of the proposed measures will ultimately depend on policy and legal reform at both domestic and regional level, the progress of harmonization and the willingness of the relevant authorities to share burdens and cooperate at a global level ideally by legally committing themselves to a forward-looking plan of action.

CHAPTER 9

The international regulation of systemic risk: the role of the leading international organizations, groups and standard-setting bodies in shaping the post-crisis reform of insurance regulation

Louise Steinberg

9.1 Introduction

Regardless of the approach a country applies when regulating its insurance market, whether it chooses to regulate by reference to principles or rules, and irrespective of the level of sophistication of its financial centre, regard must be had by it to the agenda prescribed by a cohort of powerful international organizations, government groupings and standard-setting agencies. Notwithstanding that the relevant international standards are not 'hard law', the broad international homogeneity in the regulations that apply to insurance companies bears testament to the influence of this inter-connected web of bodies.

Financial crises have been a feature of economic history over time. Government efforts to contain the impact of financial failure have gathered force as international trade and technological advances have facilitated the transfer of financial risk. Financial regulation has been alighted upon as the weapon of choice with which to address financial risk. A lack of empirical support notwithstanding, the prevailing consensus remains that provided every country is armed with the same regulatory tools applied uniformly, crises can be averted or at least contained.

There is no single international regulatory body authorized to design and implement insurance regulations across nation states. National regulators are, in principle (and subject to their commitments, for example, as members of the european Union (EU) or under the GATS[1]), free to cast their own rules for financial markets. Despite this apparently free hand, in fact the regulations that apply to insurers across nation states and the supervisory structures in place have considerably more in common than they have differences. Non-binding codes, principles and suggestions as to 'best practice' have evolved into international standards to which nation states defer. The standards that nation states have settled on are largely those promulgated by the International Association of Insurance Supervisors (the 'IAIS'). There are no material outliers.

In the absence of an international body charged with prescribing and enforcing 'hard' law (in the sense of formal, legally binding obligations that derive their authority from the sources identified by Article 38(1) of the Statute of the International

1 The General Agreement on Trade in Services.

Court of Justice), softer (but arguably no less effective) mechanisms have become the weapons of choice for setting insurance regulations that are designed to apply across nation states.[2] Since the 2007/2008 financial crisis, the 'soft' route to making law has been applied by the G20 (through the Financial Stability Board (the 'FSB'), the International Monetary Fund (the 'IMF') and the International Bank for Reconstruction and Development (the 'World Bank') in particular to tackle 'systemic risk': the key driver shaping the insurance regulation at present.[3]

Broad historical ambition notwithstanding, a review of the work of the international organisations and government groupings addressed by this chapter reveals that the threat of systemic risk has been a driver of regulatory reform long before the recent financial crisis. The 2007/2008 financial crisis has nevertheless prompted a redoubling of efforts by these bodies to shape financial regulation and to frame a regulatory template with global application.[4] The urgent need to contain what they identify as 'systemic risk'[5] is their clarion call and has been the reference point by which they have moved to secure a greater role in international governance. Perhaps mindful of the criticisms that the IMF in particular has historically faced for its weighted voting system and conditional loans[6] (alongside the ongoing issue as to the limit of its mandate by reference to Article IV), the G20 (through the FSB) has stepped in effectively above the IMF (in the global governance hierarchy) to frame the agenda that the other actors in this follow. In doing so the IMF's mandate (like that of the International Bank for Reconstruction and Development (the 'World Bank') and the IAIS) has been reinforced.

The inter-governmental groupings and standard-setting bodies ('SSBs') such as G20, the Basel Committee on Banking Supervision (the 'Basel Committee') and the IAIS are hugely influential beyond any national boundaries, despite their apparent lack of hard law-making power. The IAIS Codes and Principles increasingly shape many of the significant regulations that apply to insurance companies across the world. The influence of the government groups and SSBs has been secured by their having formed alliances between the most powerful countries, generating

---

2 Legal scholars do not agree on a definition of 'soft law' or indeed whether it exists at all. The expression 'soft law' in this chapter refers to 'non-binding normative instruments … containing principles, norms, standards, or other statements of expected behaviour' (D Shelton (2003), 'International Law and Relative Normativity', in M Evans (ed.), *International Law*, Oxford: OUP, 145 at 166.

3 C Brummer remarks that in contrast to international trade and monetary affairs, 'where global coordination efforts are led by formal international organizations, international financial law is promulgated by inter-agency forums with (at best) ambiguous legal status'. C Brummer (2010), 'Why Soft Law Dominates International Finance – and not Trade', *Journal of International Economic Law* 13(3): 623–643 at 623.

4 Interestingly, the Tietmeyer Report (see n. 52) makes many of the same proposals as the G20 recommended in response to the 2007/2008 financial crisis. In substance, that 'more of the same' is needed to avert systemic risk going forward.

5 The October 2009 report for G20 Finance Ministers and Governors (G20 Finance Ministers and Governors 'Guidance to Assess the Systemic Importance of Financial Institutions, Markets and Instruments: Initial Considerations', prepared by the IMF, the Bank for International Settlements (the 'BIS') and the FSB), found that current knowledge and understanding (as to a precise characterisation/definition) of systemic risk limits the extent to which very precise guidance can be developed and concluded that 'Assessments of systemic importance will necessarily involve a high degree of judgment'.

6 D Kalderimis (2004), 'IMF Conditionality as Investment Regulation: A Theoretical Analysis', *Social & Legal Studies* 13(1): 103–131, which argues that conditionality amounts to indirect regulation and therefore violates the states' sole right to regulate capital transactions.

consensus among members and effectively promoting those standards internationally. The lead in building this consensus has now been taken by the G20 countries[7] (through the FSB, which replaced the Financial Stability Forum ('FSF') in 2009) and the IMF. The enormous influence and reach of these organisations and groups notwithstanding, as other academics contributing to this book have emphasized, whether systemic risk can be effectively defined, averted or contained is far from clear.[8]

9.2 Setting the global standards for insurance regulation and supervision: the IAIS

Twenty years after the Basel Committee assumed its leading role in setting the international standards for the prudential regulation of banks, the IAIS made its early tentative steps towards establishing itself as a body setting the prudential standards for the regulation of insurance.[9]

The IAIS members now comprise insurance regulators and supervisors from more than 200 jurisdictions in nearly 140 countries. Collectively member countries write 97% of the world's insurance premiums.[10] A number of international organizations including the World Bank and the IMF are members of the IAIS, although they have no right to vote or join the IAIS Executive Committee.[11] The IAIS characterizes its objectives as being to: (1) promote effective and globally consistent supervision of the insurance industry in order to develop and maintain fair, safe and stable insurance markets for the benefit and protection of policyholders; and (2) to contribute to global financial stability.[12]

Although the work of the Basel Committee is not considered here, its influence in the context of the regulation of insurance is material. From the outset, the IAIS has adopted the regulatory template that the Basel Committee designed. The substance of the IAIS core principles, standards and codes closely resemble those set by the Basel Committee. The approach which the IAIS has adopted to address systemic risk likewise tracks the work of the Basel Committee and the regulation of banks.[13]

A number of committees have been established to ensure a common approach between the three SSBs (the Basel Committee, the IAIS and the International Organization of Securities Commissions ('IOSCO') including the Joint Forum that was established in 1996 (under the aegis of the Basel Committee and the IAIS) to

7 See www.g20.org/about_G20.

8 See the issue discussed in G Schinasi, 'Defining Financial Stability', IMF Working Paper WP/04/187, Washington, D.C.: International Monetary Fund.

9 For a detailed history of the IAIS, see www.nottingham.ac.uk/business/cris/papers/Grif%20-%20Ed%20Forshaw.pdf (last accessed 5 August 2012).

10 See www.iaisweb.org/About-the-IAIS/IAIS-members-31 (last accessed 12 October 2014).

11 The IAIS By-Laws Adopted 25 October 2014, Articles 6, 2(e) and (5). Article 11 recites that decisions are taken by a two-thirds majority. An assessment of the level of participation in decision making and the interplay between the SSBs and international organizations within the IAIS is hampered by the fact that few documents (including minutes of meetings) are publicly available.

12 See the IAIS homepage at www.iaisweb.org (last accessed 11 October 2014).

13 C Goodhart (2011), *The Basel Committee on Banking Supervision*, Cambridge: Cambridge University Press provides a fascinating insight into the history of the Committee and its formation. A similar analysis of the IAIS would be very valuable.

deal with common issues.[14] The Financial Stability Institute ('FSI') was created jointly in 1999 by the BIS and the Basel Committee to 'assist financial sector supervisors around the world in improving and strengthening their financial systems'.[15] The efforts of these committees mirror efforts made more widely to ensure a convergence of the regulations applied across financial sectors (as well as across nation states) to close gaps and discourage regulatory arbitrage.

Where the Basel Committee is able to claim legitimacy as a standard-setting body by reference to the G10[16] group of countries that created it, the IAIS has secured its standard-setting role over time. The IAIS has no legislative power to impose regulatory standards and codes on member countries. Its strength and effectiveness rests on the inter-linking relationship between the SSBs and international organizations. In particular, the influence of the IAIS standards and codes is secured by their place in the IMF and the World Bank Financial Sector Assessment Program ('FSAP').[17]

Following the most recent financial crisis the FSB has moved to promote global adherence to the 'international standards' on the basis that a failure to comply presented a weakness in the global financial system.[18] The influence of the IAIS has grown as a result of the clear mandate that the FSB has given it to identify sources of systemic risk in insurance. In the battle to address systemic risk, the FSB has settled on an approach to target a defined category of financial institutions, namely systemically important financial institutions ('SIFIs'). At the 2010 summit in Seoul, G20 Leaders endorsed the policy framework for SIFIs and particularly global institutions (G-SIFIs), both in promulgating and transmitting instability.[19] The IAIS was charged (by the FSB) with developing an assessment methodology for the identification of global systemically important insurers (insurers whose distress or disorderly failure would cause significant disruption to the global financial system) ('G-SIIs').[20]

At the request of the FSB, the IAIS has formulated a basic capital requirement that will, in future, apply to all group activities of G-SIIs, including non-insurance activities. G20 states have committed to introduce the enhanced regulation of G-SIIs (and G-SIFIs) by virtue of their membership. The IMF and the FSB will

14 See www.bis.org/bcbs/jointforum.htm.

15 Details of the 2015 conference can be found at www.bis.org/fsi/fsi2015.pdf.

16 See www.bis.org/list/g10publications/index.htm (last accessed 6 June 2015).

17 See www.imf.org/external/NP/fsap/fsap.aspx (last accessed 6 June 2015). Although the support of the World Bank, the IMF, the FSB and the other SSBs (the Basel Committee and IOSCO) is key to understanding the influence of the IAIS, the educational outreach programmes, as well as the technical training and support that it offers members serve to encourage compliance.

18 The FSB statement 10 March 2010. See www.financialstabilityboard.org/wp-content/uploads/r_100310.pdf?page_moved=1 (last accessed 6 June 2015). The three key financial regulatory and supervisory standards are the BCBS Core Principles for Effective Banking Supervision, the IAIS Insurance Core Principles, and the IOSCO Objectives and Principles of Securities Regulation.

19 http://www.financialstabilityboard.org/2010/10/financial-stability-baord-meets-in-seoul/ (last accessed 6 June 2015).

20 For an overview of the efforts to identify insurers who present a systemic risk, see the Geneva Association's Paper Special Contribution/SC14, D Haefeli and P Liedtke (April 2012), 'Reflections on a High-Quality G-SIFI Designation Process in Insurance'. Available at www.genevaassociation.org/media/174765/GA2012-IFSC14.pdf (last accessed 25th June 2015). See also http://www.inese.es/c/document_library/get_file?uuid=fcac524f-8efb-42ff-b85b-47d84be62fea&groupId=129513 (last accessed 25th June 2015) and the Geneva Association's Annual Report 2014/2015 at https://www.genevaassociation.org/media/919061/ga2015-annual_report.pdf (last accessed 25 June 2015).

monitor compliance. Implementation details for higher loss absorbency requirements are intended to be released by the end of this year and will apply from January 2019 to those G-SIIs identified in November 2017.[21] Although the balance of this chapter considers the significance of the IAIS through the lens of the other mutually reinforcing actors that form the key components of the international financial architecture, the most recent work of the IAIS in setting enhanced capital standards amounts to a significant increase in its influence.[22]

9.3 International organizations – an overview[23]

By virtue of their membership, the IAIS member countries commit to implement the IAIS supervisory material and undergo self-assessment and peer review.[24] Nevertheless, given that membership of the IAIS is voluntary, these standards and codes cannot be enforced. That the standards and codes have been effectively folded into national law across member countries is attributable to the inter-locking nature of global governance shaping financial law internationally. The United Nations, the World Bank, the IMF, the World Trade Organization (the 'WTO') and the EU[25] are key centres of influence.

The organizations and groups that shape the regulatory framework within which insurance and the wider financial services industry operate take many legal shapes and sizes. In the absence of a single international body able to set and enforce agreed rules that apply, global governance of the financial sector is achieved consensually by the collaboration of various bodies that have assumed responsibility for global financial stability.

There are two main types of international organizations: international non-governmental organizations (that may be profit making or not) and intergovernmental organizations. Intergovernmental organizations are broadly focused on maintaining international peace and/or stable and open financial markets. Their legal features generally include that they are established by multinational treaty[26] under international law, they are created by and their membership consists of states, they have a permanent institutional element[27] and usually (in order to avoid challenging national sovereignty) promote consensus through communication, recommendation and cooperation rather than through compulsion or enforcement.

21 See www.financialstabilityboard.org/2013/07/CoS_130718 (last accessed 25 June 2015).

22 See the IAIS Newsletter (June 2015) which provides an update on the progress of the IAIS capital-related stakeholder meetings at http://iaisweb.org/index.cfm?event=showPage&nodeId=25303 (last accessed 25 June 2015).

23 An exhaustive study of the hundreds of international organisations that exist is not attempted here. There are, of course, a panoply of other organizations and groupings that operate in the international arena and who may, on occasion, involve themselves in issues that impact on insurance. These include NAFTA, CARICOM, Mercosur and ASEAN. Their role is not addressed here.

24 The IAIS 2014 By-Laws Art. 6(5).

25 This is not to suggest that the EU is an international organization in the conventional sense.

26 Article 1 of the *The Vienna Convention on the Law of Treaties* (1969), defines a treaty as 'an international agreement between States in written form and governed by international law'.

27 N White (2005), *The Law of International Organizations*, 2nd ed., Manchester: Manchester University Press, at 1.

The key international organizations shaping financial regulation today were formed in the shadow of the Second World War when 44 countries represented at the conference at Bretton Woods in July 1944[28] formed a new wartime coalition determined to shape the international movements of capital, stabilize foreign exchange rates[29] and limit barriers to free trade and investment in the post-war world.[30] Three international organizations were conceived at Bretton Woods: the World Bank), the IMF and the International Trade Organization ('the ITO'). The General Agreement on Tariffs and Trade ('GATT') was settled in 1947 (superseding the ITO) as the organization focused on the creation of a global and open trading system. By the end of 1994, the WTO had replaced GATT in this role.

Although each of the main international organizations has a clearly defined focus which may not appear directly connected to the regulation of financial institutions (for example, the United Nations has security, the World Bank and the IMF monetary policy, the WTO has trade) it is misleading to view their impact as being limited to those narrow areas of primary concern. What the architects of these organizations had in common was a belief that peace and economic development required stable financial markets. The ongoing instability of financial markets, as evidenced by a series of financial crises, remains a key reference point.

9.4 The World Bank

The World Bank comprises the International Bank for Reconstruction and Development (the 'IBRD'), the International Development Association, the International Finance Corporation, the Multilateral Investment Guarantee Agency ('MIGA') and the International Centre for Settlement of Investment Disputes. There are presently 188 member countries.[31] The Articles of Association of the IBRD were drawn up at Bretton Woods and describe its purpose as '[t]o assist in the reconstruction and development of territories of members by facilitating the investment of capital for productive purposes ... the encouragement of the development of productive facilities and resources in less developed countries' as well as promoting 'the long-range balanced growth of international trade and the maintenance of equilibrium ...' (Article I). Article IV of the IBRD provides that 'The Bank and its Officers shall not interfere in the political affairs of any member ...'[32]

28 The United Nations Monetary and Financial Conference, Bretton Woods, New Hampshire.

29 By pinning the rates to the price of gold at $35 per ounce.

30 Under Bretton Woods, countries agreed to make their currencies convertible but they were also allowed (under Art. iv) to control capital movements. Previously (at the Brussels International Financial Conference 1920) a resolution condemning all barriers to the international movement of capital had been passed (League of Nations 1920:9) referred to in Eric Helleiner, 'Regulating the Regulators The Emergence and Limits of the Transnational Finanial Legal Order' in chapter 6 of 'Transnational Legal Orders' edited by Terence C. Halliday, Gregory Shaffer, Cambridge University Press (2015) at page 233.

31 To become a member of the Bank, under the IBRD Articles of Agreement, a country must first join the IMF. See www.worldbank.org/en/about/leadership/members (last accessed 6 June 2015).

32 See the articles at: http://web.worldbank.org/WBSITE/EXTERNAL/EXTABOUTUS/ORGANIZATION/BODEXT/0,,contentMDK:50004943~menuPK:64020045~pagePK:64020054~piPK:64020408~theSitePK:278036,00.html (last accessed 25 June 2015).

In common with the other international organizations considered here, systemic risk is an increasing focus of the World Bank. This is characterized by the World Bank as a disturbance in the financial system that is serious enough to affect the real economy.[33]

Along with the other interlocking sites of global governance, the World Bank encourages the application of macroprudential policies to address systemic risk (policies aiming to reduce systemic risks arising from 'excessive' financial procyclicality and from interconnections and other 'cross-sectional' factors in particular).[34] As part of the policy armoury (to meet 'interconnected externalities' as it sees them), it endorses the view that systemically important financial intermediaries should be identified and subjected to stricter prudential regulation depending on their systemic footprint.[35]

Macroprudential policies are not the only policies that the World Bank favours to tackle financial instability. The World Bank characterizes 'systemic vulnerabilities' as volatility in capital flows that adversely affect output and consumption.[36] In developing countries in particular, the World Bank regards the provision of insurance as a tool to address risk in this context and intervenes, through MIGA, to provide political risk insurance guarantees to private sector investors and lenders where the commercial insurance market is unavailable to underwrite risk.[37] MIGA has, for example, provided political risks insurance to promote investment in Bosnia and Herzegovina, Kenya, Sierra Leone and Lao.[38]

The World Bank's influence on the regulation of insurance is most prominent in its work with the IMF.[39] The role of the FSAP in shaping the regulation of insurance markets by reference to financial stability has gained considerable traction as a result of the international agenda-setting role assumed by the G20 in the shadow

33 A report by the Group of Ten (2001) (see www.bis.org/publ/gten05.html) defined systemic risk as 'the risk that an event will trigger a loss of economic value or confidence in, and attendant increases in uncertainty about, a substantial portion of the financial system that is serious enough to quite probably have significant adverse effects on the real economy'. For an insightful discussion, see M Dijkman (2010), 'A framework for assessing systemic risk'. Available at https://ideas.repec.org/p/wbk/wbrwps/5282.html (last accessed 25 June 2015).

34 Adopting the definition proposed by S Claessens (December 2014), 'An Overview of Macroprudential Policy Tools', IMF Working Paper, Washington, D.C.: International Monetary Fund. Available at: www.imf.org/external/pubs/ft/wp/2014/wp14214.pdf (last accessed 25 June 2015).

35 See the issue discussed at: https://openknowledge.worldbank.org/bitstream/handle/10986/10967/535450BRI0lcr0110LCR0Crisis0Briefs1.txt?sequence=2 (last accessed 25 June 2015).

36 See the World Bank paper (31 March 2008), 'Country Insurance: Reducing Systemic Vulnerabilities in LAC. Available at: http://siteresources.worldbank.org/INTLAC/Resources/CountryInsuranceFinal.pdf (last accessed 25 June 2015).

37 See www.miga.org/investmentguarantees/index.cfm?stid=1796 (last accessed 25 June 2015). See, for example, the World Bank paper (31 March 2008), 'Country Insurance: Reducing Systemic Vulnerabilities in Latin America and the Caribbean'. Available at https://openknowledge.worldbank.org/handle/10986/8010 (last accessed 25 June 2014).

38 See the World Bank's paper discussing the support provided to Bosnia and Herzegovina (paper No 13 2004) at: www.academia.edu/3879551/MIGAs_Experience_in_Conflict-Affected_Countries._The_Case_of_Bosnia_and_Herzegovina (last accessed 26 January 2015).

39 World Bank (March 2015), 'Reports on the Observances of Standards and Codes'. Available at: www.imf.org/external/NP/rosc/rosc.aspx (last accessed 25 June 2015).

of the 2007/2008 financial crisis. The detail of the FSAP and the World Bank's collaboration with the IMF and the IAIS is considered later in this chapter.[40]

9.5 The IMF

The IMF was set up in 1944 chiefly with a mandate to ensure exchange rate stability. Following the abandonment of the gold standard in 1971, the IMF has moved to establish a broader global role which it characterizes as helping to 'ensure stability in the international system'.[41] It moves to meet this role through a combination of activities including its work with the World Bank. In particular, the IMF's efforts to shape the regulation of insurance markets (as well as financial markets more widely) is undertaken through loans offered to member countries and well as technical assistance and surveillance. Article IV, Section 1 of the Fund's Articles requires members 'to collaborate with the Fund and other members to assure orderly exchange arrangements and to promote a stable system of exchange rate'.[42] This, the IMF characterizes as 'systemic stability'.[43]

The IMF (like the World Bank) is a member of the IAIS, although as minutes of the IAIS members' meetings are not available on its website, the precise nature of the role that the IMF plays in the IAIS meetings is opaque. We can nevertheless glean from the statements of the IMF, the World Bank and the G20 that those organizations largely frame the agenda that the IAIS moves to address.

9.5.1 Surveillance

A key part of the IMF's work by reference to Article IV involves monitoring member states' financial conditions and policies, a process that it calls 'surveillance'.[44] This process has significant implications for the regulation of insurance. Not least as, in the context of insurance, the IMF has moved to benchmark necessary regulatory reform by reference to the IAIS Core Principles.

The IMF's surveillance role is undertaken by reference to the mandate endorsed by member states in 1976, when they agreed to revise the IMF's Articles and add

40 The World Bank/IMF 1998 joint management statement set out the agreed principles for this collaboration.

41 See the IMF's website at www.imf.org/external/about/ourwork.htm (last accessed 6 June 2015).

42 See www.imf.org/external/pubs/ft/aa/index.htm#a4s1 (last accessed 6 June 2015).

43 See IMF, Mandatory Financial Stability Assessments under the Financial Sector Assessment Program: Update, 15 November 2013. Available at: www.imf.org/external/np/pp/eng/2013/111513.pdf (last accessed 6 June 2015).

44 The IMF's approach to surveillance is detailed in a 'Factsheet' on its website: International Monetary Fund (2014), 'IMF Surveillance'. Available at: www.imf.org/external/np/exr/facts/surv.htm (last accessed 17 January 2015). See also IMF surveillance: D Lombardi and N Woods (2008), 'The Politics of Influence: An Analysis of IMF Surveillance', *Review of International Political Economy* 15: 711; B Bossone (2008), 'The Effectiveness of IMF Surveillance: A study on global financial governance', *World Economics* 9: 27. The IMF is not the only organisation engaged in surveillance. The Organization for Economic Cooperation and Development (the 'OECD'), various United Nations agencies and regional organisations also undertake reviews that overlap with the IMF's activities. What is different about the IMF is the breadth and depth of its reach.

a new Article IV 'Obligations Regarding Exchange Arrangements.'[45] Article IV restates members' commitments to promoting economic growth and exchange rate stability and established exchange rate reporting and surveillance requirements. The text of Article IV refers to the Fund's role as being to 'oversee the international monetary system in order to ensure its effective operation' as well as to 'exercise firm surveillance over the exchange rate policies of members, and . . . adopt specific principles for the guidance of all members with respect to those policies'.[46] As a result of this provision, all 188 member states are committed by virtue of their membership to the peer review and oversight of their economy, a commitment that has allowed the IMF the opportunity to influence financial regulation.[47]

The rationale for the surveillance initiative has been summarized by the IMF as being that the global 'adoption of internationally recognized standards of good practice [would help] foster financial market stability and better risk assessment'. Compliance with standards would enable a country to 'mitigate the impact of an external crisis by supporting continued access to external borrowing', and 'help prevent crises' by reducing the cost of foreign capital so that a government could 'remain solvent in cases it otherwise might not have remained solvent'.[48] In the view of the IMF and of the World Bank 'Standards and codes are benchmarks of good practices'.[49]

The turbulence that swept through financial markets in the 1990s (including the European exchange rate mechanism crisis in 1992–93; the Mexican Crisis of 1994–95; the East Asian crisis of 1997–98; and in the Autumn of 1998, a crisis sparked by Russia's unilateral debt restructuring) prompted the IMF to move to strengthen its programme of surveillance. At a meeting on 30 October 1998, the G7 declared their intention: to support the establishment of a process for strengthened financial sector surveillance using national and international regulatory and supervisory expertise, including through the IMF's regular surveillance of its member countries under Article IV. The G7 resolved to bring together the key international institutions and key national authorities involved in financial sector stability. The aim was to encourage better cooperation and coordination in the management and development of policies to foster stability and reduce systemic risk in the international financial system and to exchange information more systematically on risks in

45 Available at: www.imf.org/external/np/exr/facts/surv.htm (last accessed 6 June 2015). The IMF's October 2014 Global Financial Stability Report is available at: www.imf.org/external/pubs/ft/gfsr/index.htm. In July 2012 the Executive Board issued a new Decision on Bilateral and Multilateral Surveillance (the Integrated Surveillance Decision) to strengthen the underlying legal framework for surveillance, and discussed the first Pilot External Sector Report. In September 2012, the Executive Board endorsed a new Financial Surveillance Strategy.

46 Available at: www.imf.org/external/pubs/ft/aa/index.htm#art4 (last accessed 6 June 2015).

47 D Lombardi and N Woods (2007), 'The Political Economy of IMF Surveillance', Centre for International Governance Innovation Working Paper No. 17, Waterloo: Centre for International Governance Innovation, p. 9.

48 C Christofides, C Mulder and A Tiffin (April 2003), 'The Link Between Adherence to International Standards of Good Practice, Foreign Exchange Spreads, and Ratings', IMF Working Paper WP/03/74, Washington, D.C.: International Monetary Fund, p. 26. Available at: www.imf.org/external/pubs/ft/wp/2003/wp0374.pdf.

49 IMF Fact Sheet at: www.imf.org/external/np/exr/facts/sc.htm (last accessed 6 June 2015).

the international financial system.[50] The G7 members reiterated the importance of the standards and codes of good practice in improving the functioning of markets.[51]

Dr Hans Tietmeyer (then President of the Deutsche Bundesbank) was charged by the G7 with consulting the relevant international bodies (in particular the IMF and the World Bank) on the reforms necessary to: (1) strengthen financial sector surveillance including through a process of peer review, and the IMF's regular surveillance of its member countries under Article IV; and (2) bring together the key international institutions and key national authorities involved in financial sector stability better to cooperate and to coordinate their activities in the management and development of policies to foster stability and reduce systemic risk.[52] On the recommendation of the Tietmeyer Report that followed, the FSF (now the FSB) was established in February 1999. The existing collaborative, mutually reinforcing relationships between the IMF, the World Bank, the IAIS and national authorities were crystallized by reference to Dr Tietmeyer's recommendations.

The World Bank and the IMF launched the FSAP in 1999 to 'help to better identify weaknesses that may contribute to economic and financial vulnerability, foster market efficiency and discipline, and ultimately contribute to a global economy, which is more robust and less prone to crisis'.[53] The FSAPs are intended to gauge the economic health and financial stability of member states in large part by tracking their compliance with internationally recognized standards and codes within twelve areas.[54] Based on their findings, FSAPs produce 'recommendations of a micro and macro-prudential nature, tailored to country-specific circumstances'.[55] FSAPs conclude with the preparation of a Financial System Stability Assessment ('FSSA'). These reports clearly aim to influence the way in which nation states regulate their financial markets.[56]

The twelve sets of standards and codes that the IMF applies in its surveillance programme fall into three main areas: policy transparency, market integrity and financial sector regulation and supervision. The IMF (and the World Bank) identify these standards and codes as representing 'benchmarks of good practice'.[57] They are characterized as being able to 'help countries identify key sources of systemic

50 For an insightful review of the how the influence of the standards and codes evolved, see D Drezner (2007) *All Politics Is Global: Explaining International Regulatory Regimes*, Princeton, NJ: Princeton University Press.

51 Available at: www.financialstabilityboard.org/wp-content/uploads/pr_981003.pdf (last accessed 26 January 2015).

52 Available at: www.bis.org/review/r990225b.pdf (last accessed 26 January 2015).

53 World Bank (2015), 'Reports on the Observances of Standards and Codes'. Available at: www.worldbank.org/ifa/rosc.html (last accessed 6 June 2015).

54 International Monetary Fund (2002), 'List of Standards, Codes and Principles Useful for Bank and Fund Operational Work and for which Reports on the Observance of Standards and Codes Are Produced'. Available at: www.imf.org/external/standards/scnew.htm (last accessed 25 June 2015).

55 Available at: www.imf.org/external/np/fsap/fssa.aspx (last accessed 25 June 2015).

56 For example, in the 2013 FSSA, the IMF recommended that proposals 'by the European Commission … to harmonize capital requirements, resolution … and insurance supervision frameworks at the EU level should be implemented promptly'. The IMF described as a 'high priority recommendation' the adoption and implementation of Solvency II. See FSSA Executive Summary for Europe 22 February 2013. Available at: www.imf.org/external/pubs/ft/scr/2013/cr1375.pdf (last accessed 25 June 2015).

57 International Monetary Fund (2015), 'Standards and Codes: The Role of the IMF', IMF Factsheet. Available at: www.imf.org/external/np/exr/facts/pdf/sc.pdf (last accessed 25 June 2015).

risk in the financial sector and implement policies to enhance its resilience to shocks and contagion'. [58] As highlighted earlier in this chapter, in the context of insurance, the standards that the IMF and the World Bank apply as representing best practice are the 'Insurance Supervisory Principles' prepared by the IAIS.[59]

Since the latest global financial crisis, with the support of the G20 (and the FSB), the IMF has announced a shift in its activities in favour of a 'systemic vision'.[60] Again the aim has been to strengthen the effectiveness (and influence) of surveillance by monitoring exchange rates and underlying macroeconomic policies, as well as global economic trends.[61] In substance the IMF has sought to widen its remit to 'strengthen the Fund's role as the guardian of systemic stability'.[62]

The changes that have been made include a delineation of institutional responsibilities between the IMF (stability assessments) and the World Bank (development assessment) and a move to clearly define the components of stability assessments (vulnerabilities and resilience of the financial system, regulatory and supervisory framework, and financial safety nets). Stress-testing has become a central aspect of the IMF's bilateral and multilateral surveillance work through the FSAP. Insurance stress-testing has played only a secondary role relative to the analysis of the banking sector risks. Since 1999, the IMF has published 22 stress tests of the insurance sector out of a total of 256 FSAP reports published (as of February 2014).[63]

Assessments of compliance with international financial sector standards (summarized in a Report on Observance of Standards and Codes) are described by the IMF as being voluntary (even in countries for which an FSAP stability assessment is a mandatory part of surveillance).[64] Nevertheless, since the FSAP was launched in 1999 after the financial crisis in Asia, 142 countries have been assessed. The IMF reports that followed made recommendations as to appropriate reforms to each country's financial sector.[65]

58 See IMF (January 2014), *Financial System Stability Assessment Report on Canada*, Washington, D.C.: International Monetary Fund, at 1. Available at: www.imf.org/external/pubs/ft/scr/2014/cr1429.pdf. See http://www.financialstabilityboard.org/what-we-do/about-the-compendium-of-standards/key_standards/ (last accessed 25 June 2015.)

59 Document A/C.6/65/L.7. See a summary provided by the UN Department of Public Information of the Sixty-Fifth General Assembly, Sixth Committee, 27th Meeting (PM) (dated 5 November 2010). Available at: www.un.org/News/Press/docs/2010//gal3405.doc.htm (last accessed 18 May 2011).

60 R Lavigne and L Schembri (2009), 'Strengthening IMF Surveillance: An Assessment of Recent Reforms', Bank of Canada discussion paper 2009–10, Ottawa: Bank of Canada.

61 For an overview, see D Lombardi and N Woods (2008), 'The Politics of Influence: An Analysis of IMF Surveillance', *Review of International Political Economy* 15(5): 711–739.

62 See D Strauss-Kahn (2010), 'An IMF for the 21st century'. Available at: www.imf.org/external/np/speeches/2010/022610.htm (last accessed 25 June 2015). This speech, by the then managing director of the IMF, addressing the Brettton Woods Annual Conference on 26 February 2010, outlined the IMF's proposal that its surveillance role going forward would enable the construction of a 'global risk map'. For an overview of the issues relevant to a review of the IMF's legal mandate, see IMF (2010), 'The Fund's mandate – an overview of issues and legal framework', IMF Public Information Notice no. 10/33. Available at: www.imf.org/external/np/sec/pn/2010/pn1033.htm (last accessed 18 March 2011).

63 See 'Macroprudential Solvency Stress Testing of the Insurance Sector', IMF Working Paper 14/33, Washington, D.C.: International Monetary Fund. Available at: www.imf.org/external/pubs/ft/wp/2014/wp14133.pdf (last accessed 6 June 2015).

64 Available at: www.imf.org/external/np/fsap/faq/index.htm#q1 (last accessed 6 June 2015).

65 *Ibid.*

In September 2010,[66] the IMF made it mandatory for 25 jurisdictions with systemically important financial sectors to undergo financial stability assessments under the FSAP every five years.[67] The list of jurisdictions for these mandatory assessments was based on the size and interconnectedness of their financial sectors.[68] For all other jurisdictions, FSAP participation continues to be voluntary.

9.5.2 Conditionality

The current reform of the IMF's conditionality is perhaps the latest development in relation to the role of the Fund in promoting financial stability and effective systemic risk management. The IMF describes a key part of its role as providing financial support to countries facing liquidity crises so that they have time to 'implement corrective policies to restore economic stability and growth'.[69] Since the 1950s, where it provides financial assistance, the IMF has required borrowing countries to sign a 'Letter of Intent' confirming their commitment to structural reform.[70] The concept of 'conditionality' was introduced on the basis that it was required by the IMF's Articles to ensure that resources are made available subject to 'adequate safeguards'.[71] It remains controversial. To some extent, the terms of the loans are a tool to shape a country's financial system and have a role in shaping the regulation of insurance markets. Although a number of countries have made regulatory reform commitments as part of the conditions attached to the loans, to the extent that the IMF intended to anchor compliance with the standards and codes to conditions, this has been resisted by a number of developing countries (including India).[72] Instead the IMF has moved to encourage compliance with the standards and codes through technical assistance, training, and support and moral suasion.

9.5.3 Technical assistance

Technical assistance is characterized by the IMF as helping countries 'develop more effective institutions, legal frameworks, and policies to promote economic

66 Available at: www.imf.org/external/np/sec/pr/2010/pr10357.htm (last accessed 17 January 2015).

67 The list was expanded to 29 jurisdictions in 2013. Available at: www.imf.org/external/np/fsap/mandatoryfsap.htm (last accessed 6 June 2015).

68 Financial Stability Board (2011), 'Mandate'. Available at: www.financialstabilityboard.org/about/mandate/ (last accessed 15 January 2015).

69 IMF's response to the Global Economic Crisis (27 March 2015). Available at: www.imf.org/external/np/exr/facts/changing.htm (last accessed 6 June 2015).

70 See A Buira (2003), 'An Analysis of IMF conditionality', G-24 Discussion Papers 22, Geneva: United Nations Conference on Trade and Development; D Kalderimis (2004), 'IMF conditionality as investment regulation: a theoretical analysis', *Social & Legal Studies* 13(1): 103–131, which argues that conditionality amounts to indirect regulation and therefore violates the states' sole right to regulate capital transactions.

71 See A Newburg (2000), 'The Changing Roles of the Bretton Woods Institutions: Evolving Concepts of Conditionality', in M Giovanoli (ed.), *International Monetary Law: Issues for the New Millennium*, Oxford: Oxford University Press. The IMF's overview of its conditionality framework is available at: www.imf.org/external/np/exr/facts/conditio.htm (last accessed 22 January 2015).

72 Which was the intention; see http://siteresources.worldbank.org/PROJECTS/Resources/imf-wb-conditionality08-22-01.pdf; www.thehindu.com/2000/09/25/stories/03250002.htm (last accessed 25 January 2015).

stability and inclusive growth'.[73] Training through practical policy-oriented courses, hands-on workshops, and seminars strengthens officials' capacity to analyze economic developments and formulate and implement effective policies is designed to 'complement to the IMF's other core functions of surveillance and lending'.[74] Through these initiatives the IMF encourages the application of the standards and codes and helps ensure consistency in their interpretation.

9.6 The FSB

Evidence that efforts to secure the stability of the financial system through internationally formulated and agreed standards and codes had failed is clear from the 2007/2008 financial crisis. Rather than abandon the approach, the G20 seized the initiative to drive forward international regulatory reform and with it regulatory convergence, again by reference to the application of the standards and codes.[75] The view seems to have been that the formula was not unsound, it just needed to be improved and more widely applied. A key failing, which the G20 identified, related to the oversight and monitoring of cross-border institutions and markets.[76]

On 13 September 2009, the FSB released its 'Charter'. Article 1 describes the objectives of the FSB as being 'to coordinate at the international level the work of national financial authorities and international SSBs in order to develop and promote the implementation of effective regulatory, supervisory and other financial sector policies. In collaboration with the international financial institutions, the FSB will address vulnerabilities affecting financial systems in the interest of global financial stability'.[77] The FSB[78] now has 42 members including all G20 countries, former FSF members, Spain, 26 representatives of national authorities for financial stability from 11 financial centers as well as the EU Commission and Council, the United Nations, the World Bank, the IMF and the WTO.[79] US Treasury Secretary Tim Geithner described the FSB's ambition as to be no less than the 'fourth pillar' of the architecture of global economic governance alongside the IMF, the World Bank and the WTO.[80]

In its Report dated 25 September 2009, the FSB stated its view that the present financial crisis has 'highlighted the moral hazards that are posed by institutions that have become too big to fail or that, by their interconnected nature, are too

73 Available at: www.imf.org/external/np/exr/facts/tech.htm (last accessed 6 June 2015).

74 See IMF Factsheet 17 September 2014 (last accessed 12 February 2015).

75 G20 Leaders' Declaration, Washington DC, 15 November, 2008. Available at: www.oecd.org/g20/meetings/washingtondc/declarationofthesummitonfinancialmarketsandtheworldeconomy.htm (last accessed 6 June 2015).

76 G20 Leader's Declaration on Strengthening the Financial System 2 April 2009. Available at: www.iasplus.com/en/binary/resource/0904g20communique2.pdf (last accessed 5 February 2015).

77 Available at: www.financialstabilityboard.org/wp-content/uploads/r_120809.pdf (last accessed 6 June 2015). Decisions by the FSB are made in plenary by consensus (which is not formerly defined, see Article 9(2)).

78 This was established as an association under Swiss law.

79 Available at: www.financialstabilityboard.org/.

80 Press Briefing by US Treasury Secretary Tim Geithner on the G20 meeting, Pittsburgh 24 September 2009.

complex too resolve'. It adds (at page 4) that the crisis had 'also illustrated the potential risks to the world economy from financial market problems, and the threat of chain reactions in the financial sector'.[81] The Report refers to the 'paramount importance of mitigating systemic risk by better understanding and alleviating the factors that cause it'. The FSB framework aims to strengthen adherence to international regulatory and prudential standards by building on IMF and World Bank assessments. The FSB member countries have agreed to lead by example in disclosing their degree of compliance. Article 5 of the FSB Charter provides that member jurisdictions commit to: (a) pursue the maintenance of financial stability; (b) maintain the openness and transparency of the financial sector; (c) implement international financial standards; and (d) undergo periodic peer reviews, using among other evidence IMF/World Bank public FSAP reports.

Although the focus of the FSB has been on banking, the regulation of insurance is being carried along in its slipstream. One of the fundamental areas for reform identified by the FSB is what it perceives as an urgent need to strengthen adherence to international supervisory and regulatory standards. In the context of insurance, those standards are those of the IAIS. The case for a harmonized set of legal standards is made by reference to 'systemic risk'.[82] In the context of insurance, the pace has been set by a number of initiatives:

(1) efforts by the G20, through the FSB and in collaboration with the IMF and World Bank in particular, to regulate, as they see it, 'systemic risk';
(2) the desire to put in place consistent rules across financial market sectors (insurance, banking and securities);
(3) to specifically regulate the activity of insurance companies that are identified as being systemically risky;
(4) to develop and apply regulations to those insurance companies which are regarded as 'too big to fail'; and
(5) shaping effective resolution regimes.

Much of the early work of the G20 and the FSF/FSB proceeded without a clear idea of the nature of the risk that the financial system faced as a result of activity in financial markets and the interdependence between nations and financial sectors. The role of the insurance sector as a source of systemic instability or a conduit is not settled. Efforts to align the regulations pertaining to insurance activity across nation states have nevertheless pushed forward.[83] These efforts are central to an understanding of what now drives regulatory convergence across nation states.

As other contributors to this book have highlighted, there are a number of

81 Available at: www.financialstabilityboard.org/press/pr_090925a.pdf.

82 A very insightful analysis of the need for harmonized laws is by D Leebron (1996), 'Lying Down with Procrustes: An Early Analysis of Harmonisation Claims', in J Bhagwah and R Hudec (eds), *Fair Trade and Harmonisation*, 2 vols, Cambridge, MA: MIT Press, vol. 1, at 41–118.

83 See the Report to G20 Finance Ministers and Governors 'Guidance to Assess the Systemic Importance of Financial Institutions, Markets and Instruments: Initial Considerations', October 2009. Available at: www.financialstabilityboard.org/publications/r_091107c.pdf (last accessed 6 June 2015).

definitions of 'systemic risk'.[84] No single one garners the support of all.[85] The FSB defines 'systemic risk' as:

> 'a risk of disruption to financial services that is (i) caused by an impairment of all or parts of the financial system and (ii) has the potential to have serious negative consequences for the real economy. Fundamental to the definition is the notion of negative externalities from a disruption or failure in a financial institution, market or instrument. All types of financial intermediaries, markets and infrastructure can potentially be systemically important to some degree.' [86]

The IAIS (with the concurrence of the Geneva Association) maintains that 'timing' must be added to the working definition in order to allow for the fact that, with respect to insurance, 'systemic risk does not typically generate immediate effects but plays out over a longer time horizon'.[87] Key to all definitions of 'systemic risk' is the risk of contagion: that as a result of financial interconnectedness, the failure of one financial institution could quickly trigger the collapse of other institutions and sectors of the financial system.

The re-branding of the FSF to the FSB was in large part the result of a desire to build an international consensus as to the reforms necessary to strengthen the international financial system by broadening the mandate and the number of participants. The membership of the FSB includes institutions from 24 countries (including emerging economies[88]). In an effort to improve its legitimacy and influence, the FSB has established regional consultative groups to strengthen the involvement of non-members in its work.[89] Members of the FSB include the IMF, the World Bank, the OECD, the European Commission as well as well as the BIS, the Basel

---

84 A good definition of systemic risk is provided by S Schwarcz (2008), 'Systemic Risk', *Georgetown Law Journal* 97: 193 at 204. Available at: http://papers.ssrn.com/s013/papers.cfm?abstract_id=1008326 (last accessed 6 June 2015). As one academic characterizes, the problem 'is not simply that financial institutions are interconnected (principally through the over-the-counter derivatives market), but equally that the risks they face are positively correlated' John C. Coffee, Jr., Columbia Law Review Vol. 111:795 'Systemic Risk After Dodd-Frank: Contingent capital and the need for regulatory strategies beyond oversight'. Available at: www.columbialawreview.org/systemic-risk-after-dodd-frank/ (last accessed 25 June 2015).

85 Over the past thirty years or more, there have been a number of studies which aim to identify sources of risk to the financial system. These include: Bhattacharya and Gale (1987), Allen and Gale (1998, 2000), Diamond and Rajan (2005) and, more recently, Brunnermeier and Pedersen (2009), Brunnermeier (2009), Danielsson and Zigrand (2008), Danielsson, Shin, and Zigrand (2009), Battiston *et al.* (2009), and Castiglionesi, Periozzi, and Lorenzoni (2009) among others. See also M Billioni, M Getmansky, A Lo and L Pellizzzoni (17 March 2010), 'Measuring Risk in the Financial and Insurance Sectors', MIT Reasearch Paper No. 4774–10, p. 8.

86 As before at: www.financialstabilityboard.org/publications/r_091107c.pdf pp. 5 and 6.

87 See www.genevaassociation.org/media/99275/ga2011-considerations_for_identifying_sifis_in_insurance.pdf. A position endorsed by the IAIS in its Report in 15 November 2011 'Insurance and Financial Stability'. Available at: http://iaisweb.org/index.cfm?event=getPage&nodeId=41633#pdf (last accessed 6 June 2015).

88 For a discussion of the issues arising from the under-representation of developing countries, see C Rustomjee (2005), 'Improving Southern Voice on the IMF board: Quo Vadis Shareholders?', in B Carin and A Wood (eds), *Accountability of the International Monetary Fund*, Ashgate: IDRC, Chapter 1. Available at: www.idrc.ca/pan/ev-85017-201-1-DO_TOPIC.html (last accessed 24 March 2011). See also N Woods and D Lombardi (2006), 'Uneven patterns of governance: how developing countries are represented in the IMF', *Review of International Political Economy* 13(3): 480–515.

89 Financial Stability Board (2010), 'Financial Stability Board meets in Seoul', the FSB Press Release 24/2010. Available at: www.financialstabilityboard.org/press/pr_101020.pdf (last accessed 6 June 2015).

Committee and the IAIS. The FSB coordinates and closely monitors the national implementation of agreed G20 financial reforms and is responsible for reporting on it to the G20. In October 2011, the FSB established a framework designed to collaborate with the international SSBs in order to intensify its monitoring and public reporting on 'priority reform' areas.[90] The FSB describes its own role as being 'to coordinate at the international level the work of national financial authorities and international standard setting bodies … in order to develop and promote the implementation of effective regulatory, supervisory and other financial sector policies'.[91]

Article 2(3) of the FSB explains how the FSB's role fits in with that of the IAIS and other standard setting bodies:

> (3) The FSB should as needed to address regulatory gaps that pose risk to financial stability, develop or coordinate development of standards and principles, in collaboration with the SSBs and others, as warranted, in areas which do not fall within the functional domain of another international standard setting body, or on issues that have cross-sectoral implications.[92]

The introduction to the recast (June 2012) the FSB Charter emphasizes the 'need to promote financial stability by developing strong regulatory, supervisory and other financial-sector policies, and fostering a level playing field through coherent policy implementation across sectors and jurisdictions'.[93] The FSB aims to promote financial stability by developing strong regulatory, supervisory and other financial policies and fostering a level playing field through coherent implementation across sectors and jurisdictions complete and consistent implementation of agreed G20/FSB financial reforms and are a means of fostering a 'race to the top' by the FSB member jurisdictions in terms of adherence to standards.[94]

9.7 Other bodies charged with regulating systemic risk

In the absence of an international regulator with power to characterize and/or address systemic risk across nation states, a wide range of organizations and groups have stepped forward. The IMF, the FSB, the EU and the United States have taken the lead. While the G20 leads initiatives at a global level to address systemic risk, many countries have launched their own efforts that largely run alongside them. It is not yet clear how these will work together. Indeed a coherent strategy for addressing systemic risk remains work in progress.

As this chapter aims to highlight by reference to the work of the IMF and the G20 in particular, the power behind the IAIS and the other SSBs are international organizations and groupings (key among them the G20) and treaty commitments (in particular the GATS and the Lisbon Treaty). In reflecting on the role and

90 Available at: www.financialstabilityboard.org/publications/r_120619a.pdf (last accessed 6 June 2015).

91 See Article 1 of the FSB Charter.

92 Ibid.

93 Available at: www.financialstabilityboard.org/publications/r_120809.pdf (last accessed 6 June 2015).

94 The FSB Handbook for Peer Review dated 12 March 2015. Available at: www.financialstabilityboard.org/2015/03/handbook-for-fsb-peer-reviews (last accessed 6 June 2015).

influence of the SSBs, the underpinning of 'hard' (treaty-based) law by reference to the WTO and the EU is often overlooked. Their role is briefly touched on here.

9.7.1 The WTO

Although the WTO has no obvious voice in the financial services standard-setting process (as it is neither a member or observer of the IAIS), the GATS does play a significant role in promoting regulatory convergence by reference to the core principles set by the international standard-setting bodies. In addition to the reference to 'equivalent regulation' used in the Annex to the GATS and to 'harmonization' in Article VII:1 GATS, the influence of the standards is through preferential trade agreements.

The SSBs and the GATS have no direct relationship. They are connected instead through the intermediation of other international organizations such as World Bank and the IMF. WTO Members have to-date been able to adopt prudential measures without interference from WTO law.[95] The GATS principle of 'national treatment' nevertheless prohibits governments, through their regulations and laws, from discriminating in favour of domestic service providers at the expense of overseas or foreign owned service providers. Article VI: 5(b) of the GATS interestingly sets out that the determination of a member's conformity with certain GATS obligations shall take into account international standards of relevant international organizations applied by that member. In this context, 'international organisations' are defined as 'international bodies whose membership is open to the relevant bodies of at least all Members of the WTO'.[96]

With Article VI:5 in mind, while the GATS does not specifically bind WTO members to use the international standards developed by the IAIS, it can be argued that the fact that the IAIS standards and codes are endorsed by the IMF suggests that domestic regulations based on the IAIS standards will be regarded as 'irrebuttably presumed consistent with the GATS' if the issue was tested'.[97] Even absent a direct link with the WTO, the reality is that the developing countries are impacted by the standards and codes, particularly where a country's pledge of adherence is linked to a conditional IMF loan.[98]

Although the GATS does not regulate the content and scope of domestic regulation, it aims to ensure that members do not put in place domestic regulations that would prove unnecessary barriers to cross-border services. Article VI requires states to ensure that where states have made specific commitments under the GATS,

95 An observation made by T Cottier and M Krajewski in E Avgouleas (ed.) (2012), *Governance of Global Financial Markets: The Law, the Economics, the Politics*, Cambridge: Cambridge University Press, at 184, 'The scope of the "prudential carve out" was and [remains] rather imprecise'.

96 See the Uruguay Round Agreement on Technical Barriers to Trade at WTO legal texts at https://www.wto.org/english/res_e/publications_e/tbttotrade_e.pdf (last accessed 21 July 2015).

97 See Bismuth at p. 14. Bismuth, Regis, Financial Sector Regulation and Financial Services Liberalization at the Crossroads: The Relevance of International Financial Standards in WTO Law (March 25, 2010). Journal of World Trade, Vol. 44, No. 2, pp. 489-514, 2010. Available at SSRN: http://ssrn.com/abstract=1578423..

98 For a discussion of the issues, see IMF (2011), 'Review of the Standards and Codes Initiative – Background Paper'. Available at: www.imf.org/external/np/pp/eng/2011/021611a.pdf (last accessed 6 June 2015).

regulations are applied in a reasonable, objective and impartial manner, are based on transparent criteria, and are not more burdensome than necessary to ensure the quality of the service.[99] So far as financial stability is concerned, the Annex on Financial Services allows WTO members to take regulatory measures that may limit cross-border trade in financial services if such measures are taken 'for prudential reasons, including for the protection of investors, depositors, policy holders or persons to whom a fiduciary duty is owed by a financial service supplier, or to ensure the integrity or stability of the financial system'. In practice, how WTO members' reliance on this provision (characterized as 'the prudential carve out') could be impacted by the commitments that nation states have made by virtue of the G20 and the IMF for example is unclear. On one assessment, the flexibility that the WTO has secured through the Annex is more apparent than real given the commitments member states have made elsewhere.

The relevance of the WTO for the regulation of the insurance industry is nevertheless clear; it allows open markets among members and allows insurance companies to compete on broadly the same terms in markets that were previously closed to them or where regulations discriminated in favour of national suppliers. A broader relevance is that it brings member countries under the umbrella of the community of international organizations that seek to influence the regulation and supervision of international financial markets.[100]

9.7.2 The EU

A consideration of the international actors involved in shaping the regulations applied to insurance markets and the impact of perceptions of systemic risk would be incomplete without mention of the EU, albeit briefly.

Broad changes to the EU regulation of insurance will be introduced from 1 January 2016 with the introduction of Solvency II,[101] which presents a revised EU framework for the regulation of insurance aimed at securing greater regulatory convergence across member states. Having concluded that the current EU minimum requirements (Solvency I) were inadequate, many countries implemented their own reforms resulting in a patchwork of regulatory requirements across the EU that were considered to hamper the functioning of the Single Market.

Solvency II is a fundamental review of the capital adequacy regime for the

---

99 Kern Alexander argues that the WTO is not an appropriate forum for establishing international standards of prudential regulation and that it should develop further institutional linkages with other international financial institutions (e.g. the IMF) to determine the extent and scope of prudential regulation. A report of the meeting of WTO Committee on Trade in Financial Services, dated 21 December 2013, demonstrates the WTO's reluctance to re-open issues regarding the application of the prudential carve out. Available at: https://docs.wto.org/dol2fe/Pages/FE_Search/.../114009/q/.../M75.pdf (last accessed 12 February 2015). See also https://wikileaks.org/tisa-financial/analysis.html (last accessed 6 June 2015).

100 Article XXVI of GATS ('Relationship with Other International Organizations') specifically provides that: 'The General Council shall make appropriate arrangements for consultation and cooperation with the United Nations and its specialized agencies as well as with other intergovernmental organizations concerned with services.'

101 Directive 2009/138/EC of 25 November 2009 on the taking-up and pursuit of the business of insurance and reinsurance (Solvency II Directive).

European insurance industry that intends to establish a revised set of EU-wide capital requirements and risk management standards with the aim of ensuring better protection for policyholders. It developed in the EU against the backdrop of the work of the other international organizations and groupings of which the European Union is a member. The framework looks very much like that of Basel II. By ensuring that insurance companies across the EU comprehensively value the risks that they face, hold adequate reserves to meet those risks and have in place robust, transparent and accountable governance systems and controls, Solvency II intends to produce a more resilient insurance system – one that is less likely to pose a risk to financial stability. Time will tell whether it is successful in this aim. Even before Solvency II leaves the starting blocks, a number of commentators have suggested that the 'framework could increase the insurance system's probability to be involved in a global crisis, thus contributing to the crisis itself'.[102]

9.8 Conclusion

Leaving aside the economic hardship and financial dislocation that followed the most recent financial crisis, the most notable outcome has been the 'lift' that it has given to the calls by international organizations, government groupings and SSBs for regulatory integration. The impact upon the framing of laws that are cast by nation-states to regulate their insurance sectors have been very significantly impacted as a result. Before the crisis, the case for regulatory convergence (in the sense of substantive equivalence) across nations was largely made by reference to the benefits that it would secure for global trade, in particular, by reducing transaction costs. Calls for substantive regulatory and supervisory convergence[103] are now largely made by reference to the security of the global financial system by reference to 'systemic risk'. The international community has, for the time being at least, largely put aside its concern as to the inevitable interference in their sovereignty as a result.

The objections of insurers notwithstanding, the regulation of insurance continues to be swept along with that of banks. At the international level there are a range of treaty organisations including the United Nations, the World Bank, the IMF and the OECD that have assumed the mantle of ensuring systemic stability. There are also international and regional government groupings including the G20, the G8,

102 See, for example, A Floreani (2013) 'Risk Measures and Capital Requirements: A Critique of the Solvency II Approach', *The Geneva Papers*, 38: 189–212. Available at: www.genevaassociation.org . Floreani argues that 'the metric used by regulators, which is based on a total risk measure such as the Value-at-Risk, is not a balanced solution between effectiveness and simplicity, but is simply wrong and could lead to significant adverse side effects, ultimately resulting in a generalised European insurance industry crisis in the case of a hard market shortfall' (at p. 211). Also M Martin (10 November 2013), 'Equity Risk Under Solvency II: Internal Models and Procyclical Effects'. Available at: SSRN: http://ssrn.com/abstract=2340430 or http://dx.doi.org/10.2139/ssrn.2340430. See also the IMF's paper discussing some of the issues ('Possible Unintended Consequences of Basel III and Solvency II'). Available at: www.imf.org/external/pubs/ft/wp/2011/wp11187.pdf (last accessed 6 June 2015).

103 The reference to 'convergence' is applied here to describe the process whereby, in the context of insurance, each country frames its domestic laws by reference to a common set of standards settled by the IAIS and the G20 (through the FSB) and endorsed by the IMF. By reference to this definition, the laws applied by individual nation states to regulate insurance markets and providers are increasingly functionally substitutional from one country to the next. This does not imply that social and cultural differences will not remain and affect markets nor that every legislative detail will inevitably be harmonized.

G7, the EU, ASEAN and the African Union among others. Those groups have themselves formed bodies such as the FSB.

Stepping forward as the guardians of global financial health, the G20 has prescribed enhanced regulatory coordination, cooperation and convergence as the remedy for minimizing 'systemic risk'. The G20 now seeks to steer the course which financial regulation takes internationally. Along with the IMF it has become a lynchpin of the international financial architecture. Working in tandem with the international organizations, government bodies and groups have formed to identify and mitigate risks to the international financial system. In the view of the G20, 'effective, robust and consistent global regulation assists in the early detection, and abatement of, potentially serious systemic issues which readily transfers risks across borders and creates global crises such as that witnessed in recent years'. There is little persuasive evidence to support this proposition but it has been accepted as a truth nevertheless across the layers of organizations and groupings each determined to have a role in identifying the sources of systemic risk and the appropriate means of addressing them through regulation.

Writing at the BIS in 1983, Borio referred to the idea of systemic risk and contagion as having an 'impeccable intellectual pedigree'.[104] Some of its more formal elements go back at least to the model of systemic risk by Diamond and Dybvig.[105] The idea of systemic risk is, therefore, not new. Nor is the attempt of regulation to address it. While the G20 leads initiatives at a global level to address systemic risk, many countries (in particular the United States and the EU) have launched their own efforts that largely run alongside. It is not yet clear how these will work together. Indeed a coherent strategy for addressing systemic risk remains work in progress.

The level of coordination notwithstanding, the 2007/2008 financial crises clearly revealed that the system of regulation had failed to secure international financial stability (on whatever basis that is defined). This has been read by governments and the majority of academic commentators as evidencing problems with the system of financial regulation (rather than an inevitable consequence of the operation of globally integrated markets). The constituent parts of the international regulatory architecture have moved to patch up what they have identified as 'fault lines' in the architecture of the financial system, shortcomings in the regulations themselves and of the approach of regulators. The changes to the topography of the regulatory landscape that followed the financial crisis revealed a shift in the regulatory focus from micro- to macro- prudential regulation (from individual firms to financial system stability). Even before the crisis, research at the BIS and the IMF had raised the need to strengthen further the macro-prudential orientation of the current prudential frameworks in order to improve the safeguards against financial instability.

There is a lack of consensus as to what defines 'systemic risk' and whether insurance companies pose a systemic risk and, if they do, how that risk should be

104 See C Borio (2003), 'Towards a macroprudential framework for financial supervision and regulation?', BIS Working Papers No. 128. Available at: www.bis.org/publ/work128.pdf

105 D W Diamond and P H Dybvig (1983), 'Bank runs, deposit insurance and liquidity', *Journal of Political Economy*, 91(3: 401–419.

addressed through regulation. Analysis as to whether financial regulation contributes to the risk rather than abates it or whether the cost of regulation is justified has hardly been started. Nevertheless, the work of the FSB in connection with systemic risk in non-bank entities is clearly a force promoting the international convergence of the regulations that apply to regulate insurance companies internationally. The FSB has expressly called for jurisdictions to 'seek convergence of their resolution regimes through the legislative changes needed to incorporate the tools and powers set out in these Key Attributes into their national regimes'.[106] This is an unequivocal call for the convergence of laws in this area that is in harmony with the sentiment of G20 members and the insurance industry itself. G20 members have reaffirmed their commitment to 'common global standards by pursuing the financial regulatory reform agenda according to our agreed timetable in an internationally consistent and non-discriminatory manner'.[107]

This chapter has not addressed whether the standards and codes are likely to abate systemic risk, even assuming that they are able to satisfactorily identify it. Its focus has instead been on the inter-locking web of actors shaping regulatory change by reference to it. In this connection, it must be noted that the constitutional freedom that national agencies have to design regulations affecting the insurance industry is limited by existing treaty obligations. In particular this is the case where states have made commitments under the GATS and/or are members of the EU but also by virtue of their membership of the Bretton Woods organizations and SSBs including the IAIS.

The processes that establish the laws regularing insurance (and the wider financial services industry) are not always easy to classify within the traditional categories of international law. Standards and codes are converted into hard law by individual nation states (and the EU). Not least as a result of the weighted voting procedures of some international government organisations, not all countries have an equal voice or level of influence. As one commentator remarks, the law in this area is 'dependent on shifting principles of prudence, policy and local centres of power, such as the opinion and disposition of specific regulators or central banks'.[108]

The overriding impression to be gleaned from a review of the international government organizations, standard-setters and government groupings is of a significant number of groupings that is more cohesive than the number of voices and interest groups might suggest. Together they have built and exported a consensus. Collectively, these organizations and groups settle rules and standards for the regulation of financial services throughout much of the world. They achieve this end where a single financial international law-making body could not. Either because it would be unpalatable to sovereign sensibilities, and/or because achieving consensus

106 Page 4 of the 'Key Attributes' document, as before.

107 25 February 2012 at: www.g20.utoronto.ca/2012/2012-120420-finance-en.html (last accessed 12 February 2015).

108 Baxter, *op cit*, p. 16.

Baxter L, 'Internationalization of Law: The "Complex" Case of Bank regulation' Duke Law School (2010) at http://scholarship.law.duke.edu/cgi/viewcontent.cgi?article=2617&context=faculty_scholarship (last accessed 25 June 2015).

on what those standards should be would be extremely difficult if all the players were represented equally at the negotiating table.

Pascal Lamy, the Director General of the WTO observed that following the 2007/2008 financial crisis, 'global governance is undergoing a major "overhaul" [and] with this increasing interdependence, the world is rightly asking now whether we have the right institutions and systems in place to govern this interdependence properly'.[109] A review of the pattern of global governance across the financial services industry, at least in the post-war years, suggests that the 'overhaul' has in practice meant a shuffling of the pack of international government organisations and other groupings, with some rebranding but much the same centres of influence as to the shape of financial regulation.[110] Even so, what has no doubt changed since the last crisis is the extent to which those shaping global governance have sought to frame the regulations pertaining to insurance markets in line with those applied to banks. The reference point for their efforts is the urgent need to stem systemic risk. Perhaps lost in the scramble for a coherent formula for the identification and management of systemic risk is the danger that could follow from a single model for the management of risk across financial sectors and nation states.

109 Pascal Lamy, at the address at the IISS Geo-Economic Strategy Summit, The Bahrain Global Forum, Manama, 16 May 2010.

110 In the *New Left Review*, 1 August 2007, Professor Robert Wade expresses the interesting view that, in so far as the West is able to get its standards of best practice accepted as 'normal' and non-compliance as 'deviant', it alters the international political economy in a manner that might be compared to global warming – away from coordinated market economies and towards a liberal market economy of the Anglo-American type. In Professor Wade's view, 'The drive for "transparency" involves not so much "removing the veil" as a massive programme of standardization around one type of capitalism, thereby reinforcing and legitimizing the power of the G7 states and multilateral organisations to intensify and stabilize financial liberalization.' R Wade (2007), 'A New Global Financial Architecture?', *New Left Review* 46: 113–129.

INDEX